ETHICS and Accountability in CRIMINAL JUSTICE

TOWARDS A UNIVERSAL STANDARD

Tim Prenzler

www.
AUSTRALIANACADEMICPRESS
.com.au

First published in 2009
Australian Academic Press
32 Jeays Street
Bowen Hills Qld 4006
Australia
www.australianacademicpress.com.au

National Library of Australia Cataloguing-in-Publication entry

Author:	Prenzler, Tim.
Title:	Ethics and accountability in criminal justice : towards a universal standard / Tim Prenzler.
ISBN:	9781921513268 (pbk.)
Notes:	Includes index. Bibliography.
Subjects:	Criminal justice, Administration of. Criminal justice, Administration of--Moral and ethical aspects. Law enforcement--Moral and ethical aspects. Law and ethics. Law--Moral and ethical aspects. Criminal law--International unification.

Dewey Number: 364

Cover and text design by Andrea Rinarelli of Australian Academic Press, Brisbane.

This book is dedicated
to the memory of

Ray Holzheimer
1929–2009

A public servant, a scholar
and a gentleman

This is a book of research and policy aimed at raising ethical standards in criminal justice practice. Around the world, corruption continues to undermine the rule of law and the application of due process rights. Misconduct by criminal justice professionals challenges democratic authority and the equality and freedom of ordinary citizens. There is an urgent need for academics, advocates and policymakers to speak with one voice in articulating universal ethical standards and, most importantly, in prescribing systems and techniques that must be in place for criminal justice to be genuinely accountable and as free from misconduct as possible.

The focus of the book is on the core components of the criminal justice system — police, courts and corrections — and the core groups within this system: sworn police officers; judges, prosecutors and defence lawyers; and custodial and community correctional officers. The ethical challenges these groups face and the accountability standards that apply to them also apply broadly to the very wide range of associated occupations. For simplicity's sake the focus of the book is on the core groups.

Ethics and Accountability in Criminal Justice: Towards a Universal Standard begins by establishing general ethical standards and principles of accountability that apply to the criminal justice system as a component of the public sector. The emphasis here is on democratic authority and the implications of democracy for the impartial execution of duty by politicians and public servants. The book then deals, in order, with the police, courts and corrections, systematically working through the topics of ethical issues, misconduct case studies and corruption prevention methods. The book proposes a series of policy 'solutions' to ethical issues and a program for translating these positions into practice through comprehensive integrity systems. The result is a basic checklist that can be used to assess the ethical quality and accountability of the criminal justice system in any jurisdiction.

Tim Prenzler

SECTION ONE   Police

SECTION TWO   Courts

SECTION THREE   Corrections

Chapter 1

Ethics and Accountability in the Public Sector and Criminal Justice System

This chapter introduces the main principles of public sector ethics. It begins with a discussion of the nature of ethics and the two major secular ethical systems: ethical formalism and utilitarianism. It then introduces the concept of accountability and examines how ethics and accountability apply to government, particularly in the context of democracy. The types of ethical standards and accountability mechanisms that should apply to all government-related activities are then set out based on key United Nations (UN) documents. Next, a series of examples of corrupt, unethical or ethically questionable conduct by politicians and public servants is provided. The chapter concludes by briefly drawing out major implications for the criminal justice system as a public sector institution. The primary argument in this chapter is that the legitimacy of the criminal justice system depends on the degree to which government is substantively democratic, and that an impartial service ethic is the key to ethical standards in criminal justice.

Background

Imagine the following scenario:

> Maria Bloggs runs a small law firm. A lawyer leaves and Maria replaces this person with her son Jimmy (who has a law degree). Maria then gets a job in the government sector in the Department of Justice managing a specialist unit. When one of the lawyers in the unit resigns, Maria replaces the person with Jimmy.

Was it right for Maria to employ Jimmy in her business? Was it right for Maria to employ Jimmy in the Department? These are typical ethical questions, and the answers to these questions go to the core of the issue of public sector ethics. Modern societies make a fundamental distinction between standards of behaviour in the private and public sectors. In her private business Maria would normally be legally entitled to employ her child — subject to some constraints in order to protect third parties from incompetence, such as the need for the relevant qualifications and professional registration. The fact that Maria has established this business and taken on the risks of running a business entitles her to a great deal of freedom about how she manages it. Broadly speaking, she is entitled to employ whomever she chooses. Were Jimmy lazy and incompetent, one might question the ethics of keeping him. But that is a secondary issue.

The employment of a family member, or a friend, in the public sector involves quite different criteria. The department is not Maria's property. It is 'owned' by the citizens of the relevant jurisdiction. Not only do these citizens have a right to apply for the job vacancy, they also expect to be served by the best person available for that job. Consequently, the employment process should be governed by strict rules of open advertising, open application, appointment by merit and the application of objective selection criteria. Were Jimmy to apply, Maria would be obliged to declare a conflict of interest and absent herself from the selection process. Any attempt by her to influence the selection panel in her son's favour would be considered extremely unethical. In fact, favouritism towards relatives or friends in a public sector context is usually considered a type of corruption — described, respectively, as nepotism and cronyism.

The Nature of Ethics

Ethics, as a system of thought, is concerned with moral judgments about right and wrong, good and bad. One way to conceptualise this is through the 'fact–value' distinction. While people might agree on certain alleged 'facts', they are more likely to evaluate those facts in different moral terms. For example, a group of people might agree with a government health department statistic about the number of abortions each year in a particular locality. The group might agree to accept the statistic as roughly accurate. However, they might be bitterly divided about whether abortion is moral or immoral. Some will support it as an unfortunate but justifiable necessity involving 'the greatest good for the greatest number'. Others will deem it murder and immoral under any circumstances. There will also be a range of more complicated opinions over issues such as late terminations or tolerance of terminations following rape.

'Normative ethics' usually involves support for a range of positive values and moral principles, including honesty, fairness, equity, rights, responsibilities and duty (Pollock, 2007, p. 35ff). Normative ethics lies behind the law in that it provides the rationale for laws, but it is also beyond the law in that it posits higher duties above 'the letter of the law'. A good example of this concerns Good Samaritan Laws. One aspect of these laws is that they do *not* require people to come to the aid of others. This is designed in part to protect would-be rescuers from harm. However, in many situations we would expect that helping other people in emergency situations is the right thing to do and that people *should* do this. Similarly, disobeying the law might also be considered the right thing to do in some situations. Environmental protestors argue it is necessary to violate public order laws in order to bring attention to the greater problem of environmental destruction. This is an example of the 'end–means disjunction' in ethics, when bad means are justified in terms of good ends.

One problematic aspect of ethics (and accountability) is the assumption of people's responsibility for their actions. In order to judge a person's behaviour as morally right or wrong there is usually an assumption that their actions are freely chosen. The idea of free will is therefore central to ethical reasoning and judgment. However, we really do not know what free will is. Scientific research, both psychological (concerned with nurture) and biological (concerned with nature), tends to increasingly show that human behaviour is highly determined — or strongly influenced — by factors that appear to be outside people's will (Pollock, 2007, pp. 74–88). In fact, some scientists argue that free will might be a complete illusion; that all behaviours are determined, and that free will is only something we assume when we do not know the causes of behaviours (Pollock, 2007, pp. 10–23).

Despite these problems with the concept of free will, it appears impossible to escape ethical reasoning and ethical judgments in our lives. People continuously judge each other's behaviour in moral terms, and we assume that a great deal of behaviour is somehow a choice that people make (Pollock, 2007, p. 11). When people do 'the wrong thing' we also appear to have a collective urge to punish them and stop them repeating the behaviour in the future. This is of course the purpose of criminal justice, organised on a collective basis.

Ethical dilemmas are another aspect of ethics that are difficult to escape. A dilemma involves an emotionally or intellectually difficult choice, sometimes between competing 'goods' or competing 'evils'. Just getting out of bed in the morning can involve a dilemma between the 'good' of sleeping in and staying out of the traffic and the 'good' of getting to work on time. Government policymaking also often entails ethical dilemmas around human interest priorities in areas like health and education — where an increase in funding in one area necessitates a decrease in another. Saving a forest might involve making forestry workers unemployed. The list seems almost infinite.

Studies of ethics often employ scenarios to illustrate dilemmas. A typical example follows:

> You are in a lifeboat along with four others. You have only enough food and water to keep four alive for the several weeks you expect to be adrift until you float into a shipping lane and can be discovered and rescued. You definitely will all perish if the five of you consume the food and water. There is the suggestion that one of you should die so that the other four can live. Would you volunteer to commit suicide? Would you vote to have one go overboard if you choose by straws? Would you vote to throw overboard the weakest and less healthy of the five? If you were on a jury judging the behaviour of four who

3

did murder a fifth in order to stay alive, would you acquit them or convict them of murder? (Pollock, 2007, p. 65)

We will return to this dilemma soon.

Ethical Systems

Ethical systems have been developed to try to solve ethical dilemmas in ways that employ consistent guidelines intended to appeal to, and be accepted by, all people. Their ultimate goal, usually, is to resolve human conflicts by means that are considered fair by everyone, or at least the large majority of people. In her book *Ethical Dilemmas and Decisions in Criminal Justice*, Jocelyn Pollock (2007) describes a number of ethical systems that have developed over time. The main ones we will consider here are religious ethics, ethical formalism and utilitarianism, with some attention to the idea of a hierarchy of moral reasoning. Religion has been a major source of ethical principles and deserves some discussion. The present study, however, makes use of formalism and utilitarianism as major reference points. It also focuses its arguments on a separate, partly composite, system of modern public service ethics. Formalism and utilitarianism provide foundation frameworks for a secular morality with universal application, and have a variety of relevant principles and concepts for public service and criminal justice. Both systems are highly problematic, but they do provide criteria that feature prominently in modern thinking about law, punishment, government, ethics and professional ethics. A public service ethic is a critical component of the larger 'social democratic' political system that is slowly being adopted around the world, and provides for core consensus positions on government and criminal justice.

Religious Ethics

Historically, ethics has been closely aligned with religion. Religious systems usually involve complex ethical positions and rules of behaviour. Nonetheless, despite often emphasising principles of equity, justice, compassion and love, religion appears to divide rather than unite people. Of particular concern is the fact that the basis of ethical authority — the existence and power of God — is both arbitrary and impossible to demonstrate. In that regard the irrationality of much religious thinking is summed up in that honest but naive bumper sticker: 'God said it, I believe it, and that settles it'.

Close analysis of the ethics of major religions, like Christianity and Islam, reveals hopelessly muddled and contradictory principles (Pollock, 2007, pp. 42–46). Christianity, for example, simultaneously advocates poverty and wealth, and war and passivism, as moral imperatives. Christians usually support a state legal system, but the New Testament component of the *Bible*, on which Christianity is based, provides no grounds for criminal justice whatsoever because it argues that vengeance is the exclusive province of God. Christians are also explicitly prohibited from involvement in politics, including, by implication, making and enforcing laws (Prenzler, 1990). Unfortunately, this has not stopped many Christians imposing their beliefs on others by the force of law and war.

Contradictions in Islam have received international attention in the last decade because of the growth in Islamic terrorism. While some followers of the *Koran* find a justification for terrorist violence in selected passages, other Muslims reject this and find pacifist meanings (Venkatraman, 2007). In another example of fuzzy but dangerous religious ethics, the modern Catholic church prohibits contraception on moral grounds — because it denies God's purpose for sex — despite the fact that human over-population represents the greatest threat to the wellbeing of the planet and that without contraception many women would die from pregnancy-related complications (United Nations, 2006, 2007).

These disagreements demonstrate the impossibility of developing a consensus ethic from a set of ancient patriarchal tribal texts. Both Islam and Christianity have also historically been used to support authoritarian governments and provide little in the way of support for modern principles of democracy, human rights and justice. The justice systems produced by world religions have generally been arbitrary and brutal. Ironically, perhaps the greatest present threat to world peace comes from the 'War on Terror' and the 'War by Terror', which are closely linked to the conflict over occupation of the 'Holy Land' of Palestine. This conflict involves the seemingly irreconcilable interests of fundamentalist Islam, Judaism and Christianity.

Historical religions, like Hinduism and Judaism, often include traditional elements that are particularly repugnant to modern morality. Some strains of Hinduism advocated the hideous practice of widow burning (sati), and supported gross social inequalities on the basis that one's present social position was the result of actions in a previous life. The Jewish holy books require a range of practices that can only be described as grotesquely unjust, cruel and bizarre in the extreme (Dawkins, 2006). They include the stoning of female adulterers, the forcible marriage of an unbetrothed virgin who is raped to the man who raped her, and the punishment by death of an extended family for the crimes of one family member. According to the *Bible*, the original establishment of a Jewish kingdom was the result of a war of genocide against the indigenous peoples carried out under orders from God (see the books of *Deuteronomy* and *Joshua*).

Formal religion therefore provides little of value in developing a widely acceptable public ethic for government, criminal justice and the professional ethics of criminal justice practitioners. Let us turn elsewhere to examine secular attempts to solve ethical problems.

Ethical Formalism

Ethical formalism is a system of ethics that is described as 'absolutist'. That is, it attempts to identify universal rules that apply in all situations without exception. It is somewhat like religious ethics but without God. It was developed during the Enlightenment period in 18th century Europe and represents an attempt to devise an alternative to religious ethics. Its most famous exponent was the philosopher Emmanuel Kant. Kant believed that principles of right and wrong apply to all human behaviour in all cultures and can be deduced by reason. There were several key components to his theory, paraphrased here (Pollock, 2007, pp. 37–40):

- People's motives should be judged as moral or immoral, not the consequences of their actions.
- An action must be freely chosen in order to be subject to moral judgment.
- People should only be treated as ends in themselves, not as the means to an end.
- Whatever action you take you must be willing to accept that all people can do the same.

The latter point is often referred to as the 'categorical imperative'. 'Categorical' means without exception, and 'imperative' means an essential duty. Kant defined the categorical imperative as follows: 'Act only on that maxim by which you can at the same time will that it should become a universal law' (2002, p. 222). This is very much the basis for the idea of the equality of all people before the law. In theory, what happens to one happens to all, because what has been done to one person can therefore be done to all people. A person who steals from one person also steals in principle from themselves and everyone else (Kant, 1996, p. 105). This is very similar to the golden rule found in many religious texts: 'Do unto others as you would have them do unto you' (Pollock, 2007, p. 43). Pollock uses the example of cheating on a test to explain the categorical imperative: 'A student might decide to cheat on a test, but for this action to be moral, the student would have to agree that everyone should be able to cheat on tests' (p. 37). This is unlikely because it would mean there was no such thing as a fair test.

Kant believed in intrinsic moral values, even if harmful consequences follow from doing the right thing. Formalists would respond to the lifeboat dilemma (earlier in this chapter) by arguing that taking a life is always wrong, and even an extreme situation like this will not justify it. Each person will have an argument about why their life should be spared or why one of the others should be the one to be sacrificed. And, in any case, the consequences are too unpredictable: 'In reality, it is not known whether anyone will survive. The fifth may be murdered, and five minutes later, a rescue ship appears on the horizon' (Pollock, 2007, p. 41).

Formalism emphasises fairness in terms of equitable treatment of all people. It encourages us to question people who would make exceptions to rules — including questioning people who would place themselves above the law. It challenges hypocrisy and double standards, and it challenges people who claim they can justify questionable actions based on a higher good achieved in the future. At the same time, it does consider people's motives in a way that might partially excuse apparent bad behaviour in some cases because the person 'meant well'.

There are of course criticisms of formalism. An obvious one is that it is overly rigid and intolerant. It fails to recognise the relevance of people's different circumstances or the fact that sometimes rules need to be broken in the interests of a greater good. For example, formalism appears to argue that lying is always wrong, whereas we can probably think of many situations where telling a lie might be considered the right thing to do: to save a life, for instance. Modern criminal law is formalist in many of its basic requirements, but it is usually tempered by various defences or excuses that are meant to be taken into account when determining guilt or penalties. Another problem with formalism is that interpretation can be difficult when it is applied to practical ethical issues. For example, Kant supported a principle of equity, or forfeiture, in punishment — that is, 'an eye for an eye'. He stated simply that anyone who commits murder must die (1996, p. 106). But he was opposed to the infliction of physical pain and supported punishments such as imprisonment, solitary confinement and penal labour. Kant's support for the death penalty seems at odds with his emphasis on the intrinsic value of life (Pollock, 2007, p. 39).

Utilitarianism

Utilitarianism also developed in Europe, a little later than formalism, and it also represents an attempt to develop a fully secular ethical system, that is, one that does not entail threats from God. Two major exponents were Jeremy Bentham and John Stuart Mill. In contrast to formalism, utilitarianism explicitly focuses on the consequences of actions and is explicit in recognising pain and pleasure as the real concerns of people. According to Bentham, 'Nature has placed mankind under the governance of two sovereign masters, *pain* and *pleasure* ... They govern us in all we do' (1996, p. 11). Mill describes utilitarianism as follows (1966, p. 157): 'Utilitarianism, or the Greatest Happiness principle, holds that actions are right in proportion as they tend to promote happiness, wrong as they tend to produce the reverse of happiness. By happiness is intended pleasure, and the absence of pain.'

There are two primary principles in utilitarianism (Pollock, 2007):

- What matters in making a moral judgment is not the motive of the person but the effects of their actions in terms of benefits and harms.
- Where moral issues involve more than two people what matters is the 'greatest good for the greatest number'.

Consequences are conceptualised by utilitarianism in two forms. 'Act utilitarianism' is concerned with the immediate effects of a decision. For example, a decision to drive above the speed limit might not result in any injury and therefore might be considered 'okay' because 'no-one was hurt'. In the lifeboat scenario, act utilitarians might accept the calculations about survival of the majority to justify murder (Pollock, 2007, p. 41). 'Rule utilitarianism', however, examines the effects of actions in terms of the precedent they set. What would happen if everyone ignored speed limits? The obvious answer is that enormous harm would result. It might also be used to reject killing one survivor in the lifeboat scenario because it could lead to killing the majority of survivors one by one — 'the slippery slope' argument.

Utilitarianism is valuable for focusing attention on the consequences of actions and considering the wider social benefits and harms of any action. It also drives much of the modern concern with quantifying the effects of government policies. However, it does have problems. Act utilitarianism can arguably be used to justify extreme abuses, such as selecting a minority group for medical experiments that will benefit the majority. Rule utilitarianism, however, would reject this because the precedent threatens all people. It therefore holds to strong universalist and egalitarian principles.

A Hierarchy of Moral Reasoning

One helpful way to think of ethics is in terms of levels of moral reasoning. Lawrence Kohlberg famously proposed a six-part theory of moral reasoning that follows stages of childhood development and adult maturity. The hierarchy is set out here in its most basic form (adapted from Kohlberg, 1976):

Level I 'Pre-Conventional'
Stage 1: Obey rules to avoid punishment. Egocentric.
Stage 2: Obey rules to benefit self. Self-interested, 'individualistic'.

Level II 'Conventional'
Stage 3: Obey rules for group approval and harmony; 'interpersonal conformity'.
Stage 4: Obey rules because of belief in social order; 'societal point of view'.

Level III 'Post-Conventional'
Stage 5: Obey rules because of formal social contracts for mutual benefit. Practical 'contractual commitment', 'greatest good for the greatest number'.

Stage 6: Obey rules that embody egalitarian universal values and rights. 'Personal commitment', 'Persons are ends in themselves'.

We can use these stages as criteria to assess different types of moral arguments, in part in terms of their commitment to self-interest or universal human values and interest. Formalism and utilitarianism, for all their faults, aspire to Level III universal values and reasoning.

Public Service Ethics

We now come to the ethical system that frames the arguments in this book. Public service ethics involves a set of beliefs and rules governing conduct in the public sector. The focus is usually on government employees, but the majority of principles apply equally to elected officials. A key criterion is that of 'public interest'. A 'public interest test' is a universal test that should be applied to all the actions of public servants. Hence actions that benefit public servants outside their remuneration, such as graft and gratuities, usually fail a public interest test. A key value of the criterion is that it can be used to address the question of who benefits from government decisions by applying formalist notions of equity and utilitarian notions of human needs. Public service codes involve a number of other important principles such as commitment, impartiality and competence — principles that are developed in more depth in a later section of this chapter.

At the beginning of this chapter there was a discussion of the differences between private sector and public sector ethics. However, there is also an observable trend towards converging ethical standards. Increasing responsibilities are being placed on corporations to act responsibly as members of a wider community with obligations beyond making profits for their shareholders. And many traditionally private commercial transactions are being questioned from a public interest standpoint. A good example is the outcome of the 1999 'cash for comment affair'. An Australian Broadcasting Authority (2000) inquiry found that Sydney commercial radio presenters John Laws and Alan Jones had dishonestly presented opinions about major companies — including Qantas, Telstra and major banks — as their own personal and independent opinions. In reality, they had secretly been paid many millions of dollars to make favourable comments. The Australian Broadcasting Authority's report recommended that in the public interest a legal requirement should be introduced that the funding of commentary be disclosed on air.

Accountability

'Accountability' is a slightly awkward word that is probably best translated as 'responsibility'. It implies a relationship between at least two people. One delegates a task. The other receives the task. The process entails an obligation, or contract, on the second person to fulfil the task in the way intended. The second person is accountable to the first. The classic example is an employer giving an employee a task that will be performed out of sight of the employer. This entails a grant of power (the capacity to affect things), an assumption of responsibility (that the person is capable of the task) and usually some discretion (the capacity to exercise personal choices about how something is done). But because the person delegating the task is not omnipresent there needs to be a mechanism for checking the work of the nominee and correcting any errors. A full accountability process therefore involves the following steps:

1. Delegation of a task
2. Articulation of performance measures
3. Disclosure of work done
4. Reward/punishment depending on quality of work
5. Repair when work is inadequate
6. Reform to prevent future failings.

The primary question is how to make people accountable? Various sub-questions involve performance measures, the apportionment of degrees of responsibility and the appropriate rewards ('carrots') and sanctions ('sticks') required to make a system work optimally.

Accountability can also be considered in terms of two main areas of institutional functioning: *performance*, in terms of the product of that agency; and *conduct*, in terms of the ethical behaviour and integrity of members in generating that product. We can think of police accountability, for example, as being about both crime minimisation and law enforcement on the one hand, and ethical conduct on the other. The two are closely related but can be separated. One can think of a police force that is highly efficient and effective in terms of preventing crime and bringing offenders to justice, but that achieves this by terrorising citizens and violating suspects' rights. On the other hand, one could think of a highly ethical police department free of corruption but losing the fight against crime because it uses outmoded techniques. The focus of this book is on the question of accountability for ethical conduct, but with a view to that commitment entailing efficiency and effectiveness.

Accountability in Government

Criminal justice is part of government and therefore part of a political system. Political systems are macro-level accountability systems. They entail a source of authority, delegated authorities and mechanisms of accountability back to the source. The best-known contemporary system is parliamentary democracy. The theory of democracy is that the will of the people is the only viable source of authority for government (Mill, 1966, p. 453ff). The support and welfare of all citizens are the ultimate tests of government legitimacy. Even non-democratic theories of government — such as monarchy, communism and fascism — posit human welfare as the ultimate goal and usually also set some mechanism by which the people transmit their authority to the unelected leadership. Monarchists tend to revert to the old theory of divine authority, but still accept the principle that monarchs must serve the interests of their subjects. Fascists resort to mystical theories of leaders as embodiments of their racial group, while communists assume their party acts as the agent of the masses. In reality, non-democratic governments resist direct accountability, act primarily as self-serving elites and usually employ torture, murder and terror to maintain power.

Since the end of the Cold War in 1990 the world has seen the expansion of democracy as the main form of government in most countries, despite many compromises in practice (Puddington, 2008). 'Liberal democracy' describes the mix of constitutional liberties constraining elected governments. Constitutional freedoms are designed to protect individuals from capricious or oppressive governments that might garner majority support for a period, overturn basic rights, persecute particular groups and permanently monopolise power (Mill, 1966, p. 454). These liberties include the right to vote, freedom of expression and belief, equality before the law and the right to trial by jury. The following is a selection of exemplar rights from the 30 articles of the UN *Universal Declaration of Human Rights* (1948):

1. All human beings are born free and equal in dignity and rights ...
2. Everyone is entitled to all the rights and freedoms set forth in this Declaration, without distinction of any kind, such as race, colour, sex, language, religion, political or other opinion, national or social origin, property, birth or other status ...
3. Everyone has the right to life, liberty and security of person.
4. No one shall be held in slavery or servitude ...
5. No one shall be subjected to torture or to cruel, inhuman or degrading treatment or punishment.
7. All are equal before the law and are entitled without any discrimination to equal protection of the law ...
8. Everyone has the right to an effective remedy by the competent national tribunals for acts violating the fundamental rights granted him by the constitution or by law.
9. No one shall be subjected to arbitrary arrest, detention or exile.
10. Everyone is entitled in full equality to a fair and public hearing by an independent and impartial tribunal, in the determination of his rights and obligations and of any criminal charge against him.

12. No one shall be subjected to arbitrary interference with his privacy, family, home or correspondence, nor to attacks upon his honour and reputation …

17. (1) Everyone has the right to own property …
    (2) No one shall be arbitrarily deprived of his property.

18. Everyone has the right to freedom of thought, conscience and religion …

19. Everyone has the right to freedom of opinion and expression …

20. (1) Everyone has the right to freedom of peaceful assembly and association …

21. (1) Everyone has the right to take part in the government of his country, directly or through freely chosen representatives.
    (2) Everyone has the right of equal access to public service in his country.
    (3) The will of the people shall be the basis of the authority of government; this will shall be expressed in periodic and genuine elections which shall be by universal and equal suffrage and shall be held by secret vote …

29. (2) In the exercise of his rights and freedoms, everyone shall be subject only to such limitations as are determined by law solely for the purpose of securing due recognition and respect for the rights and freedoms of others and of meeting the just requirements of morality, public order and the general welfare in a democratic society …

These 'rights' are of course aspirational and not without problems. For example, how much property is fair in terms of the right to own property? However, issues like these can be addressed through the democratic mechanisms advocated by the declaration. In its pure form democracy involves the direct say and vote by all members of a community on matters that concern it. Hence modern complex democratic systems retain an idealised image of ancient Athenian democracy, where citizens attended the assembly in person, freely debated proposals and voted by a show of hands. Athenian democracy functioned even with many thousands of participants. It was necessary, nonetheless, to delegate administrative functions to particular individuals so the assembly's decisions could be put into practice (an early type of public service). Furthermore, some citizens were much more active, influential and in fact domineering than others. One practical problem for direct democracy in the Athenian model was that work commitments, illness or military service were disenfranchising in that citizens had to be present at the assembly to vote. And the proper fulfilment of one's democratic duties could be time consuming and laborious (Claster, 1967).

In most modern democracies these practical issues are addressed through representative democracy. Representatives are elected to act on behalf of citizens in a parliament of manageable proportions. If the representatives fail to carry out the will of the electors they can be replaced at the next election. Some countries, including Australia, have a specific form of representative democracy called the Westminster system, based around ministerial responsibility.

Ministers are elected members of parliament who head government departments and are responsible for implementing the decisions of the parliament in their portfolio area. They also participate in an inner circle of ministers — the cabinet — that decides on core policy initiatives and legislative changes that are taken to the parliament for debate and voting. The system of ministerial accountability involves a chain of delegated authority. Authority is passed from citizens to the parliament, on to ministers, and from ministers to the public service, which delivers government services to citizens. Therefore, what citizens want should come back to them, as they are the ultimate recipients of the process.

Faults in the System

The ideal of direct participatory democracy inherited from the ancient Athenians had its own deep contradictions. While there was considerable equality in rights of speaking and voting among citizens, citizenship was restricted to adult males. Women and slaves were excluded, and the slave labour freed citizens from work so they had time to attend the assembly. Modern democracies often appear to be highly egalitarian and open, but closer inspection can reveal distortions that are subversive of basic principles of equality and transparency. A variety of factors are responsible for this, but the main ones are set out here.

A genuinely egalitarian representative electoral system requires 'one vote one value' and majority rule. These principles are distorted through unequally sized electorates and through single member geographically based electorates that do not provide for overall proportional representation of voters. For example, imagine a system of proportional representation with a single large electorate and 100 members of parliament. An election results in Party A receiving 51% of the vote and Party B receiving 49%. This translates into 51 seats for Party A and 49 seats for Party B. Now imagine a parliament with 100 members elected from 100 single member electorates. In each electorate Party A receives 51% of the vote and Party B receives 49% of the vote. Party A wins in each electorate and therefore takes 100% of the seats. The single member system allows major parties to dominate parliaments, such as the lower houses of parliament in Australia at the federal and state level. The system excludes minor parties whose overall proportion of the vote does not translate into seats and fair representation. ('Optional preferential' voting arguably gives the best consensus outcome.)

Many electoral systems try to counter this distortion by adding an upper house elected by proportional representation. But even here things can go badly awry. In Australia, for example, at the federal level the whole of Australia does not form a multi-member electorate for the Senate (the upper house). Instead, a concern for states' rights means that each state and territory constitutes an electoral district. The states have 12 representatives each. To use the most extreme cases, as reported by the Australian Bureau of Statistics (ABS), this means that Tasmania, with a population of 490,000, has the same number of representatives in the Senate as New South Wales, with a population of 6,800,000 (2008, p. 181).

All sorts of other bizarre distortions can exist in electoral systems for anachronistic historical reasons. The United States presidential system is a prime example. Voters do not directly elect the President. They express a preference in a popular vote, but the real vote is made by a much smaller electoral college of persons elected (or appointed in some cases) on a state basis. One potential consequence of this is that the college vote does not match the popular vote. For example, in the year 2000 the winner in the election (George W. Bush) received 50,456,002 popular votes or 47.87%. The runner up (Al Gore) received 50,999,897 votes or 48.38% (Federal Election Commission, 2001).

Another distorting factor is the discipline of political party machines. Electors vote for individuals, not parties. But most candidates belong to parties that require loyalty in return for support. In some cases — such as the Australian Labor Party — representatives will be expelled from the Party if they do not vote in parliament according to the predetermined Party vote. Voting along popular lines or on scientific advice can lead to isolation and subsequent loss of a seat without Party support.

Candidates and elected representatives also hold personal agendas that they seek to put into practice through law and policy. This is an inversion of the idea of representation. In other words, politicians do not act as representatives of the people but seek to obtain sufficient votes to win power and then use the system to advance their own ideology.

Secrecy in government is a violation of the principle of democratic transparency. A genuine vote must be an informed vote. Voters cannot evaluate a government's performance, or a representative's performance, if they do not know how the government made decisions, what information was used, and how representatives argued and voted. Under cabinet government, especially in the Westminster system, cabinet is the real engine of government where the real decisions are made. These decisions are then usually ratified by the caucus (all members of parliament in the governing party), and the debate and vote in parliament is a mere formality. In many countries, cabinet and caucus proceedings are completely secret. Violations of cabinet secrecy are punishable by law.

A final example of electoral distortion occurs in constitutional monarchies that are blended systems of democracy and absolute monarchy. These systems often leave a reserve power to the monarch, but these reserve powers in law can be dictatorial. In Australia, an unelected hereditary monarch residing on the other side of the world (or their representatives) has the power over common-wealth and state parliaments to appoint and dismiss ministers (including the Prime Minister), appoint judges, veto parliamentary decisions, overturn laws, dissolve parliament, dismiss the Prime Minister, and command the military (*Commonwealth of Australia Constitution Act*).

Public Service Ethics

Modern ideas about large-scale bureaucratic public services derive from Imperial China via the Napoleonic centralisation of state power after the French Revolution. Post-revolutionary France removed inherited positions in government, replacing this with the idea of a dedicated professional public service and 'the career open to talent'. A key document in the development of public service standards was the Northcote–Trevelyan report of the mid-1800s in the United Kingdom (Northcote & Trevelyan, 1854). The inquiry that led to the report was prompted by a widespread sense that public admin-istration was corrupt, in a state of chaos and highly inefficient — most evi-dently in Britain's disastrous prosecution of the Crimean War. (The negligent treatment of wounded soldiers led to the legend of Florence Nightingale and the establishment of modern nursing.) The report noted that the public service was a refuge for many incompetent and unhealthy persons who did little work and lacked any vision for social improvement. The bureaucracy was plagued by delays, inaction, inefficiency and excessive sick leave.

The Northcote–Trevelyan report was also concerned with establishing 'a permanent civil service' to avoid major changes of staff when governments changed. A change of government should not require significant changes in public service personnel, and public service positions should not be used as rewards for supporters of political parties. The report recommended replacing patronage (appointment through a personal benefactor) with appointment by merit. Initial employment, the report observed, usually occurred as follows: 'The chief of the department … will probably bestow the office upon the son or dependent of some one having personal or political claims upon him, or perhaps upon the son of some meritorious public servant' (1854, p. 6).

Promotion occurred largely by a mechanical process of seniority. People moved up salary scales and simply took their turn to fill higher vacancies as they arose, or senior vacancies were filled from outside largely through patronage. There was little in the way of objective testing of abilities and previous achievements. Staff also tended to stay within narrow sections, with no internal transfers and little flexibility in moving people from redundant areas to new areas of demand. The recommendations regarding appoint-ment by merit involved selecting the best candidates on a competitive basis using standardised examinations, requiring medical certificates and ensuring probationary reports were more rigorous. The report emphasised how:

> To obtain full security for the public … none but qualified persons will be appointed, and … they will afterwards have every practicable inducement to the active discharge of their duties …
>
> The Government of the country could not be carried out without the aid of an efficient body of permanent officers, occupying a position duly subordinate to that of the Ministers who are directly responsible to the Crown and the Parliament, yet possessing sufficient independence, character, ability, and experience to be able to advise, assist, and, to some extent, influence, those who are from time to time set over them. (p. 2)

Public servants embody the power of the state. They are the hands, the muscles, and also the ears and eyes of government. Public service ethics are important because public servants have significant power to affect people's lives in beneficial or harmful ways — in the delivery of welfare payments and health and education services, in decisions about public transport and workplace safety, in issuing permits and licences, in enforcing the law and providing emergency assistance, and in setting regulatory standards and requirements in food, transport and medicines, to name some basic functions. In exercising this power, public servants frequently use considerable discretion. They have to interpret rules, and they can act zealously and responsibly or go as slowly as possible and be as uncooperative as possible. Public servants are not only responsible for putting government policy into action, but politicians are also frequently dependent on them for advice. In this capacity, public servants can act honestly and conscientiously, or they can hide information or give misleading information in a way that will benefit their own partisan purposes. Many readers will be familiar with the British television comedy series Yes Minister, which illustrates this problem. The plot revolves around the continual subversion of the good intentions of the elected official (Minister Jim Hacker) by the appointed permanent head of the department (Sir Humphrey Appleby).

In light of these issues, public service codes of ethics and rules have been developed and refined over the centuries. Core principles of modern public service normally include the following:

- impartiality
- efficiency
- transparency (while maintaining confidentiality with personal and commercial information)
- appointment by merit
- a prohibition on the use of office for personal gain.

The following illustrates these principles from an exemplar code: the UN *International Code of Conduct for Public Officials* (1996). The sections cover many of the topics expected in a code: public interest, democratic authority, lawfulness, attitudes, gratuities, information management, conflicts of interest and the political activities of public servants.

I. GENERAL PRINCIPLES

1. A public office, as defined by national law, is a position of trust, implying a duty to act in the public interest. Therefore, the ultimate loyalty of public officials shall be to the public interests of their country as expressed through the democratic institutions of government.

2. Public officials shall ensure that they perform their duties and functions efficiently, effectively and with integrity, in accordance with laws or administrative policies. They shall at all times seek to ensure that public resources for which they are responsible are administered in the most effective and efficient manner.

3. Public officials shall be attentive, fair and impartial in the performance of their functions and, in particular, in their relations with the public. They shall at no time afford any undue preferential treatment to any group or individual or improperly discriminate against any group or individual, or otherwise abuse the power and authority vested in them.

II. CONFLICT OF INTEREST AND DISQUALIFICATION

4. Public officials shall not use their official authority for the improper advancement of their own or their family's personal or financial interest. They shall not engage in any transaction, acquire any position or function or have any financial, commercial or other comparable interest that is incompatible with their office, functions and duties or the discharge thereof.

5. Public officials, to the extent required by their position, shall, in accordance with laws or administrative policies, declare business, commercial and financial interests or activities undertaken for financial gain that may raise a possible conflict of interest. In situations of possible or perceived conflict of interest between the duties and private interests of public officials, they shall comply with the measures established to reduce or eliminate such conflict of interest.

6. Public officials shall at no time improperly use public moneys, property, services or information that is acquired in the performance of, or as a result of, their official duties for activities not related to their official work.

7. Public officials shall comply with measures established by law or by administrative policies in order that after leaving their official positions they will not take improper advantage of their previous office.

III. DISCLOSURE OF ASSETS

8. Public officials shall, in accord with their position and as permitted or required by law and administrative policies, comply with requirements to declare or to disclose personal assets and liabilities, as well as, if possible, those of their spouses and/or dependants.

IV. ACCEPTANCE OF GIFTS OR OTHER FAVOURS

9. Public officials shall not solicit or receive directly or indirectly any gift or other favour that may influence the exercise of their functions, the performance of their duties or their judgment.

V. CONFIDENTIAL INFORMATION

10. Matters of a confidential nature in the possession of public officials shall be kept confidential unless national legislation, the performance of duty or the needs of justice strictly require otherwise. Such restrictions shall also apply after separation from service.

VI. POLITICAL ACTIVITY

11. The political or other activity of public officials outside the scope of their office shall, in accordance with laws and administrative policies, not be such as to impair public confidence in the impartial performance of their functions and duties.

These code positions blend formalist and utilitarian ethics. The ideas of impartiality, non-discrimination and lawfulness are essentially formalist. The emphasis on the public interest and democratic obligations appear more utilitarian. The UN code is a relatively short example. Other codes add sections on reporting misconduct (whistleblowing), whistleblower protection, secondary employment, supervisor accountability, political campaigning, tendering processes and public–private partnerships, communications with clients, dealing with lobbyists, and public comment (e.g., Australian Government, 2008; Council of Europe, 2000).

Strengthening Democratic Accountability

Codes of conduct for public servants provide one mechanism for enhancing democratic accountability, especially when the codes are enforceable through disciplinary tribunals and other mechanisms. As we have seen, equity in electoral systems is also essential to establishing democratic accountability. However, were the operations of democracy confined to these two pillars — regular elections and codes of conduct — accountability would still be very limited. Politicians could engage in all sorts of unpopular and destructive actions in their term of office and then be cast out, but significant and irreparable harm could have been perpetrated in the meantime. Consequently, there are a variety of supplemental mechanisms that are essential to buttress the core electoral process to ensure permanent accountability in government:

- A 'separation of powers' is required across key institutions to prevent the monopolisation of power. The primary separation is between the legislature, executive and judiciary. The legislature makes the law, while the executive (primarily the public service) carries it out and the judiciary interprets it.
- Community input is required outside elections through consultative committees and open forums, public opinion surveys, opportunities to make submissions on current issues, and referendums on key issues.
- An appeals system allows citizens who are aggrieved by a public service decision to seek independent review. Forums include internal departmental boards, ombudsman departments and the court hierarchy.
- Departments need to be subject to regular independent financial audits.
- Freedom of information legislation allows citizens access to information held on them, as well as information relevant to administrative decisions that affect them and more general information related to government decisions.
- An independent anti-corruption agency is essential to monitor ethical issues in government departments with a substantive capacity to investigate matters and engage in disciplinary decisions and prosecutions.

A Rogues' Gallery: Unethical Conduct in the Public Sector

We have already seen many of the ways in which democracy can be deeply subverted by distortions in electoral systems. Public service can also be abused and distorted, both legally and illegally. The Northcote–Trevelyan report of 1854 was cited earlier in this chapter as a progressive watershed report. But it only ever envisaged the employment of men in the public service. The existence of women was not even acknowledged. For centuries, public service entailed a deep injustice by legally excluding half the population. The Northcote–Trevelyan report, opposed as it was to patronage, was also blind to the class bias entailed in its recommendations for open examinations. In the 20th century the British public service was increasingly seen as a 'closed shop'. The working class was poorly represented, with the public service dominated by the graduates of private schools and elite universities (Dodd, 1967). Hidden biases like these involve examples of structural discrimination or 'systemic abuses'. Other abuses involve acts by individuals or small groups that are more patently illegal or unethical and result in some type of conviction in a judicial proceeding or condemnation in an official report. The following provides a list of types of 'integrity violations' that are normally prohibited in codes of conduct and laws governing public service (as cited in van Delden, Van de Wouw, & Van der Veer,

2008, p. 192). They articulate the negative side of the coin of public service ethics. The list is used by the Integrity Bureau of the City of Amsterdam.

- *conflict of (private and public) interest:* personal interest (through assets, jobs, gifts, etc.) interferes (or might interfere) with public interest;
- *fraud and theft:* improper private gain acquired from the organization (with no involvement of external actors);
- *corruption:* bribing: misuse of public power for private gain; asking, offering, accepting bribes;
- *misuse and manipulation of (the access to) information:* lying, cheating, manipulating information, breaching confidentiality of information;
- incompatible functions/activities;
- *improper use of authority (for noble causes):* to use illegal/improper methods to achieve organizational goals (within the police for example illegal methods if investigation and disproportionate violence);
- *waste and abuse of resources:* failure to comply with organizational standards, improper performance, incorrect or dysfunctional internal behaviour;
- *discrimination and sexual harassment:* misbehaviour towards colleagues or citizens and customers;
- *private time misconduct:* excessive serious misconduct in one's private time which has repercussions on one's job, and/or harms the public's trust in the administration/government.

The following snapshots provide a very small number of examples of misconduct, or alleged unethical conduct, by politicians and public servants from Australia and overseas, covering many of these categories. They partially illustrate the breadth of misbehaviour and something of the audacity of many offenders.

- On his last day of office in 2001 US President Bill Clinton used his executive authority to issue 140 pardons to persons convicted for offences that included drug trafficking, fraud and corruption. One of the beneficiaries was his half-brother, Roger Clinton, who had been convicted of drug offences. Other beneficiaries were on the run from authorities and some had made donations to Clinton's campaigns. Although legal, the pardons were widely condemned as unethical. (Schorr, 2001)
- In 2005 the Deputy Mayor and acting Mayor of San Diego, Michael Zucchet, and a Councillor, Ralph Inzunza, were found guilty in a federal court of accepting a bribe from a strip club owner. The owner of Cheetahs Totally Nude Club, Michael Galardi, wanted the law changed to allow nude dancers to touch clients. FBI phone taps revealed that the bribe was made in the form of a US$23,000 campaign donation in return for a commitment to seek to alter the regulations. (Perry & Marosi, 2005)

- In 1995 Secretary-General of NATO Willy Claes was forced to resign after he was accused of bribery in relation to a military contract when he was economics minister in the Belgium government. He, and former Belgian defence minister Guy Coeme, were later found guilty of corruption. The court determined that donations of approximately US$3 million made to their Socialist Party from aviation companies Agusta SpA and Dassault were in return for contracts worth US$520 million. (Trueheart, 1998)

- In early 2009 Rod Blagojevich was sacked as Illinois Governor by the state senate after he was arrested on multiple corruption charges in an influence peddling 'pay-to-play' scam. His scheming allegedly included an attempt to sell the senate seat vacated by the incoming US President Barack Obama. On one secretly recorded telephone tap, referring to the senate vacancy, Blagojevich was recorded saying, 'I've got this thing and it's f...king golden, and, uh, uh, I'm just not giving it up for f...king nothing'. (Goldenberg, 2008)

- In 2007 Paul Wolfowitz was forced to resign as president of the World Bank after it was revealed that he had arranged for his partner, Shaha Riza, to be promoted within the bank with a large tax-free salary increase. While at the bank he launched a campaign against corruption but was accused of repeatedly overriding appointment processes to install like-minded colleagues in key positions. He was allowed to exit with a US$400,000 performance bonus. (Donnelly, 2007)

- A 1992 report on 'travel rorts' by the Queensland Criminal Justice Commission found that in one state parliamentary term 54 members had been involved in 225 journeys of a questionable nature. The majority of members under suspicion were unable to recall what they did or provide any reasonable explanations for the trips. Many of the journeys were transparently for personal reasons such as family holidays. One of those involved, Terry Mackenroth, travelled with his wife to Sydney at taxpayers' expense in order to coach his netball team who were playing in a national competition. He later became state treasurer. (Criminal Justice Commission, 1992; Targett, 2001)

- A 2008 report by the New South Wales Independent Commission Against Corruption (ICAC) found that two project managers in the New South Wales fire department, Christian Sanhueza and Clive Taylor, had acted corruptly. The men manipulated tendering processes to ensure that a company controlled by Sanhueza won contracts for maintenance and capital works. Between them the two made a profit of approximately AU$2.4 million. (ICAC, 2008)

- In 1992 the ICAC found that New South Wales Premier Nick Greiner and Minister Tim Moore acted corruptly by offering a plum public service directorship to Terry Metherell in exchange for his resignation from a safe Liberal seat that the government hoped to regain. Greiner and Moore were obliged to resign from their portfolios and then from their seats. (ICAC, 1992)

- In 1997 *The Courier-Mail* revealed that heads of Queensland government departments had repeatedly flouted public service standards and accepted gifts from companies tendering for work. Kevin Davies, Director-General of the Public Works and Housing Department, 'accepted free tickets to the Three Tenors concert from Telstra and was accused of later granting the telecommunications company a AU$200,000 contract' (Metcalf, 1997, p. 3). Davies was also accused of using his departmental credit card to pay for accommodation in Melbourne while attending the performance. Despite a promise by Premier Rob Borbidge (Murray, 2004, p. 21) to tighten the rules, a 2004 investigation by *The Sunday Mail* used freedom of information law to obtain details of numerous gifts paid to senior public servants. Denis Luttrell, Director of the Police Service's Information Management Division, received 82 gifts in five years — including numerous free golf games, theatre tickets and tickets to sporting events — all from companies seeking business with the police.

- In 2009 *The Australian* revealed that former federal minister Larry Anthony was paid AU$65,000 a year as a director on the Board of failed childcare company ABC Learning. His private consulting company was also paid AU$235,000 to lobby governments. As Minister for Community Services, and then Children and Youth Affairs, in the Howard government Anthony had been responsible for the policy of privatisation that allowed ABC Learning to use taxpayer-funded vouchers, worth billions of dollars, to rapidly expand its operations before it collapsed in 2008. (Bita, 2009)

Implications for Criminal Justice

Criminal justice is a subset of government and therefore subject to the same basic standards and accountabilities that apply to the whole public sector. However, it could be argued that public service ethics are most imperative in this component of government. Most government departments require people to act in certain ways, but often the process is persuasive or coercive. In criminal justice there is much greater reliance on direct force. Criminal laws and related legislation authorise government agents to deprive people of their liberty, to subject them to trial and judgment, and forcibly punish or coercively treat them — often for extended periods of time. Some systems even authorise the execution of offenders. Clearly these are enormous powers with significant potential consequences for good or ill for ordinary citizens.

Another area of difference between the main body of the public service and criminal justice agencies is in the degree of line control by a minister. Criminal justice departments or units, especially the police, courts and public prosecutors' and defenders' offices, generally require a greater degree of independence from politicians — or a separation of powers — than other government departments (Prenzler & Sarre, 2009, pp. 262–263). Police commissioners are more likely to have a leading role than other department heads, where the minister will be more prominent. With so much at stake in the courts, it is particularly important that decisions by judges and magistrates are made independently of any perceived or real influence from ministers or other politicians. The same applies to public defenders' officers. Most decisions about prosecutions should also be independent of government, although in some cases ministers have a right to direct prosecutions or appeals in the public interest.

The responsibilities and accountabilities that apply to criminal justice professionals occupy the remainder of this book. The democratic chain of delegated authority and public service ethics are fundamental to understanding the requirements and complexities of criminal justice ethics.

Conclusion

Criminal justice personnel are authorised to use direct force against citizens. They have the capacity to shame people with the label of criminal guilt, to extract monetary fines or impose compensation orders, and to deprive people of their liberty, often for extended periods of time. Inevitably the only source of legitimacy for these powers is the whole body politic. Consequently, legitimacy in criminal justice is dependent on legitimacy in government, and legitimacy in government requires the clear consent and participation of the body politic. In larger human groupings there is a practical rationale for representative government, but its legitimacy requires equal and fair votes and high levels of direct input by citizens. Other conditions include transparency, a strict and enforceable public service code of conduct that emphasises neutrality in service, independent administrative appeals and financial audit systems, freedom of information, and a well resourced, independent and capable anti-corruption commission.

SECTION ONE

Police

Chapter 2

Police Ethics

This is the first of three chapters on the police. The present chapter focuses on ethical issues and standards. Subsequent chapters deal with police corruption and corruption prevention. Policing is an occupation fraught with temptations and pressures for misconduct that present practitioners with numerous difficult choices in their day-to-day work. The chapter begins by briefly discussing what police do, the value of that work to society and the importance of police doing their job properly. The discussion is set within the framework of police political legitimacy. The chapter then identifies the different types of dilemmas police face, the competing issues involved and the principles developed to guide police conduct. The dilemmas are grouped around the topics of discretion, due process, bribes and gratuities, loyalty, use of force, confidentiality, personal conduct and cooperation between agencies.

The standards generally accepted as applying in these cases are taken from well-known codes from the UN and the International Association of Chiefs of Police (IACP). These codes emphasise the importance of impartiality in the allocation of police services and in enforcement of the law, compliance with due process, rejection of graft and gifts, the necessity of internal whistleblowing, use of minimum force, maintenance of confidentiality, high personal standards and willing cooperation. The chapter also makes some suggestions for improving these codes to more precisely define expected behaviours and cover more issues.

The Importance of Police Ethics and Accountability

The role of police is usually summarised in terms of enforcing the law, preventing crime, maintaining order and providing emergency assistance. This means that police are charged with the responsibility of protecting people from assault, sexual assault, murder, robbery, theft, extortion, kidnapping, fraud and many other types of threats to their property and wellbeing, as well as assisting at accidents and other emergencies. Police also have a duty to assist in minimising people's fear of crime, because concern about crime can have a constraining effect on people's liberty and their state of mind. This function is sometimes referred to as 'reassurance policing' (Innes, 2004). In a modern democracy that values personal freedom police provide an essential service. They are a truly vital institution in the realisation of universal human values of security, safety, freedom, equity, justice and the right to enjoy the fruits of one's labour.

Public sector policing of the type we know today is only a very recent invention. A key date is 1829, when the 'New Police' were established in London. Before then governments lacked any general capacity to provide consistent crime prevention and law enforcement services to citizens. Ad hoc or customary arrangements — such as nightwatchmen, militia or sheriffs — were usually uneven, discriminatory, highly inadequate and often corrupt and even brutal (Johnston, 1992). Now, in many countries, a person can pick up a phone and have a police officer rush to their location to provide assistance. The speed and quality of responses is highly variable, but the basic service is in place as a mainstay of public safety in any modern civilised society.

Police are given a variety of tools to do their job. They obviously have a power of arrest and a right to use force. However, this authority is based in citizen powers. Generally speaking, what makes police different to ordinary citizens is that they can usually exercise these powers with a higher level of protection if they make mistakes, and they can usually intervene with a lower level of evidence of criminal acts or the intent to commit criminal acts (Leaver, 1997, p. 131ff). It is easy to believe police have enormous discretionary authority, given television dramas that show police in high speed pursuits through city streets, threatening suspects or entering property at will. However, there are numerous legal and regulatory restrictions on police, which in part underlie the dilemmas they face. What is possibly the most significant aspect of police work is not so much any powers they hold above those of ordinary citizens, but the fact they are specifically tasked with law enforcement — that is, they are employed, trained and equipped to enforce the law. They carry weaponry that can be used to threaten, restrain, incapacitate, injure and kill. They are required to locate, arrest (or summons), detain and prosecute offenders. They are tasked with responding rapidly to calls for assistance, and they are expected to develop strategies for preventing crime. Their actions therefore have enormous impacts on people's freedoms and on the experience of justice of numerous stakeholders, including victims of crime, suspects, witnesses and the general public.

At the same time that police are required to multi-task and follow strict regulations, they inevitably exercise significant discretion (Pollock, 2007, p. 205ff). For example, they must prioritise competing requests for assistance in regard to variable harms and threats, while operating under resource limitations. They must decide whether or not to put additional resources into unproductive inquiries or focus on fresh cases. They must decide whether or not to prioritise street crime over white-collar crime or vice versa. There are innumerable other choices like this that need to be made on a daily basis and on a long-range strategic basis.

At the same time, it must be kept in mind that, in theory at least, police carry out these tasks as agents of the whole community. They are public servants whose authority to act comes from citizens and the democratic process. They are part of the chain of delegated authority by which authority is transmitted from the people to the parliament, to the government, police minister, police chief, the police department and front line officers, and back to the people. Police therefore operate with 'authority', combined with 'power' and 'discretion', and this sets the context for ethical issues and the need for tight accountability systems (Pollock, 2007, pp. 193–195). Authority can be abused. Discretion can be exercised in a biased fashion. Added to this, as the next chapter shows, policing is arguably unique in the variety of temptations and pressures for misconduct that occur in routine work: in offers of bribes, for example; in the temptation to fabricate evidence; in provocations to engage in assault; or in the build-up in frustration and disillusionment that can lead to neglect of duty and acceptance of illicit perks.

Policing in Unequal Societies

The legitimacy of the police resides in their democratically delegated authority, premised on a principle of equal service to all citizens, mediated through a 'triage' system by which more harmful and urgent crime threats are prioritised over others. In theory, all citizens should receive equal protection relative to risk. The problem, however, is that modern societies are far from equal in the amount of property and power held by citizens, and therefore the amount of protection they receive from police. Concepts of police legitimacy are deeply challenged by social inequality. Left-wing critics argue that traditional policing misdirects state resources away from the social causes of crime, and that police persecute the poor and marginalised who turn to crime as a consequence of poverty and alienation (White, 1998). Worse still, while police may go about their day-to-day activities responding to calls from ordinary citizens, they in fact have a dual role as a reserve army for the ruling class. In modern liberal democracies the ruling class consists mainly of the owners of private capital. When their power is threatened by strikes and demonstrations police are called in to repress dissent and short-circuit reform by breaking up public protests and locking up demonstrators.

Does this mean we should turn our backs on police as lacking any genuinely useful purpose for ordinary citizens? The situation in many societies is much more complex than this and does not justify a simple denunciation of police as exclusive agents of ruling elites. Although deeply flawed, liberal democracies include complex processes for re-setting equality of opportunity and preventing poverty through wealth transfers, public education and health, and social services. Poverty and inequality are key predictors of crime (van Dijk, 2008, chap. 5). At the same time, opportunity and individual psychological motives are also important (Gabor, 1994). Consequently, different types of opportunity reduction, incapacitation-oriented and deterrence-oriented techniques, which involve different types of police in frontline or back-up roles, remain important for preventing crime and protecting ordinary citizens.

Police are also engaged in one of the most egalitarian and direct forms of democracy in responding to calls for assistance regardless of the status of the caller. In these terms Michael Buerger (1998) makes a useful argument about the *variability* of police legitimacy. Drawing on the social contract theory of government (see chapter 8 of this book), he argues that: 'Police authority is weakest when officers act on their own initiative, and strongest when they act on behalf of citizens requesting assistance' (Buerger, 1998, p. 93). We can in fact evaluate police work in this regard by analysing the nature and origins of calls to police and the speed and outcomes of police responses. Overall, police authority, public dependence and police discretion make accountability an issue of critical importance. The more policing is biased in favour of one group, or the more police abuse their position to benefit themselves, the less legitimate and the more harmful they become.

Police in non-democratic societies face a particular dilemma in that their position has no formal authority from the people. While in many cases they may appear to have a mission to serve citizens equally, in reality their first duty is much more explicitly and tangibly to serve the ruling elite by acting against opposition groups and popular demonstrations and revolts. Police are clearly more in position as the enemies of the people than the servants of the people. However, even in these circumstances, Buerger's concept of variable legitimacy has application. Individual police and police managers in non-democratic states can seek to exercise what discretion they have in the interests of equitable crime prevention and law enforcement. In addition to exercising discretion in this way, police in authoritarian states also at times defy their masters and support popular movements when conditions are right. One of the most recent examples of this was the removal of the Milosevic regime in the '5th of October Overthrow' in Serbia in 2000. Police allowed protestors to overrun the parliament building and popular support forced the government's collapse (Glenny, 2000). Nonetheless, the capacity of police in non-democratic societies to act 'democratically' is highly variable and insecure, and in some repressive regimes choosing to work as a police officer might not be ethically justifiable at all.

Ethical Dilemmas in Policing

Policing is considered an occupation characterised by diverse ethical dilemmas and it is also described as an occupation where ethical dilemmas are most intense at the bottom ranks of the organisation (Findlay, 2004, p. 75). Ethical dilemmas in policing are difficult to avoid. Even when officers are determined to reject corruption, dilemmas still arise from competing choices about how to act in different situations. As we have seen in chapter 1, a dilemma, by definition, involves a difficult choice, with competing principles at play and competing goods and/or competing harms at stake. In some cases police may have to decide which is the least worst outcome. A good example is a hostage situation where delaying action may result in deaths but storming the location might also result in deaths. An estimation might have to be made about which strategy will result in the least deaths. Scholars have identified a set of classical ethical dilemmas for police (Pollock, 2007) that are outlined in the following sub-sections. Each sub-section includes a summary code position that reflects the generally accepted standards that should apply to police when negotiating these issues. The two codes used here are the UN *Code of Conduct for Law Enforcement Officials* (1979) and the *Law Enforcement Code of Ethics* from the IACP (2002).

Discretion

Figure 2.1 provides a model of a police discretion continuum that charts the main options for action usually available to police when they observe a probable offence. Also following is a scenario of a potential dilemma of discretion for police. The discretionary options are then applied to the scenario.

Discretion scenario

Two undercover officers in a downtown district are engaged in a crackdown of organised street solicitation for prostitution. Efforts are focused on organised prostitution. On the street they are accosted by a young woman who offers them sex for money. When the officers attempt to arrest the woman, she attacks them, hitting one of the officers across the face. After she is subdued she breaks down and starts crying. She says she is a heroin addict. Her boyfriend got her hooked and her parents threw her out of home. She is homeless and

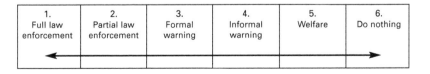

1. Full law enforcement	2. Partial law enforcement	3. Formal warning	4. Informal warning	5. Welfare	6. Do nothing

Figure 2.1 Police discretion continuum (Prenzler, 2006, p. 127). Reproduced with permission from Pearson Education Australia.

cannot keep a job because of her addiction. She does say, however, that her parents have agreed to pay for her to attend a private reha-bilitation clinic and she is booked in for the following week. Her ID shows she is 17, which means she is young but subject to prosecution as an adult. (Adapted from Prenzler, 2006, p. 127)

The contexts in which frontline officers are free to make decisions across the discretion continuum will vary in relation to this scenario. Theoretically, dis-cretion will be removed by direct orders to arrest all offenders or specific wording in legislation requiring arrest. But this does not mean a decision not to arrest will lead to a charge of breach of duty. Because the officers are acting without direct supervision the outcome of the encounter can remain confi-dential between the three individuals involved. With these caveats in mind we can consider the six options from the discretion continuum:

1. The officers might engage in full law enforcement by arresting the woman for solicitation, resisting arrest and assault of a police officer (one version of the colloquial expressions 'ham, cheese and tomato sandwich' or 'trifecta').

2. Alternatively, the officers might decide that the latter two charges were minor matters and simply arrest for solicitation.

3. They might decide, however, that arrest is a harsh and unproductive response given the woman's circumstances, the fact she is operating alone and the cost to taxpayers of the legal process. Or it might simply be that they do not want to have to be bothered with processing the case at the end of their shift. They could therefore decide to issue a warning, emphasising that a reoccurrence of the behaviour will automatically result in arrest. The caution might be official, with the woman's name going on a register.

4. Or the caution might be informal, without a record. The officers might simply tell the woman they will arrest her if they see her soliciting again.

5. Alternatively, the officers could decide that the best thing to do is to provide a 'harm minimisation' welfare response by immediately taking her to a nearby government clinic where her condition can be diagnosed with various treatment or management options made available, includ-ing a supervised injection program. The government clinic could also then liaise with the private clinic.

6. A final option is to do nothing, given that the woman appears to be outside the target of organised prostitution and that she has declared she is about to attend a private treatment program — or, again, because the officers want to go home.

Each of the six options available to police in the solicitation scenario carry dif-ferent potentially positive and negative consequences. Formalist ethics emphasises the need for the systematic rule of law and the importance of a retributive response to satisfy the demands of impersonal justice. The exercise of discretion allegedly results in inequalities and confusion. Hence in option 1 the categorical imperative demands that all breaches of law are prosecuted to ensure equal treatment for all persons and to prevent discrimination and favouritism. Option 2 is also formalist but watered down somewhat by reference to situational and mitigating factors. However, formalism is often considered inflexible, failing to take into account different personal circumstances, thereby creating injustices, and creating an impossible burden for the criminal justice system in prosecuting all breaches of the law.

The other options are primarily utilitarian. (There are also some self-interested aspects.) Those who take a utilitarian or situational approach to the scenario will consider the specific circumstances of the case and the consequences — especially in terms of public interest criteria. They might consider that anyone in the woman's position is as much a victim as a perpetrator of wrongs and should be provided with a welfare response. Some might argue that, in the long term, society is unlikely to benefit from prosecution and more likely to benefit from the treatment of drug addiction by way of improved public health and reduced crime and public nuisance behaviours. But how utilitarians apply these criteria, subject to evidence about the likely effects of different actions, might result in full law enforcement.

As noted in chapter 1, a complication with a utilitarian approach involves the difference between act and rule utilitarianism. Where officers' reasoning is governed by act utilitarianism they may feel that no immediate adverse consequences will follow from not arresting the woman. However, if they are more cognisant of the precedent — or rule — set down by their actions, they might feel that the general deterrent effect of prosecution is more important for public order, and for public welfare and the suppression of vice. Simply doing nothing out of self-interest is likely to put the woman back on the streets, only benefits the officers in the short term, and does not provide for either equity or 'the greatest good for the greatest number'.

Similar dilemmas of discretion apply across the range of police work: booking motorists for traffic offences, for example; or following up with possible witnesses to crimes and claiming overtime. Some support for formalist arguments against police officer discretion can be found in research. For example, as part of an attempt to improve ethics in the Queensland Police Service in the 1990s an ethical climate survey was conducted that surveyed police views on ethical issues. One set of questions concerned police responses to a discretion scenario involving a cafe owner who provides gratuities to local police and then is observed breaching a traffic law:

> Frank is a uniformed police officer in an under-resourced high crime area where officers on the night shift are particularly appreciative of the friendly service and free coffee and food provided by 'Teddy's shop'. Having been robbed twice in the past, Ted is appreciative of the regular police presence he receives. One night at 3.30am Ted is pulled over by Frank for running a red light. Frank is a regular at 'Teddy's' and the two have developed a good relationship. Ted apologises for the traffic breach and says 'Hey, you're not going to give your old mate here a ticket for a little thing like that are you?' (Adapted from Cohen & Feldberg, 1991, p. 110, as cited in Macintyre & Prenzler, 1999, p. 187)

This is a challenging scenario to evaluate. On the one hand, it would seem petty to ticket Frank at a time when there are likely to be few cars on the road and little likelihood of a crash. On the other hand, violations of traffic laws produce enormous suffering. Research suggests that law enforcement needs to produce a habit of compliance, even when 'no-one is watching'. The law in Queensland was clear that running a red light was a serious offence and that police were duty-bound to ticket all serious violations. However, what was of significance in the survey responses was that police were deeply divided over what they said they would do in response. A minority of 43% said they would write the ticket, while 57% said they would not. There was further divergence within these response categories. Of those who said they would write the ticket, some said they would continue to accept the hospitality, some said they would stop going to the shop and some said they would keep going to the shop but would start paying. Some who said they would not write the ticket said they would give a warning, others said they would not. Some of them said they would keep accepting the hospitality, others said they would not. Overall, this does not make for consistent application of the law or consistent police–community relations.

On the issue of the exercise of police discretion, the IACP code emphasises the centrality of the guiding principle of impartiality:

> A police officer shall perform all duties impartially, without favour or affection or ill will and without regard to status, sex, race, religion, political belief or aspiration. All citizens will be treated equally with courtesy, consideration and dignity. Officers will never allow personal feelings, animosities or friendships to influence official conduct. (IACP, 2002, p. 36)

What does this mean for the street solicitation scenario outlined earlier? The code allows for the exercise of discretion and does not promote the idea of a robot-like formalist prosecution of all offences. At the same time, it does not provide an off-the-shelf answer, but develops some important sub-principles that apply in such situations, including concepts of acting responsibly in the public interest with consistency and with an eye to maintaining community confidence in the police. By implication, these public service principles do not permit actions motivated by selfishness or laziness, but they emphasise the importance of taking mitigating and aggravating factors into account up to a point, along with a range of potential consequences:

> A police officer will use responsibly the discretion vested in his position and exercise it within the law. The principle of reasonableness will guide the officer's determinations, and the officer will consider all surrounding circumstances in determining whether any legal action shall be taken.
>
> Consistent and wise use of discretion, based on professional policing competence, will do much to preserve good relationships and retain the confidence of the public. There can be difficulty in choosing between conflicting courses of action. It is important to remember that a timely word of advice rather than arrest — which may be correct in appropriate circumstances — can be a more effective means of achieving a desired end. (IACP, 2002, p. 36)

In relation to the gratuities scenario — Teddy's shop — it is also difficult to assert only one course of action that follows from these principles. Given the earlier point about the importance of a habit of compliance with traffic laws, it could be argued that ticketing Ted is the right thing to do and a course of action that satisfies both formalist and utilitarian criteria. A registered formal warning might also be considered defensible if a second violation automatically triggered a ticket. At the same time, it is certainly the case that a decision influenced by the personal relationship and obligation related to gratuities is not acceptable for any exercise of discretion in Ted's favour.

Due Process, Including Deception and Entrapment

This is one of the best-known types of dilemmas in policing and provides a regular plot device in police dramas — usually by making a hero out of the 'can-do' officer who flouts the rules (Pollock, 2007, p. 274ff). The 'Dirty Harry syndrome' or 'noble cause corruption' occurs when officers adopt illegal or ethically dubious methods to obtain justice of some sort. Examples include coercing or torturing a suspect into admitting to a crime or revealing the whereabouts of a kidnapped person. Variants of this occur when police engage in deception — such as through pretending they have a right of entry to a premise or that suspects are required to cooperate with them. Undercover work is another example. Although usually legal for police, and something generally taken for granted as a legitimate component of policing, it does involve lying to people, including people who are not suspects. Another variant is that of 'stings'. These are often used when strong suspicions against a person cannot be proven by conventional investigative methods. Police will then resort to a simulation — such as using an undercover officer to offer drugs to a suspect — to catch them in the act with covert recording devices.

The issue of torture committed by 'the good guys' has come to prominence internationally in the post-9/11 War on Terror, mainly through the adoption of 'extraordinary rendition' techniques by security agencies in countries allied to the United States of America. Interrogation techniques — including hypothermia, sleep deprivation, nudity, stress positions, and partial drowning (waterboarding) — were justified in terms of saving innocent lives. Human rights groups branded the techniques as torture, and illegal under international agreements (Human Rights Watch, 2007, p. 531ff). A 2008 report by the US Senate Armed Services Committee (USSASC) found that President George W. Bush and White House Counsel and later Attorney-General, Alberto Gonzales, had authorised the torture program (USSASC, 2008). The value of the information gained by extraordinary rendition has never been openly reported. However, in a normal court of law any evidence obtained by such means would be inadmissible. This is partly for utilitarian reasons — to deter police and related security agencies from using illegal methods — but also because the veracity of any statement made under torture is highly questionable, given that the subject's main motivation is to end the pain and not necessarily to tell the truth. Article 5 of the UN code is unambiguous and categorical about rejecting 'torture' and any rationalisations for torture:

> No law enforcement official may inflict, instigate or tolerate any act of torture or other cruel, inhuman or degrading treatment or punishment, nor may any law enforcement official invoke superior orders or exceptional circumstances such as a state of war or a threat of war, a threat to national security, internal political instability or any other public emergency as a justification of torture. (UN, 1979, p. 2)

The UN code reflects a formalist position that prohibits all such actions because coercion cannot be made into precedents for normal human relations. The same can be said for deception and entrapment. People may be willing to apply it to others but do not want it applied to them. It follows that policing needs to proceed by a standard investigative process that values the presumption of innocence and does not use torture or deception or put temptation in people's way. Utilitarians, on the other hand, are likely to argue that the higher goals of justice and public safety may justify some breaches of common ethical standards — such as the dishonesty entailed in undercover operations — under strictly controlled conditions that emphasise minimising risks of both a physical and emotional nature.

Most police ethicists argue that any benefits to be had from illegal means — such as finding the location of a serious criminal by torturing an accomplice — are difficult to justify and entail the potential for serious miscarriages of justice (Kleinig, 2008). Thus Article 4 of the IACP code, 'Utilization of Proper Means to Gain Proper Ends', also states categorically that:

The law enforcement officer shall be mindful of his responsibility to pay strict heed to the selection of means in discharging the duties of his office … The employment of illegal means, no matter how worthy the end, is certain to encourage disrespect for the law and its officers. If the law is to be honoured, it must first be honoured by those who enforce it. (2002, p. 38)

Contrary to this, some ethicists, such as John Kleinig (2008), concede that situations might arise where serious harms can only be averted by the less serious harm of a degree of torture inflicted on an individual or small number of persons. An example is the question of intervention in a 'ticking bomb' scenario — when urgent action is needed to save lives. Kleinig argues, however, that law and policy should disavow this option in terms of any kind of 'advance directive' (p. 46) because that could open the door to the use of torture as a common, even routine, police practice, which, by extension, would threaten the safety of all persons.

Bribes and Gratuities

A police officer may be offered cash with the explicit purpose that they will not prosecute the person supplying the money. This is clearly a bribe, prohibited by criminal law. However, an officer who is normally conscientious and honest might be tempted if (1) the protection money relates to a seemingly innocuous offence such as low level illegal gambling or small time prostitution, and (2) the officer feels they are deserving in some way — such as having a chronically ill spouse and a large family to support. In such cases there is a conflict between a formalist duty to uphold the law 'without fear or favour' and a utilitarian principle regarding relative benefits and harms to different groups of people. However, a rule utilitarian approach is likely to reject any type of corruption because minor corruption opens up 'a slippery slope' in the form of a precedent for further and more serious forms of corruption. Minor bribes also add up over the long term to make for large amounts of money. and there is usually a question mark over the alleged 'harmlessness' of any activities protected by graft. Codes therefore follow an absolutist formalist position that is also consistent with a utilitarian position: 'Law enforcement officials shall not commit any act of corruption. They shall also rigorously oppose and combat all such acts' (UN, 1979, p. 4).

A police officer may also be offered a discount meal by a cafe or restaurant owner in a situation where the intentions of the person offering the benefit are more ambiguous. The intention might simply be to express appreciation for the fact police do a difficult job (a genuine gratuity), or it might entail the expectation that police will exercise discretion in their favour by overlooking offences by the cafe owner or providing better security by frequenting the cafe (something more like a bribe). Ethically, the idea of showing appreciation is used to justify the arrangement. But the research evidence shows that the intention behind many types of gratuities offered to police is usually to obtain cheap security in violation of the principle of equitable service (Macintyre & Prenzler, 1999). One study in the United States found that stores offering gratuities received a disproportionate, if limited, amount of police presence (Wells & DeLeon-Granados, 1998). According to public opinion surveys, gratuities create a perception of biased or potentially biased policing in favour of the people providing the benefits. The public limit their tolerance to very minor and incidental gifts, such as a drink of water or cup of coffee outside a commercial context (Jones, 1997; Prenzler & Mackay, 1995; Sigler & Dees, 1988). Gratuities are also seen as an unfair 'private or special advantage' that derives from the 'official status' of police (IACP, 2002, p. 7).

A related area of ethical consideration is that of corporate gifts. Sponsorships and donations can be a means of boosting police resources in the public interest but they need to be carefully vetted to ensure there are no real or apparent obligations on police. Gifts related to tendering processes, on the other hand, are completely unacceptable. Police are large customers of private sector suppliers in areas such as motor vehicles, computers and weapons (Ayling & Grabosky, 2006). Common commercial practices of companies 'wining and dining' clients and offering gifts, such as theatre tickets and seats at sporting events, are transparently intended to court personal preferences (see chapter 1, pp. 18 and 22). As a public service agency, police must absolutely stand above such influence peddling. Offending gift givers is a small price to pay for probity.

With considerations like these in mind, the IACP position on gifts and favours is uncompromising, based on the assumption that the giving and receiving of gifts always creates a bond between the two subjects. Article 9 states that:

> The law enforcement officer … shall … guard against placing himself in a position in which any person can expect special consideration or in which the public can reasonably assume that special consideration is being given. Thus, he should be firm in refusing gifts, favours, or gratuities, large or small, which can, in the public mind, be interpreted as capable of influencing his judgment in the discharge of his duties. (IACP, 2002, p. 39)

The wider implication of this position is that the appearance of a conflict of interest must be avoided as much as possible, not just conflict of interest that results in any type of neglect of duty (Davids, 2008, p. 252).

Loyalty

Police work is one of those occupations where danger and stress create a special bond between members of the inside group. Police officers need to rely on colleagues to protect them in the variety of life-threatening situations that police can encounter. More generally, the fact that many of the people they deal with are hostile means that they need to look to each other for emotional support. Loyalty to colleagues therefore readily becomes a subcultural ethical principle that overrides the rule of law and the public interest (Mollen, 1994, p. 51ff). Informing on colleagues entails a breach of the informal subcultural ethical standard and police can readily become torn between pressure from colleagues to keep silent and their duty to reveal the truth and help stop corruption. The pressure to remain silent can be extremely intense and can mutate from normal peer pressure (often unspoken) to deliberate ostracism, physical intimidation and threats (Fitzgerald, 1989, pp. 202–205).

Article 8 of the UN code emphasises the need for police to report all suspected misconduct:

> Law enforcement officials who have reason to believe that a violation of the present Code has occurred or is about to occur shall report the matter to their superior authorities and, where necessary, to other appropriate authorities or organs vested with reviewing or remedial power. (1979, p. 4)

Although this is presented as a categorical imperative, the code recognises the various risks that police might face from making disclosures. The risks include the fact that the persons receiving the report might be corrupt themselves or might leak the information to corrupt cronies. The code therefore allows an option of reporting to the media when officers do not trust government agencies. The code also stresses the need for management to ensure that no repercussions occur against the whistleblower.

Use of Force

Police may be required to apply forms of physical restraint to apprehend offenders, protect people or affect a lawful direction. These actions can range from yelling, pushing or grabbing; through pinning arms or tackling people, applying capsicum spray or a taser charge, hitting with a baton or engaging in a high speed vehicle pursuit; up to the use of deadly force — usually by shooting a person. If insufficient force is used, offenders can escape justice and victims of crime or police themselves can be hurt. Censure is likely to follow. But it is also easy to use too much force, also resulting in hurt or even death. Excessive force may attract criticism and disciplinary action. The split-second nature of many of these decisions makes them particularly acute.

Given the significant risk of excessive force in police work, and that force directly contradicts the principle of individual freedom, codes of conduct stress the importance of police always using minimal force, proportionate to the threat or gravity of the offence, and using force as an absolute last resort. Article 3 of the UN code states that:

> Law enforcement officials may use force only when strictly necessary and to the extent required for the performance of their duty.

(a) This provision emphasizes that the use of force by law enforcement officials should be exceptional; while it implies that law enforcement officials may be authorized to use force as is reasonably necessary under the circumstances for the prevention of crime or in effecting or assisting in the lawful arrest of offenders or suspected offenders, no force going beyond that may be used. (1979, p. 2)

The code also singles out firearms as a type of weapon that requires particular restraint:

The use of firearms is considered an extreme measure. Every effort should be made to exclude the use of firearms, especially against children. In general, firearms should not be used except when a suspected offender offers armed resistance or otherwise jeopardizes the lives of others and less extreme measures are not sufficient to restrain or apprehend the suspected offender. In every instance in which a firearm is discharged, a report should be made promptly to the competent authorities. (1979, p. 2)

Confidentiality

Another area where police might be tempted to break the rules relates to the protection of confidential information. Consider the following scenario: a police officer's good neighbour is suspicious about their child's babysitter and wants to know if they have a police record in relation to child abuse and paedophilia. Should the officer look up the person on the police computer? It would seem that privacy is less a consideration here than child safety. However, open access to police data contains numerous risks. Data can be misused to harass people or pursue a vendetta, or to discriminate unfairly against people. Consequently, strict protocols on access and dissemination are required. The commentary on Article 4 of the UN code states that:

Law enforcement officials obtain information which may relate to private lives or be potentially harmful to the interests, and especially the reputation, of others. Great care should be exercised in safeguarding and using such information, which should be disclosed only in the performance of duty or to serve the needs of justice. Any disclosure of such information for other purposes is wholly improper. (1979, p. 2)

While we might think of exceptional cases this is not an area where police should be allowed an 'advance directive' to make disclosures. Public access to criminal records is a larger policy issue that should be dealt with through an officially structured process, not left to the discretion of individual police officers.

Personal Conduct

Should police be subject to a higher standard of personal behaviour as custodians of the law and role models to the community? For example, should a police officer who is caught committing serious traffic offences off duty be dismissed from their employment? A formalist notion of equal justice would say 'no'. But the argument that police hold a special position in the community is used to justify additional sanctions, including dismissal for actions deemed to bring the profession into disrepute. The IACP is uncompromising on this issue:

> Police officers will behave in a manner that does not bring discredit to their agencies or themselves. A police officer's character and conduct while off duty must always be exemplary, thus maintaining a position of respect in the community in which he or she lives and serves. The officer's personal behaviour must be beyond reproach. (2002, p. 37)

An example of this issue occurred in an Australian country town in 1989, attracting national and international media attention. Two New South Wales police officers attended a fancy dress party with a 'bad taste' theme in the town of Eromanga in south-west Queensland. The off-duty officers had blackened their faces, wore imitation nooses in a parody of Aboriginal deaths in custody, and referred to themselves as Lloyd Boney and David Gundy. Boney had committed suicide in a police cell and Gundy had been shot dead in a police raid. A private video of the party, which surfaced in 1992, stirred outrage in many quarters. Critics labelled the officers' behaviour as deeply offensive, and called for their sacking as an example to all police that racism would not be tolerated. However, the President of the Police Association of New South Wales defended the officers. He said they should apologise, but that their actions were symptomatic of lack of government action on social problems. He also said that critics were overreacting to a 'misguided comedy sketch', and that this type of humour was a way of relieving the high levels of stress experienced by police. Following an investigation, the officers were transferred to Sydney and ordered to undergo a training program and two years of close supervision (Cornwall, 1992; *Straits Times*, 1992).

Cooperation Between Policing Agencies

Another staple plot element of police dramas is conflict between police agencies, such as local police and the FBI in the United States. There is some basis to these fictional scenarios, and rivalries and lack of communication between agencies have been responsible for major law enforcement disasters (Prenzler, 2009, chap. 1). The problem is partly manifested in attempts by one agency to monopolise a crime problem and claim the credit. But it can also involve 'buck-passing', where no-one wants responsibility for a crime problem. Hence the IACP code states that: 'Police officers will cooperate with all legally authorized agencies and their representatives in the pursuit of justice … It is imperative that a police officer assist colleagues fully and completely with respect and consideration at all times' (2002, p. 37).

Miscellaneous

Police also face a range of other dilemmas. Going on strike may entail a conflict between support for a legitimate industrial demand versus exposing the public to danger by withdrawing police services. Moonlighting is another. Police may wish to improve their income by working in private security, as one example, but this may present conflicts of interest in the form of temptations to use confidential information or exercise police powers when working in a private capacity. The treatment of prisoners can also present dilemmas. Officers might be tempted to deny basic necessities to inmates who they dislike or they may feel they have more pressing priorities. 'Sweating' a prisoner by denying them necessities and information can be designed to weaken their resistance to interrogation. Special care needs to be taken to prevent prisoners committing suicide. Because of the power differential involved between the two groups — police and prisoners — and the risks of harm in custody, the UN code has a separate Article stating that: 'Law enforcement officials shall ensure the full protection of the health of persons in their custody and, in particular, shall take immediate action to secure medical attention whenever required' (UN, 1979, Article 6). The section includes a requirement for police to defer to the opinion of medical professionals on prisoner health and welfare issues.

Updating Codes

This chapter has drawn on two well-known international codes of conduct for police. These are codes that have considerable longevity and universal application. However, they are not immune from the need for some refinement. The UN code is particularly in need of updating in light of the post-9/11 War on Terror. For example, the definition of torture employed in the code is weak, confined to 'severe pain or suffering' (1979, p. 3). The codes also do not address issues of labour strikes, secondary employment, and whether or not police can legitimately remain anonymous when informing on colleagues.

Conclusion

This chapter has discussed the main ethical dilemmas faced by operational police and police managers. It has highlighted the range and complexity of these areas of often very difficult decision-making. The next chapter on police corruption elaborates on the negative aspect of police ethics: when police make the wrong ethical choices. The chapter after that, on police integrity management and accountability, sets out practical strategies to ensure ethical behaviour is a matter of normal practice for police. That mission begins with the establishment of clear standards about the conduct expected of police, as set out in this chapter.

Chapter 3

Police Corruption and Misconduct

In 1975 an English court sentenced Gerry Conlon, aged 21, to life imprisonment for murder in a terrorist bombing. Surrey police officers held Conlon in custody without charge, deprived him of sleep and the basic necessities of life, repeatedly threatened his family and beat him until he signed a false confession. His conviction was overturned and he was released from jail in 1989 (see chapter 6). Conlon's troubles with the police had started when he was a young man growing up in an anti-government republican family in the strife-torn city of Belfast, where police formed a powerful anti-republican force. In his autobiography he described one of his encounters with the local constabulary:

> When I was thirteen I was standing in the hall of a chemist's shop in the Falls Road with a boy called Gerry McAnoy. We were waiting for a friend by the name of Kieren O'Neill to arrange a football match with him, and it was pissing down with rain. Suddenly this big black Zephyr car drew up and two RUC [Royal Ulster Constabulary] men got out and asked us what we were doing. When we told them, they said, 'No, we think you're loitering with intent [to commit a crime].' And I said, 'What does loitering mean, mister?' I really didn't know the word. But it can't have helped matters, and they arrested us. We were taken down to Hastings Street barracks and they asked our names and addresses, and what we were doing. We told them again, but they wouldn't believe us, and they were pushing us around, one of them pulling Gerry around by the ears. I said, 'I'm going to tell my ma and dad about you.' And he just punched me in the nose. Immediately there was blood pouring out of it. Then he hit me a great kick up the arse. After about an hour and a half they'd had their sport and they threw us out on the street. We went straight to Gerry's sister's house, and I remember her saying as she tried to clean the blood off my shirt, 'them dirty black-bastards, never leaving people alone.' That was how we felt about the police. (Conlon, 1993, p. 25)

How is it possible for members of a supposedly professional police department to kidnap children, hold them in a police station and torture them, with impunity?

The answers to this question are complex, and the many abuses perpetrated by British police in this period were not, unfortunately, out of the ordinary. Police corruption is a universal phenomenon. Even advanced democracies, with relatively sophisticated integrity systems, suffer from recurring corruption scandals. In many jurisdictions police misconduct has been inter-generational and endemic, with rampant violence by police, entrenched corruption of the investigation and prosecution process, and police working hand-in-glove with organised crime. The drug trade now presents a particularly lucrative and insidious source of corruption in almost every country. More generally, policing is subject to very high volumes of complaints and allegations of misconduct that are difficult to prove but keep recurring. And formal complaints represent only the tip of the iceberg of public dissatisfaction with police. The upshot of this is that policing appears to be an occupation that carries an extreme high risk for misconduct and conflict. This chapter examines types of police misconduct, a variety of prominent case studies from different jurisdictions around the world, and explanations for the problem put forward by police scholars.

Case Studies in Police Conduct Issues

Knapp Commission

Perhaps the most significant corruption inquiry globally was the Knapp Commission in New York City, from 1970 to 1972. It marked a turning point in public and political recognition of the problem of misconduct in policing. One important factor in the Commission's profile was the international media focus and unrelenting reporting of the revelations emanating, often explosively, from the hearings. The problem in New York City was also dramatised in two high profile books and films, *Serpico* (Maas, 1973) and *Prince of the City* (Daley, 1978). The Knapp Commission revealed a deeply entrenched, 'horizontal', highly organised system of graft. Knapp described corruption as 'an extensive, Department-wide phenomenon, indulged in to some degree by a sizeable majority of those on the force' (1972, p. 61).

Knapp (1972) also categorised two types of police involved in corruption. The majority were described as

> … grass-eaters … who accept gratuities and solicit five- and ten- and twenty dollar payments from contractors, tow-truck operators, gamblers, and the like but do not aggressively pursue corruption payments. (p. 65)

Most of these officers also received regular payments from a designated 'bag man' who delivered cash to precinct officers according to their position in the bureaucratically organised corruption system. A good deal of this money came from the protection of illegal gambling operations, drugs and vice. There were also scams associated with commercial parking and construction permits, and payoffs from corrupt lawyers for officers to change their testimony. There was daily indulgence in free or discounted meals and alcohol through an extensive system of extortionate gratuities applied to restaurants and business owners. Knapp also described a smaller number of police as

> … meat-eaters … who spend a good deal of their working hours aggressively seeking out situations they can exploit for financial gain, including gambling,

narcotics, and other serious offenses which can yield payments of thousands of dollars. (p. 65).

These officers also engaged in shakedowns of criminals, mainly drug traffickers, by stealing cash and drugs from them during raids and searches.

Wood Commission

Many of the findings of the Knapp Commission were mirrored in the Royal Commission of Inquiry into the New South Wales Police (Wood Commission) that ran from 1994 to 1997. Although corruption in this case was not as organised as it was in New York, it was nonetheless described as 'serious ... widespread ... long-standing ... systematic and entrenched' (Wood, 1997, p. 161). Many of the problems were concentrated in pockets of corruption. There was an extensive problem with the protection of vice, with the fabrication of evidence and related tampering with evidence, and theft of money and property from suspects. 'Perhaps most disturbing of all', wrote Wood, 'was the extent to which police admitted to being directly involved in the supply of cocaine, heroin and cannabis' (p. 133). One area of investigation by the Commission revealed that the police Physical Surveillance Branch engaged in systematic falsification of duty records and logs. Officers were absent, playing golf among other things, while claiming to be working. In New South Wales the flow of gratuities to police included sexual favours as well as free meals.

Both the New York and New South Wales reports identified problems with the sale or disclosure of confidential information, theft from dead bodies, kickbacks from tow truck operators, internal corruption in overtime and sickness benefits, extensive abuse of alcohol while on duty, and interference with internal investigations. The Wood Commission reported that drinking while on duty 'and covering for police affected by alcohol while on duty, was an entrenched and expected practice' (1997, p. 98).

Fitzgerald Commission

The Fitzgerald Inquiry in Queensland, from 1987 to 1989, revealed widespread police malpractice. At the centre of the problem was a racket, called 'the Joke', involving the protection of gambling dens and brothels. The police commissioner sat at the peak of this system of 'vertical corruption'. He was eventually sentenced to 14 years' jail. Fitzgerald (1989) also identified institutional sex discrimination and a highly politicised police force that traded overt support for the anti-democratic state government for virtual immunity from accountability. Starting with the problem of corruption, Fitzgerald's report moved to a devastating critique of the whole management of police operations:

> The Queensland Police Force is debilitated by misconduct, inefficiency, incompetence, and deficient leadership. The situation is compounded by poor organization and administration, inadequate resources, and insuffi-

ciently developed techniques and skills for the task of law enforcement in a modern complex society. Lack of discipline, cynicism, disinterest, frustration, anger and low self-esteem are the result. The culture which shares responsibility for and is supported by this grossly unsatisfactory situation includes contempt for the criminal justice system, disdain for the law and rejection of its application to police, disregard for the truth, and abuse of authority. (1989, p. 200)

Other Cases

Around the world we can witness a variety of other cases of police misconduct that have come to light and received intense media and public scrutiny. The following are snapshots of a number of cases:

- In 2006 Felipe Calderon took over as President of Mexico and declared war on the enormous trade in drugs flowing from Columbia to the United States via Mexico. Calderon's campaign brought to international prominence a problem well known to many Mexicans: the illicit trade thrived on police protection. Police had allowed the trade to flourish to such an extent, and were so compromised by their involvement, that the government called in over 36,000 troops to assist in the crackdown. In 2008 alone it was estimated that 5,300 people had been murdered in turf wars. In February 2009 troops arrested the chief of the Cancun Police and 35 other officers over the torture and murder of former General Mauro Enrique Tello, who headed up an anti-drugs army unit. Cancun Police have also reported that 800 of the city's 2,100 operational police are under investigation. Police involvement in the drug trade and gang murders was only the apex of the police corruption that has been embedded in society for so many decades it is considered 'normal'. (Anozie, Shinn, Skarlatos, & Urzua, 2004; 'Mexico Nets Seven-Tonne Cocaine Haul', 2009, p. 8; Cortazar, 2009)
- In the 1960s Thailand became a rest and recreation destination for American troops fighting in Vietnam. Brothels were a major attraction, and from the 1970s Thailand developed a reputation as a haven for child prostitution and paedophilia-related sex tourism. Estimates of the number of victims under 18 years of age vary enormously between tens of thousands and hundreds for thousands. However, there can be little doubt that there has been a thriving trade in children for sexual exploitation, including sexual slavery. Many of the victims are trafficked into major cities from impoverished country areas. Available evidence indicates that a major facilitating factor is graft accepted by local police to protect local prostitution syndicates. (Burke & Ducci, 2005)
- The 1960 Sharpville Massacre drew international outrage against the racist apartheid regime of South Africa. The massacre by police was in response to a protest against pass laws that required all non-whites to

carry pass books authorising them to travel within the country. In the town of Sharpville demonstrators marched to the police station and made a symbolic gesture of offering themselves for arrest for not carrying their pass books. By most accounts the protest was peaceful. The organisers made public commitments to non-violence. Protestors sat down and began singing hymns. Police ordered the crowd to disperse but upwards of 5,000 people remained. Police reinforcements arrived and about 300 police lined up beside armoured vehicles. Accounts differ over what triggered the shootings. Police argue that stones were thrown from the crowd and some less experienced officers immediately began firing. Some members of the crowd, however, reported that they saw police being given a signal to fire. What is clear is that police started shooting into the unarmed crowd without any warning and continued to fire as the crowd scattered. The majority of victims were shot from behind. The death toll was 69, with more than 300 injured. A number of children were included among the dead and injured. In the aftermath police refused to provide medical assistance to the injured and arrested many of them. (Truth and Reconciliation Commission, 1998, pp. 533–537)

- Police departments in central and south American countries — including Honduras, Mexico, Guatemala, El Salvador and Brazil — have operated death squads that engage in summary executions of suspected members of youth gangs from ghetto areas of major cities. Special police patrols operating at night — referred to by one journalist as 'hunting expeditions' — executed young men on the spot on the basis of identifiers such as tattoos, or kidnapped their victims and executed them on the city outskirts where they disposed of the bodies. (Bermúdez, 2005)

- In 1992 the reunited German government opened the files of the former East German Stasi (the secret police of the former communist government). Many of the files were saved when protestors stormed the Stasi headquarters in Berlin in 1990 while former officers were shredding documents. The Stasi were responsible for monitoring the political activities and ideas of citizens and for repressing any anti-government actions or sentiments. They created what is probably the most extensive regime of close surveillance of a population that has ever existed. At the time it was disbanded in 1989 it had 91,000 staff engaged in investigations, physical and electronic surveillance, interrogations, torture and occasional executions. There was one officer for every 180 citizens. Their work was supplemented by a network of secret informants numbering about 600,000 in total between 1949 and 1989. The files revealed what many suspected: colleagues, friends, even relatives and spouses had regularly informed against them. The files also revealed that the Stasi had supported terrorist cells in the former West Germany. (BstU, 2009)

- In Florida in 1985 the Key West Police Department was declared a 'criminal enterprise' under the US government's Racketeering Influenced and Corrupt Organizations Act (RICO). The Chief of Detectives and Deputy Chief of Police were convicted on 17 counts, including bribing a witness and cocaine possession with intent to distribute, and jailed for 30 years. Two other senior police, eight drug traffickers, and an attorney and his wife also received convictions. Regular deliveries of cocaine were made to the Deputy Chief in his office in City Hall. According to the main witness's testimony the deliveries were made 'in Burger King bags and Chicken Unlimited boxes'. ('3 Ex-cops Get Prison Terms in Key West Cocaine Case', 1985, p. a10)

- In Los Angeles in 1991 a citizen covertly videotaped the bashing of a Native American, Rodney King, who had been chased by police while speeding in his car. Although King had allegedly attacked police after being apprehended, the film showed him lying unmoving and defenceless on the ground while being repeatedly kicked by four officers. He was also hit with batons and tasered. Another group of officers stood by and watched. The bashing led to the creation of an inquiry, the Christopher Commission, which identified widespread brutality and racism in the Los Angeles Police Department (LAPD), and systematic extra-legal 'punishment' of suspects by police. (Christopher, 1991)

- In 1997 in the state of Victoria, Australia, an investigation by the Ombudsman — codenamed 'Operation BART' — revealed a system of illicit payments to police who bypassed a roster system for assigning emergency repairs to burgled premises. The system was believed to have been operating for at least 20 years. Approximately 550 serving officers were implicated. (Ombudsman, 1998)

- In 1996 authorities in Belgium rescued two girls held in a secret dungeon by a criminal, Marc Dutroux. The bodies of four other girls were also discovered. All the girls, aged between 8 and 19, had been kidnapped, tortured and raped. Some had been filmed during their ordeal. Two were murdered, and two starved to death while their torturer spent some time in jail for other offences. A parliamentary inquiry found that Dutroux had been part of a paedophile ring that operated under the noses of incompetent and negligent police. Earlier searches for the missing girls might have saved their lives had police been more thorough and shared vital intelligence. More than 250,000 people marched in Brussels in protest against police and the justice system. (Landuyt & T'Serclaes, 1997)

- In 2006 two retired New York City detectives were convicted of eight murders. The convictions resulted from the dogged investigations of another New York detective who pieced together evidence that revealed the men worked for decades as informants and hitmen for a major New York crime group, the Lucchese family. Detectives Stephen Caracappa and Louis Eppolito — dubbed 'the Mafia cops' — received monthly payments for information that stymied police investigations into organised crime and large payments for Mafia-ordered executions. (Lawson & Oldham, 2006)

Definitions and Typologies of Police Misconduct

The cases in the previous section illustrate a variety of different types of police misconduct and corruption. These are terms that are often given different meanings in different contexts. 'Misconduct' is at times used broadly to cover all unethical behaviour, or it can be used to describe unethical behaviour other than 'corruption'. 'Corruption' in this latter sense refers to a more narrowly conceived behaviour in which police accept some kind of benefit, such as a cash payment, for not doing their duty, such as arresting and charging an offender (i.e., bribery). The UN code of police ethics provides the following description of corruption in this sense:

> Corruption … should be understood to encompass the commission or omission of an act in the performance of or in connection with one's duties, in response to gifts, promises or incentives demanded or accepted, or the wrongful receipt of these once the act has been committed or omitted. (1979, p. 4)

However, the two terms are also used interchangeably. Misconduct can be used to encompass all unethical behaviour. Corruption can also be used to describe any kind of deviation from ethical standards, and there is probably little to be achieved by trying to insist on strict usage.

Following is a six-part typology of police misconduct (from Prenzler, 2009, chapter 2). The typology is designed to cover all possible forms of deviance, while also allowing for a separate focus on clusters of behaviours. However, it should be kept in mind that people have produced other typologies that readers might find useful (e.g., Barker, 1983). In addition, laws establishing ethical standards for police normally have their own particular language. Statutes often make use of three levels of misconduct according to a hierarchy of seriousness. At the top might be something like 'official corruption', followed by an intermediate level with something like 'official misconduct', with 'disciplinary offences' at the bottom.

1. Graft, Bribery or Classic Corruption

With graft, bribery or classic corruption an officer misuses their position for personal benefit in the form of cash, property, sex, drugs, food, promotion or preferred assignment. Graft can be highly organised. In a protection racket, for instance, a regular payment is made to police by a gambling den, brothel or other illegal establishment for not raiding the premises and prosecuting the offenders. Graft can also be disorganised. Examples of opportunistic corruption of this type include not charging a motorist who has committed an offence or a drug user caught in possession of drugs. Classic corruption is often consensual, in that both parties willingly enter into the transaction. However, it can also be extortionate. This involves police intimidating citizens or criminals into making payments. In a shakedown, police aggressively demand money or steal cash, drugs or property from criminals. Corruption also covers the sale of confidential information held by police and the onselling of drugs stolen from traffickers or stolen from police exhibit storage rooms. Gratuities, such as free or discounted food and drink, have also been referred to as 'petty corruption' (Sigler & Dees, 1988).

2. Process Corruption

Process corruption involves any kind of interference with the process of gathering and presenting evidence. 'Perverting the course of justice' can occur by police obtaining evidence illegally (such as by a search without a warrant when a warrant is required), by lying in court, by withholding evidence that supports the accused or by coercing arrested persons into making confessions.

3. Brutality or Excessive Force

Brutality or excessive force involves unjustified force against persons. As noted in the chapter 2 on police ethics, police are expected to use minimal or proportionate force in carrying out their duties, especially when arresting offenders. Brutality can include a very wide range of actions including abusive language, rough handling, assault and unlawful killing.

4. Unprofessional Conduct or Miscellaneous Misconduct

Unprofessional conduct or miscellaneous misconduct is a broad area focused on other forms of misconduct directed towards the public where there is no clear personal benefit to police. Inaction in relation to calls for assistance is one example, as is the common problem of racial or sexual discrimination, as well as negligent treatment of victims of crime or persons in police custody, and misuse of the office of constable to intimidate persons in civil disputes.

5. Internal Corruption or Workplace Deviance

Internal corruption or workplace deviance includes behaviours such as harassment and sexual discrimination directed against colleagues, and cronyism and nepotism in promotion and assignments. In some cases internal corruption can even include police buying promotions and assignments. It also covers embezzlement; fraud in overtime, sick leave and workers compensation payments; as well as personal use of departmental equipment and being under the influence of drugs or alcohol on duty.

6. Off-Duty Unprofessional Conduct

Unprofessional conduct off duty includes criminal conduct off duty and other behaviour considered to reflect poorly on the office of constable and the police department, including drunk driving, fights and foul language.

Extent of Police Misconduct

Major inquiries into police misconduct often describe the problem as 'pervasive', 'entrenched' or 'endemic'. Certainly it would seem that whole police departments can be almost entirely corrupt for long periods of time, with the very large majority of officers engaged either directly or indirectly in diverse types of misconduct. However, it must be kept in mind that police misconduct is also extremely variable. A department that was once deeply corrupt can be cleaned up, with serious and organised forms of misconduct largely eliminated over the longer term. A department that had a reputation for integrity can deteriorate rapidly following a change in leadership. Within nation states as well, an inter-jurisdictional perspective shows that corruption can vary significantly between departments. Even within departments, some sections might be deeply corrupt while others are considered largely free of corruption.

The really key point is not that policing is intrinsically and hopelessly corrupt, but that policing is a very high-risk occupation for misconduct. And within policing, certain areas are extremely high-risk, such as vice and narcotics. An additional point to note is that policing is not at all unique in terms of occupations that are prone to corruption. Most areas of public service are prone to abuses, as we saw in chapter 1. The same is true for business and the professions; including areas thought to attract persons of high moral calibre and dedication to service, such as medicine (Friedrichs, 2007). Some areas of employment that are notable for misconduct include door security staff at nightclubs in relation to assaults, and building inspectors and purchasing agents in relation to bribery. Policing includes a combination of these order maintenance, law enforcement and even purchasing functions. What is possibly distinctive about policing, however, is the multiplicity of opportunities for corruption combined with intense pressures for misconduct (see the section following on causes of police misconduct).

Effects of Police Misconduct

Police misconduct has highly variable effects. Vice operations that attract police protection, such as prostitution and gambling, are sometimes described as 'victimless crimes'. While this may be true up to a point, and it might be argued that police corruption actually facilitates needed services, these activities are often highly exploitative. Prostitution can involve coercion, and gamblers can be indebted to loan sharks. Furthermore, vice operations protected by police usually involve organised crime groups that may also be involved in extortion, torture and murder.

If police are involved in corruption they often have less time to protect the public. The Knapp Commission pointed out that in some high crime areas in New York police were drinking in bars when they should have been patrolling the streets and investigating offences (1972, p. 146). Police process corruption also leads directly to miscarriages of justice, including the conviction and sentencing of innocent persons and the failure to convict guilty persons — a topic covered in greater depth in chapter 6. Excessive force by police can also lead to injury and death. Repressive policing tactics and racist harassment at times provoke destructive riots such as the notorious 1981 Brixton riot in London (Scarman, 1986). In 1992 three of the officers charged over the Rodney King beating were acquitted by what many thought was a stacked white jury. Los Angeles then erupted in three days of rioting that resulted in thousands of injuries, 53 deaths, and vandalism and arson attacks that caused US$1 billion in damage (Parks & Smith, 1999).

Public alienation and lack of confidence are also negative effects of police misconduct. A recent public opinion survey in Australia (Murphy, Hinds, & Fleming, 2008, p. 136) found that

> Views about police legitimacy do influence public cooperation with the police, and ... those who view the police as more legitimate are more likely to assist police to control crime. The key antecedent of legitimacy is procedural justice. (p. 136).

Surveys also show that ethnic minorities are frequently very distrustful of police and therefore less likely to cooperate in police efforts to protect their communities (Weitzer, 2004).

Many of the costs of police corruption and mismanagement fall on taxpayers through damages payouts to successful litigants, informant protection costs, multi-million-dollar inquiries and the costs of complex anti-corruption systems. One of several inquiries into how the FBI handled the 1993 siege at Waco, in which 75 persons were burnt to death, '... lasted 14 months, employed 74 personnel, and cost approximately [US]$17 million. The Office of Special Counsel interviewed exactly 1,001 witnesses, reviewed over 2.3 million pages of documents, and examined thousands of pounds of physical evidence' (Danforth, 2000, p. 4). The Rodney King civil suit resulted in a payout of US$3.8 million from the City of Los Angeles (BBC News, 2002).

Corruption can also have a poisonous effect on the workplace through stress, secrecy, suspicion, guilt and ostracism (Daley, 1978; Maas, 1973). Exposés of corruption often result in suicides, resignations, sackings, jail terms, and a trail of ruined careers and damaged families (Barron, 2007).

Causes of Police Misconduct

An understanding of causes is essential to put in place systems that will effectively prevent the development or continuation of misconduct in the future. There has been a great deal of research about the causes of police misconduct. Some of this has been by academics and some has been carried out as part of the wider brief of judicial inquiries. The findings from this research do not ascribe a single cause, but can be divided into two broad areas of explanation termed 'structural' (or 'structural–functional') and 'cultural' (Prenzler, 2009, chap. 2). Structural explanations refer to the 'task environment' of policing and the organisation of police work (Bennett, 1984). Cultural explanations refer to values, beliefs, symbols, traditions and habits that involve the transmission and reinforcement of governing beliefs and behaviours between generations of police. The following sections elaborate on these themes of structure and culture in understanding the problem (based primarily on Alain & Grégoire, 2008; Barker, 1983; Fitzgerald, 1989; Human Rights Watch, 1998; Mollen, 1994; Reuss-Ianni, 1983; Scarman, 1986; Sherman, 1977; Skolnick, 1994; Wood, 1997):

Structural Explanations

Classic corruption derives from the law enforcement function of police and the opportunity structure this creates for a trade in benefits. Criminals will offer money and other benefits to police for protection from prosecution. Large amounts of cash from the drug trade or smaller regular payments from vice operations can generate almost irresistible temptation. This is an 'economic' demand-and-supply equation. It can be activated opportunistically and inconsistently, for example, between a traffic police officer and a motorist in a single incident, or on a highly organised, routine and long-term basis, for example, in a protection racket.

At a higher level of analysis the historical problem of police protection of vice has been related to political processes. In democracies, vocal conservative minorities lobby politicians to enact laws prohibiting the 'pleasures' they abhor, partly for intrinsic 'moral' reasons and partly because of the harms they associate with them. These pleasures include liquor, prostitution, pornography, drugs and gambling. Abortion has been another topic of protest. These activities are in considerable demand from sections of the population and the situation creates a demand-and-supply conflict. Police act as a circuit breaker. They step in as brokers of an arrangement whereby an underground supply is permitted, the occasional real or engineered overt supply arrangements are publicly shut down in token raids, the conservatives are placated, the politicians keep the support of the conservatives and the police augment their income through illicit payments. These arrangements can continue for decades and include large numbers of persons, including lawyers. They are often concentrated in and around inner-city red-light districts.

Politicians can also be part of protection rackets (at the top of the payment pyramid), in which their role is to deflect calls for inquiries into corruption or hobble inquiries with inadequate powers or resources. Even when they are not directly involved, politicians can be part of the problem by turning a blind eye — either because they think that exposure will reflect poorly on them, or in return for police political support and repressive action against political enemies.

An important contributing factor to the proliferation of graft is the highly dispersed nature of frontline policing. Patrol officers and detectives cannot be supervised like workers on a factory floor. They necessarily 'roam the streets', responding to dispatches or following leads with limited scope for direct supervision by middle managers. This gives them significant opportunity to engage in bribery and escape detection. At the same time, a consistent finding of corruption inquiries is that managers have failed to even attempt to supervise operational police or require that they account for their movements.

The jurisdictional structure of policing can also facilitate rivalries and non-cooperation through the creation of parallel and hierarchical police agencies, with uncertain responsibilities or separate performance measures.

A structural perspective is also useful for understanding variations in corruption and misconduct across different types of policing tasks and police organisational units. Larger police organisations have developed an often highly segregated division of labour with different squads and units. Detectives are more likely to engage in process corruption in order to achieve their goal of successfully prosecuting suspects. Within some specialist squads, such as drug squads and armed hold-up squads, there is a particular tendency for officers to participate in high-stakes corruption involving large amounts of cash and valuables and for them to develop relationships with hardened criminals. Organised graft is more likely to involve licensing branches or vice squads, with police working with mafia-style organised crime groups. Patrol officers might be excluded from the more lucrative forms of corruption but face shifting opportunities and temptations across lower-level corruption areas, such as theft from crime scenes or unprofessional conduct through inaction. Temptations to use excessive force can come from patrol officers' routine encounters with members of the public who are prone to verbally abuse police, spit, scratch and throw punches; but also with more specialist order maintenance duties such as controlling demonstrations.

Police violence can also serve as a fallback mechanism to the problem of policing high crime areas and public disorder problems where due process constraints are seen as a tying of police hands. It can develop as part of a standard operating routine for police in the exercise of 'stop and search' powers targeted at suspects based on racial or cultural identifiers. Harassment and assaults are designed to intimidate potential troublemakers and show them 'who's boss'.

A structural–functional analysis also helps with understanding process corruption and associated miscarriages of justice. Political and community pressure to solve crimes and bring offenders to justice puts enormous pressure on police, particularly in relation to more horrendous and shocking crimes such as terrorist attacks. This creates a temptation to cut corners in an investigation by coercing suspects into making confessions, pressuring other persons into making false or misleading witness statements, and finding scientists who will place misleading interpretations on forensic data.

Process corruption is both stimulated and facilitated by key aspects of due process rights, such as suspects' right to silence and procedures under the adversarial justice system (see chapters 5–7). The courtroom process can devolve into a contest to persuade a jury or magistrate, as opposed to a fair and open inquiry into the truth. Police and police prosecutors are therefore tempted to underplay or hide exculpatory evidence and present falsified evidence supporting their case.

Process corruption can also be stimulated by the over-reliance on crime clearance rates as a performance measure for police. (Scandals over the under-recording of crime reports are also part of this.)

Cultural Explanations

Corruption research has also focused on the occupational culture — or 'subculture' — of policing. All institutions, workplaces and human groups tend to take on governing beliefs, values and practices. Traditional police departments are noted for their tendency to close ranks and protect corrupt colleagues behind a 'blue wall' or 'blue curtain' of silence. The New South Wales Wood Commission reported that:

> One of the greatest obstacles identified by the Royal Commission has been the code of silence and solidarity in the face of any form of criticism of the Service or prospect of internal investigation. In some quarters this has been referred to as the brotherhood which supports those who close ranks and punishes viciously those who place duty first. It has become so powerful a feature of the police culture that it rarely requires express enunciation. Rather, it has been understood, accepted and blindly followed without regard to the harm to the Service it causes, or to the risks it creates for honest police. (Wood, 1997, p. 134)

The negative aspects of a traditional police culture have their origins in male dominance, and in recruitment and training methods that emphasised physical prowess and the use of force. In divided, especially colonial and post-colonial, societies police were often drawn from the white ruling class (as a working-class sub-element) or other dominant ethnic group. Education was undervalued or even treated as a handicap, and police were encouraged to blindly follow orders. According to this account, in a traditional police department, a fit young idealistic recruit, perhaps carrying some bigoted tendencies, was rapidly transformed into a 'normal' officer who was overweight, a heavy smoker and drinker, under-educated, sexist, racist, ethnocentric, homophobic, foul mouthed, deeply cynical, corrupt, violent, defensive and paranoid! Many of these conformist and reactionary aspects of policing were reinforced by shared jokes and derogatory language; and by military practices such as drills, 'hazing' of recruits and formal officer dinners (Fitzgerald, 1989; Prenzler, 1997; Reuss-Ianni, 1983; Wood, 1997).

Conclusion

At the beginning of this chapter a question was posed about how police can engage in fairly blatant and systematic abuses of their authority. The answer involves a complex combination of a large number of factors. Government neglect and complicity set the context for a corrupt culture. The fact that police in many locations have engaged in blatant and systematic abuses cannot be denied. Local conditions will vary, but understanding the broad high-risk profile of policing for misconduct is essential in taking on the challenging task of establishing misconduct prevention systems: the subject of the next chapter.

Chapter 4

Police Integrity Management and Accountability

The previous two chapters covered the role of police in society, the ethical issues police face, conduct standards for police, and the nature and causes of police misconduct. The present chapter focuses on techniques for preventing misconduct, creating an ethical culture and ensuring police are fully accountable. What is crucial here, following on from the key point in the previous chapter, is to effectively match regulation to risk. Policing, it was argued, is a high-risk occupation for misconduct. This means that police misconduct prevention requires a large, complex and expensive integrity management infrastructure. The diversity of types of police misconduct and the complex causes of misconduct mean that the solutions will also be complex. There is no single nor simple way of ensuring police behave ethically.

What follows then is a checklist of strategies that can be used to ensure any police department is properly organised to maximise ethical and lawful behaviour. The chapter describes a broad set of conditions that make for an appropriate accountability context. These elements often exist in rudimentary forms in many societies and are often in need of extensive reform. They include fair elections, governmental transparency, the rule of law and a free press. A set of minimal police integrity strategies is then outlined. Some of these have been part of policing for much of its modern history, but often in rudimentary forms, and include recruit screening and investigations and discipline. The chapter then elaborates on a number of more advanced strategies, many of which have been introduced and trialled in the more recent post-Knapp period, including early intervention systems and covert tactics (Prenzler, 2009).

Poor Integrity Management

We can think about good integrity management by briefly considering what counts as poor integrity management — a topic touched on in the previous chapter on the causes of corruption. One aspect of a culture of denial and neglect in the police force has been the failure to take complaints and disclosures seriously, including complaints or information from criminals. Inquiries have repeatedly found that police have ignored complaints or persecuted complainants and this has allowed corruption to flourish unchecked. Another key aspect has been the failure of police management and other relevant authorities to be proactive. In a traditional police department, anti-corruption measures are largely passive, relying on complaints to come in before anything is investigated. Even with a conscientious response to complaints this can mean that hidden and consensual forms of corruption never come to light. Difficulties in substantiating complaints also means they are of limited value, especially when pursued through traditional investigative and adversarial models.

Lack of supervision has been another deficiency. While we might think of traditional policing as highly authoritarian and militaristic, in fact middle and upper middle managers frequently fail to closely monitor the behaviour of police on the job and set clear standards, including in their own behaviour. For example, the New South Wales Police Integrity Commission, in its 2004 *Operation Florida* report on major police drug corruption in Sydney's northern suburbs, found that:

> Supervision or lack of it was an obvious issue … Unsurprisingly, it was shown that where a supervisor condones the corrupt actions of those he supervises, or takes part in them, corrupt activities will continue unchecked, whether corruption prevention plans are in force or not. The Commission considers that a high trust model of supervision is inadequate and inappropriate for corruption prevention, and that police officers at the operational level must take a greater responsibility for ensuring that corrupt officers are exposed. (p. xv; emphasis added)

Another weakness in traditional models of police integrity has been the failure to use information strategically, especially with a view to detecting early warning signs of misconduct. With no central repository for collecting and analysing misconduct indicators, 'problem officers' who avoid high profile disciplinary convictions can move around within a department under the radar (Walker, Alpert, & Kenney, 2001).

Accountability Contexts

The first point to be made in regard to an adequate accountability system is that the political context needs to be right. Governments that operate police departments and set the general direction for policing strategies need to be fairly elected and consultative, so that the policing policy framework is representative and balances community concerns wherever possible. Given the potential for the politicisation of policing, there also needs to be a high degree of operational independence of police from the government, and there needs to be genuine freedom of information so citizens can know how decisions about policing are being made and by whom. For example, if citizens cannot see cabinet agendas, minutes and documents regarding policing issues, then there is no baseline accountability to the electorate for policy decisions.

A second point relates to police remaining the subject of law. Police are granted some 'immunities', which are partial immunities that give police protection from, or some tolerance in, civil or criminal prosecution when they make 'human errors'. At the same time, there should not be any general protection of police from criminal law. Where there is evidence that police have committed criminal offences they should be charged the same as any citizen.

Civil law, for all its limitations, is a vital potential source of accountability that is open to all citizens (Ransley, Anderson, & Prenzler, 2007). For many this will be an action of last resort, given the likely personal expense and risk of failure. Nonetheless, citizens are normally free to sue police for injuries and harms that constitute either negligent or intentional torts. Successful litigation can result in an order for compensatory damages and even exemplary or punitive damages designed to deter police from acting the same way in the future. Normally police departments will pay for a defence, if they see merit in defence, and cover the cost of damages. This is a mechanism to give officers confidence in the support of their department. However, where departments feel employees have been particularly reckless they may in turn sue the officer for losses. Torts are wide ranging and can include assault, false imprisonment, slander and emotional stress.

If police commit breaches of administrative or regulatory law they should also be charged and punished when found guilty. Examples include breaches of traffic regulations, and sexual or racial discrimination. In some countries citizens can also sue police for breaches of their constitutional rights. The law can also be used not just as a 'remedy' for a harm perpetrated by a police officer, such as an assault, but also to enforce a right. For example, citizens can usually sue a police department in relation to discrimination in recruitment or lack of action to protect them if they are threatened. The judgment can entail the court ordering a police department to comply with the law. Courts can also issue injunctions that specify actions police departments must or must not take, with penalties for noncompliance. In some countries, most notably the United States, police departments have often been obliged to comply with consent decrees that specify actions — such as the recruitment of minority groups and women or the creation of anti-corruption measures such as an early warning system. A related device is contempt of court. While in criminal trials police officers have a right to silence, under administrative processes if they refuse to answer a question or give a false answer they can be charged with contempt of court (Human Rights Watch, 1998).

Another important aspect of the legal accountability of police is judicial scrutiny in the courts (Sarre, 1989). This operates when judges and defence lawyers examine the quality and sources of police evidence. Evidence obtained illegally, such as through an illegal search or illegal telephone intercept, is usually subject to the exclusionary rule as a deterrent to illegal conduct. The courts should also be alert for possible fabrications of evidence, false evidence and the suppression of exculpatory evidence.

A judicial inquiry is another traditional mechanism of accountability. Judicial inquiries are enacted by parliaments to inquire into serious allegations of police misconduct. Often called 'commissions of inquiry', they are usually headed by judge or former judge. Historically, judicial inquiries have often been constrained by limited terms of reference, limited time frames and limited resources or powers (Lewis, 1999). An inquiry of substance will need to be able to compel testimony, 'turn' corrupt officers to act as undercover agents or accept an indemnity from prosecution in exchange for testimony, and engage in covert tactics and telecommunications intercepts.

Finally, a free press is essential to police accountability (Human Rights Watch, 1998). At times journalists will ignore police corruption because of their dependency on police for crime stories. In other cases the news value of a corruption story will attract journalists' interest. The wide reach of the press — for example, through print, television and the internet — means that cases of police misconduct can be brought to a wide audience, which can facilitate pressure for action by governments, including commissioning an inquiry. Investigative journalism — where journalists engage in in-depth research, sometimes of a covert nature — is particularly important for exposing hidden forms of police corruption.

Beyond this, systems of police integrity management can be modelled in terms of minimal and advanced strategies.

Good Integrity Management: Minimal Strategies

The following briefly outlines the core elements of a basic police integrity system. All police departments, even in the most impoverished countries, need to be subject to this regime to ensure that the more blatant forms of misconduct are prevented or detected and stopped, and that citizens have somewhere to take their grievances against police and obtain a reasonable hearing.

Internal Chain of Command

The chain of command and internal discipline are systems through which police organisations delineate lines of authority so that responsibility can be assigned at different levels and officers ordered by a commanding officer to comply with law and regulations. There must be a genuine threat of disciplinary action for disobeying a reasonable lawful command to ensure a basic level of internal compliance.

Complaints Investigation and Discipline

Policing attracts large numbers of complaints. Many of these lack any probative value — that is, the evidence involved is weak. The police involved deny the allegations. There might not be any independent witnesses or forensic material to corroborate the complainant's version of events. However, when properly investigated some complaints provide evidence of genuine misconduct, even when they are made by people who have committed crimes. Complaints also represent conflict or misunderstanding between police and the public where a resolution is desirable. Surprisingly perhaps, the large numbers of complaints that flow in daily to larger police departments are generally only the tip of the iceberg. There is in fact a 'dark figure' of undisclosed dissatisfaction in citizen encounters with police. Up to 90% of people who have felt dissatisfied do not complain (Maguire & Corbett, 1991, pp. 53–55). At the same time, some complaints are malicious and vindictive. So, trying to provide a fair response to the many stakeholders in this process is a major challenge.

'Complaints' is often used as a catch-all phrase for all reports, disclosures and information about possible police misconduct, as well as genuine grievances. A person might observe police engaging in misconduct and report the matter even though they are not personally affected. What is important, however, is that all this incoming material is objectively and competently evaluated for initial probative value, and then follow-up investigations undertaken where appropriate. These investigations need to be undertaken with the same rigour and the same techniques as normal crime investigations. Where complaints are substantiated an appropriate penalty or remedial intervention needs to be consistently applied. The best way to ensure confidence in this process is to establish a disciplinary matrix (Walker, 2003), developed in consultation with stakeholders about what constitutes offences and appropriate sanctions.

Proper complaints investigation and discipline is essential to ensure public confidence in police and ensure justice in police operations. It should also send a message to operational police about what is and is not acceptable. Many complaints against police are not about graft or abuses like assaults, but about a lack of professionalism in providing basic policing services. A recent Commonwealth Human Rights Initiative report on police accountability asserted that:

> Perhaps the greatest public resentment over bad policing is reserved for impunity — the safety from punishment provided by authorities and supervisors to errant police and the lack of accountability. In addition, it includes a boundless tolerance for poor performance in delivering safety and security and protecting the rule of law. (2005, p. 9)

And a recent United States National Institute of Justice study, *Enhancing Police Integrity*, found that 'Officers learned to gauge the seriousness of various types of misconduct by observing their department's diligence in detecting and disciplining those who engaged in police misconduct' (2005, p. 3).

It is also essential that the lodgement of complaints is easy and that complainants are not intimidated into withdrawing. Both complainants and accused officers expect the matter to be processed quickly and they expect the agency to communicate with them. To ensure these basic processes are properly undertaken there is a range of assessment measures available, including quality audits of case files by a panel of experts (Prenzler & Lewis, 2005).

Internal Affairs and External Oversight

Police integrity management is now recognised as a specialist field where consistency in approach and the integration of knowledge is essential. As a consequence, larger police departments have professional standards units (often in the past known as 'internal affairs') that hold an exclusive mission to detect and prevent misconduct. This means a total focus on integrity, with no distractions. It is also intended to ensure a comprehensive, department-wide approach to the management of police behaviour, with the central processing of all complaints and intelligence about misconduct.

Unfortunately, internal affairs units on their own were almost always an abject failure — deeply compromised by internal loyalty and the code of silence and often staffed by officers with histories of corruption. Their real function was to deflect complainants and hide corruption. Consider the following extract from the Queensland Fitzgerald report:

> The Internal Investigations Section has been woefully ineffective, hampered by a lack of staff and resources and crude techniques. It has lacked commitment and will and demonstrated no initiative to detect serious crime … The Section has provided warm comfort to corrupt police. It has been a friendly, sympathetic, protective and inept overseer. It must be abolished. (Fitzgerald, 1989, p. 289)

This is an almost universal finding of commissions of inquiry and it has led to the creation of external police integrity agencies tasked with the oversight of police complaints and discipline. 'Oversight' is in fact what most of these agencies have done, with often very limited capacity to be directly engaged in investigations and discipline. Most of the currently existing agencies could best be described as weak review agencies, primarily engaged in paper assessments of police responses to complaints and associated conduct issues, perhaps on occasions engaging in independent or joint investigations of very serious cases.

Dissatisfaction with this model has led to the gradual introduction of a greater role for some of these agencies. This includes investigating cases where a complainant has made an appeal against a police decision, automatically conducting independent investigations for more serious matters and having greater input into disciplinary decisions (Prenzler, 2009, chap. 10). Two particularly notable agencies in that regard are the New South Wales Police Integrity Commission and the Police Ombudsman for Northern Ireland. Both these agencies employ non-police investigators and hold a wider remit for assessing the corruption prevention strategies of the departments they regulate.

Applicant Screening

Testing of applicants is another standard mechanism for attempting to prevent misconduct (Police Education Advisory Council, 1998). Tests are designed to screen in recruits who display traits that appear to make them resistant to corruption pressures and to screen out applicants who show evidence that they might be prone to corruption. A variety of tests are applied in relation to integrity. Most departments automatically exclude applicants with a criminal record, partly because a record may indicate a pre-disposition towards repeated criminal conduct, but also because having officers with previous criminal convictions is likely to reduce public confidence. A number of personality tests are also employed in recruitment, including the *Minnesota Multiphasic Personality Inventory* (MMPI) and the *Sixteen Personality Factor Questionnaire* (16PF). These tests have been subject to repeated tests for validity and are useful for detecting a range of positive and negative traits, including honesty, emotional stability, impulsiveness, aggressiveness and defensiveness, as well as signs of mental illness. Personality tests are generally used to flag areas of concern that can then be investigated by recruiting staff. Other screening mechanisms include panel interviews, where questions about personal ethics and ethical scenarios can be presented, referee reports, drug tests, and even home visits and financial reviews. Screening should also be used when officers apply for a position in high-risk squads and promotion to key management roles.

Ethics Training

Judicial inquiries that discover systemic abuses in police departments usually find that training in ethics is non-existent or highly inadequate. This is despite the responsibility on the police command to clearly communicate the ethical standards of the organisation. There is also a responsibility to prepare recruits for managing the kinds of dilemmas they will face on the job, including pressure to conform to misconduct and the requirement to inform on colleagues (Kleinig, 1990). This should in part involve behavioural training where recruits practise responses in simulations, such as scenarios involving offers of gratuities or provocative behaviour from members of the public. Recruits also need a broad sociological understanding of the corruption problem in policing and the rationales behind the anti-corruption system they have to work under. It is also essential that ethical competencies are maintained through in-house training and testing — given the well-known rapid deterioration in officer attitudes and the onset of cynicism (Alain & Grégoire, 2008). As officers move further up the ranks they also need a more specific practical knowledge about corruption prevention methods.

System Controls

There are a number of high-risk areas in policing where strict procedural controls need to be put in place and monitored to ensure compliance. These include the following:

- A tough vehicle pursuits policy is required to minimise injuries and deaths from crashes. Reviews have recommended that pursuits only be engaged in relation to serious crimes, with speeds limited to 30–40% above the posted limit, radio supervision of drivers by a superior officer and termination of pursuits at the first signs of any danger (such as the presence of bystanders; Hoffman, 2003).

- Strict access controls are required on all police information technology systems to prevent misuse of information. Access should be limited to 'need to know' criteria, by password only, with a requirement that officers state the reasons for all inquiries. All access must be able to be tracked, regularly audited and subject to alerts when unauthorised access is attempted. Highly sensitive data, such as informant registers, should be on separate databases (Commissioner for Law Enforcement Data Security, 2007).

- Criminal informants are often a source of undesirable influence on their police 'handlers' and the idea that a criminal associate is an 'informant' is a favourite excuse of corrupt police. Strict protocols need to be in place for the management of informants, including senior officer contact and authorisation, documentation of identity, regular assessments of the informant's value, approval for all meetings, and the recording of all meetings and payments (ICAC, 1994).

- Protections against process corruption need to include audio-taping or videotaping of all interviews, signed statements by interviewees that they have been informed of their rights, an internal police policy that down-grades confessional evidence and uncorroborated eye witness testimony, access to independent legal counsel for accused persons, high security and strict access controls for all storage of evidence, and a limit of 24 hours for holding suspects without charge (see chapter 7).

Good Integrity Management: Advanced Strategies

Recurring relapses into corruption on the part of reformed police departments have stimulated interest in more radical integrity management techniques. Some of these are highly intrusive and have drawn controversy, but they have mainly derived either from successful techniques adopted by judicial inquiries (such as covert tactics), or because the inquiries have identified major problems that need to be addressed by more intrusive measures (such as drug and alcohol testing). These advanced strategies, set out here, are also designed in many cases to be highly proactive, in that they involve going out and looking for misconduct and putting in place routine checks and tests, rather than simply responding to complaints as they come in.

Measuring Integrity

Police corruption is often highly secretive, and the nature of frontline policing means it is difficult to monitor officer conduct. A number of social science techniques have therefore been developed to assemble misconduct and integrity indicators in order to try to obtain as complete a picture as possible about ethical challenges and behavioural issues across the department (Brereton, 2002). Time-series analyses can also provide a picture of changing issues and emerging problems. The following sources are now being used routinely by many departments or oversight agencies:

- Ethical climate surveys ask police officers questions about their attitudes to ethical issues, often using the scenario-type questions. These surveys can provide valuable information about attitudes that support misconduct, the willingness of officers to report on colleagues and their views on integrity strategies.

- Public opinion surveys provide measures of public confidence in police integrity. Questions addressed to people who have recently been involved with police can provide more specific information about how police handle requests for assistance and other interactions with the public.

- Surveys or interviews with people who have been arrested by police can also provide useful information about how they were treated in relation to a wide range of issues including use of force, information about rights, treatment in custody and interview methods.

- Analyses of complaints data and other misconduct indicators, such as disciplinary convictions, can also provide important information about problem areas of policing that may need to be addressed with more effective management strategies.

Early Intervention Systems

Allegations against police are notoriously difficult to prove in a court of law or even in an administrative disciplinary forum. A traditional approach that emphasises due process and the presumption of innocence has tended to ignore all complaints that were not proven. However, this means that patterns of complaints are not identified, even when these may be strongly indicative of patterns of misconduct. A common finding of judicial inquiries has been that, just as a small number of offenders is often responsible for a large number of crimes, a small number of police are often responsible for a large number of complaints. In a famous example, the Christopher Commission on the Los Angeles Police Department that followed the Rodney King bashing found the following:

> Of approximately 1,800 officers against whom an allegation of excessive force or improper tactics was made from 1986 through 1990, over 1,400 officers had only one or two allegations. But 183 officers had four or more allegations, 44 had six or more, 16 had eight or more, and one had 16 allegations … Of nearly 6,000 officers identified as involved in use of force reports from January 1987 through March 1991, more than 4,000 had less than five reports each. But 63 officers had 20 or more reports each. The top 5% of officers ranked by number of reports accounted for more than 20% of all reports, and the top 10% accounted for 33%. (Christopher, 1991, p. 36)

Similar findings have been made in Australia. In a special study in 2002 the New South Wales Ombudsman found that over 200 officers had complaints histories suggesting they posed 'a significant risk to the police service and community' (p. 8; see also Legosz, 2007).

Ignoring officers who have unsubstantiated complaints pile up against them is one problem. A related problem is ignoring, or even rewarding, officers who develop a heavy record of complaints that have been substantiated in one form or another. Research by the Kolts Commission on the Los Angeles County Sheriff's Department identified 62 officers with large numbers of complaints against them. Within this group, 17 were responsible for 22 lawsuits that resulted in over US$3 million in payments to litigants (Kolts, 1992, chap. 9, p. 160). In a detailed investigation of these 62 officers the Commission found that their personnel records almost completely ignored their complaints history while lauding their achievements, and that there was no evidence that their complaints histories held them back from promotion.

These problems have led to the introduction of computer-based early intervention systems. These systems flag officers who attract a number of points above a threshold — such as two complaints in a six-month period. The flagged officers attend a meeting where their performance is discussed and a range of remedial options is considered. This process of integrity pro-filing and review can be triggered by other incidents and reports, such as use-of-force incidents, injuries, motor vehicle accidents, negative supervisor reports and excessive sick leave. Interventions can include warnings, counselling, retraining and close supervision (Walker et al., 2001).

Program evaluations have shown this approach can be very successful in reducing complaints. In one of the earliest examples, in Miami-Dade in Florida, the system introduced in 1981 flagged an average of 37.5 staff per quarter. This fell to an average of 7.6 per quarter in following years (Charette, 1993). Case study assessments in Minneapolis and New Orleans also found citizen complaints against profiled officers fell by two-thirds one year after intervention (Walker et al., 2001).

In Australia, a study of the Victoria Police early intervention system tracked complaints against a sample of 44 officers who were profiled and subject to remedial interventions (Macintyre, Prenzler, & Chapman, 2008). In the 16 quarters prior to being profiled the sample received an average of 15.1 complaints per quarter. Following profiling there was a 72% drop to 4.3 complaints per quarter across eight quarters. Given the high cost of complaints management infrastructure and investigations it was estimated that the interventions saved AU$3.2 million over two years.

Not only do some officers attract more complaints than others, but some police stations and squads attract more complaints than others. The Macintyre et al. (2008) study in Victoria also identified a 58% reduction in complaints following profiling and intervention of a sample of nine policing 'units', including five 'uniform' units and four CIB (detective) units. Interventions included revised management styles. As with the individual profiles, the data showed that complaints were on the increase before the interventions and then continued to decline following the interventions.

Alternative Dispute Resolution

The large majority of complaints against police are not substantiated, even in the most sophisticated complaints and discipline systems that have a high degree of independence (Ede & Barnes, 2002). As well as this, surveys indicate that complainants are generally unhappy with formal investigations of their complaints, even when the complaint is substantiated and the officer disciplined. Surveys also show that complainants do not usually want the officer involved punished but that they want to be able to communicate their dissatisfaction to the officer and the department and see systems improved in the future. Many are satisfied with an apology. And, as noted, many complaints are not about serious misconduct but lower-level customer service issues. All of this adds up to a strong case for the use of alternative dispute resolution techniques for dealing with complaints. The main types of alternative dispute resolution are as follows (Ede & Barnes, 2002):

- *Informal resolution* is sometimes referred to as 'conciliation'. It involves a third party to a dispute who acts to resolve the allegation. The third party is usually a senior officer, who establishes some basic facts about the matter and then communicates with the complainant in a way designed to mitigate their concerns, such as through an explanation or an apology on behalf of the department.

- *Mediation* brings the two parties together in a conference managed by a trained and independent mediator with a view to finding an agreement that will satisfy everyone involved. 'Agreeing to disagree', but without malice, might be one outcome.

- With *managerial resolution* — sometimes called 'local resolution' — police middle managers provide a response both to the concerns of the complainant and to any associated conduct or competence issues involving the subject officer. Both informal resolution and mediation can be involved here, but the focus is on improving systems and the future conduct of officers through options that can include re-training and close supervision.

These responses can be very successful in terms of complainant and even police officer satisfaction. When matters are formally investigated typically about 10–40% of complainants are satisfied with the process and outcome, but with alternative dispute resolution satisfaction rates can be as high as 60–75%. While subject police officers report much higher satisfaction rates than complainants for investigations, they report even higher satisfaction rates for informal resolution procedures, in the order of 75–85% (Prenzler, 2009, chap. 7). Alternative dispute resolution is also much quicker and cheaper than formal investigations. An example of a fairly successful mediation process from the complainant's point of view is provided here:

> An officer was ticketing a car parked on the wrong side of the street when the owner came out of her house to complain. The officer ran the woman's name through the computer and found that a person matching her description had an outstanding warrant. The officer (a female) pat searched the woman and asked her to wait in the back of the cruiser. The officer then received more information indicating the woman was not the same person, so she released her. The woman filed a complaint because she felt the officer had embarrassed her in front of her children. The officer, in turn, was angry she had to mediate the issue because she felt that, having done nothing wrong, the department should have told the woman the case was closed. At the session, the mediator sat between them and asked them to decide who would talk first. The officer did, asking, 'Was I rude?' 'No.' 'Did I act professionally?' 'Yes.' The officer then explained why she had asked the woman to sit in the car, showing her the printout that indicated a person fitting her description — approximate age, race, gender, and same last name — had a warrant out for

her arrest. The officer said, 'I can understand why you were embarrassed, but if I was going to have you sit in the back of my cruiser, I needed to make sure you weren't carrying a gun that you could shoot me with in the back of the head.' The woman became less frustrated and ended up satisfied with the officer's explanation. (Finn, 2001, p. 78)

While alternative dispute resolution is often highly successful, there are risks. Resolution of complaints can hide systemic misconduct issues and be used to placate individual complainants while police carry on with 'business as usual'. Surveys also show that complainants prefer mediation, and that subject officers are willing to participate, but very few integrity systems offer proper mediation services and prefer the cheaper options of informal resolution and managerial resolution.

Covert Tactics

The kind of undercover methods used by police against organised crime have also been found to be successful when turned inwards against police (Marx, 1992). A particularly effective technique has involved judicial inquiries bringing in corrupt officers, presenting them with evidence against them, and then 'turning' them by sending them back to work 'wired' with covert recording devices (Daley, 1978). This then provides more powerful evidence against corruption networks. Covert tactics can also include physical surveillance, telephone intercepts and the installation of listening devices or video cameras.

The downfall of Roger Rogerson exemplifies how covert tactics can augment conventional investigations. Roger 'the Dodger' Rogerson was Australia's most notorious police officer. At his peak as a detective in Sydney in the 1970s and 1980s authorities repeatedly failed to prove powerful suspicions against him of 'green lighting' armed robberies and heroin trafficking, as well as murder, conspiracy to commit murder, bribery and evidence tampering. In the latter part of the 1980s a person made a report to police after overhearing Rogerson discussing secret bank accounts. A hidden camera was placed in a bank and showed Rogerson operating accounts of approximately AU$110,000 under a false name. He was dismissed from the force by a disciplinary tribunal over the offence (Whitton, 1990). Although the source of the monies was never established and the more serious suspected offences never proven, a lesser victory was achieved in removing a tainted officer.

Another example of the successful use of cameras occurred recently in Victoria. In 2005 the newly formed Office of Police Integrity (OPI) received a complaint from a criminal alleging he had been seriously assaulted by members of the Armed Offenders Squad. Similar allegations had been received before but had not been pursued or were difficult to prove. The OPI then installed a hidden camera in the ceiling of the Squad's interview room and began public hearings into the allegations. When members of the Squad denied the assault allegations they were shown footage from the hidden camera. The film showed detectives questioning a suspect about the location of jewellery and a gun used in a robbery. The suspect was threatened and then repeatedly slapped around the face while being questioned. One officer threatened to rip off his bleeding ear. The suspect was also repeatedly struck in rhythm to the words, 'F…ing … armed … robbery … squad'. The suspect was tackled to the ground and held down while being kicked. When he requested a telephone call he was hit with a phone and told, 'Want a phone call? Here it is. Here's ya f…ing phone call. Want to make another one?' During the video showing, one of the officers involved collapsed in the witness box and was carried from the room. The three detectives visible in the footage pleaded guilty to assault and were charged with lying to the OPI hearing (Collins, 2008; McKenzie & Berry, 2006).

Integrity Testing

Integrity testing is closely related to undercover tactics and often involves undercover officers in created corruption opportunities designed to test suspicions that officers might be corrupt. This is usually done in a targeted form against officers for whom traditional investigations have failed to allay strong suspicions or where traditional investigations (interviews, for example) might drive the corrupt officers underground (Prenzler & Ronken, 2001).

Integrity tests can require some special legislation, primarily to allow undercover agents to engage in illegal activities such as offering illicit drugs for sale. Tests are unlikely to attract a defence of entrapment as long as they do not involve coercive tactics. In order to be fair, the simulated situation is usually closely allied to the suspected corruption. The limited research evidence available suggests integrity tests have value for uncovering corruption and provide for something of a win-win outcome. Cases where officers 'fail' the test show that corruption is being detected. Cases where the tests are 'passed' provide reassurance that officers are not corrupt (Prenzler & Ronken, 2001). Two examples of integrity tests are provided here, one from New South Wales and one from Los Angeles:

> Gregory Joseph Sweeney thought he'd landed a handy [AU]$270 bonus to brighten the graveyard shift. But at the end of the night the senior constable had succumbed to one of the [New South Wales] Police Service's first stings on its own brethren. The sting … had involved more than a dozen police, including two female police who had masqueraded as night-clubbers. The test began when a Nissan sedan was reported stolen to Senior Constable Sweeney from Taree police. He was told also a vanity bag in the missing car contained a sum of cash. The stolen car was recovered by Senior Constable Sweeney who was then videotaped removing $270 cash from the vanity bag

and placing it in his pocket. Nearing the end of his shift a plain clothes detective stopped and searched Sweeney. The $270 was recovered and the constable admitted the theft. Sweeney was charged with stealing and convicted. Placed on a two-year good behaviour bond, Sweeney is one of at least 20 officers who have failed integrity tests since the integrity testing unit was established in February ... As with other targets, Sweeney was on the integrity testing unit hit-list of suspects, based on intelligence sent to the command by local area commanders and internal affairs spies. ('Anatomy of an Integrity Test', 1997, p. 4)

In Los Angeles a tip from an FBI informer passed on to the police led to the setting of a trap that caught two members of a special burglary unit. After an initial investigation, a fake burglary situation was created and the suspects took the bait and were arrested. They were part of a special burglar alarm response unit. After responding to the alarms, the officers would then pilfer the stores themselves. They were believed to trip the alarms of stores specializing in expensive electronic equipment and then respond to the alarms. Investigators turned the tables and set off the alarm at one such store. They then watched as the two made several trips carrying out cash and expensive goods which had been treated to leave an indelible, invisible mark on anyone who touched them. In later searches of their homes and those of several other suspects, authorities seized almost a truckload worth of electronic equipment. (Marx, 1992, p. 160)

Drug and Alcohol Testing

By most accounts, for many decades detectives in Sydney spent a good deal of their time on duty drinking in hotels and many were intoxicated while working (Padraic, 2005; Wood, 1997). The problem was largely eliminated by a very simple mechanism: random breath testing applied to police (Prenzler & Ronken, 2001). Low levels of positive test results for both alcohol and drug tests in New South Wales have been interpreted as a strong deterrent and a valuable quality assurance mechanism. Drug testing is a more intrusive technology than alcohol testing. The most reliable tests require both urine and hair samples (Mieczkowski & Lersch, 2002). Drug testing has not typically been applied on a random basis but in a targeted fashion when police are involved in traffic accidents or incidents resulting in serious injury or deaths, or when supervisors express concern about their behaviour. Tests are also often mandatory for police applicants and recruits. The practice with positive drug and alcohol test results for serving officers often involves offers of therapy and personal assistance before invoking more drastic actions such as employment termination. Given the significant risks to policing from the illicit drug trade some departments have introduced random testing. A recent review of the New South Wales system by the Police Integrity Commission recommended increasing the number of officers tested from 3–4% each year to 15% to develop a stronger deterrent effect (PIC, 2005).

Risk Management

The previous chapter outlined how policing is a high-risk occupation for misconduct, with particular heightened risks in certain areas, such as drug law enforcement or public order policing. As part of a more advanced approach to maximising ethical practice a number of police departments and oversight agencies have developed risk management protocols designed to identify emerging problems and put in place mitigation measures. Police should also be continuously evaluating all areas where conflicts or injuries occur as a result of police operations, with a view to reducing adverse consequences. The system controls described earlier in this chapter in the areas of high speed pursuits, data management, informant management and process corruption have all been developed by research using a variety of standard social science research tools.

A good example of an area where risk management is required is that of litigation against police. Research has shown that successful litigation is increasing in many jurisdictions (Ransley et al., 2007). A traditional police department would tend to follow a set practice of contesting cases, at considerable cost to the taxpayer, and then paying out on unsuccessful cases without any follow-up research on the causes of the problem. A smart department, on the other hand, will adopt a policy of litigation minimisation by analysing the nature and causes of all cases with a view to changing procedures that will measurably reduce both problematic police behaviours giving rise to litigation and the costs associated with responding to litigation. A good example of this approach in practice is provided by the Los Angeles County Sheriff's Department. In 2003 it implemented a Strategic Risk Management program in the area of litigation. The program:

1. systematically investigated and vigorously contested cases considered to be lacking in merit, especially if they appeared to involve potentially high payouts;

2. expedited settlements where the litigant appeared to have a strong case; and

3. where possible, identified and addressed behavioural patterns and procedural problems that triggered litigation.

The outcomes were very positive: 'The fiscal year 2003–4 statistics, when compared to the previous fiscal year, revealed that the active caseload decreased 17.8 percent, that new lawsuits decreased 26.9 percent, and that judgment and settlement costs decreased more then 55 percent' (Jones & Mathers, 2006, p. 126).

Miscellaneous

A number of other preventive strategies have been recommended by inquiries and reviews or introduced by police. One is the rotation of personnel through high-risk squads on a basis of five to seven years to prevent the establishment of corrupt habits and networks (Mollen, 1994, p. 124). A second is the requirement that police negotiate with the organisers of demonstrations to seek agreements about march parameters, the use of crowd marshals, and what behaviours police will and will not tolerate, in order to limit public disorder and police brutality. Another is the recruitment of more women, given that women tend to be more conciliatory than males and attract significantly less complaints (National Center for Women and Policing, 2001).

Conclusion

This set of strategies makes for a complex integrity system that is certainly not cheap. Most larger police departments, especially those with a recent history of systemic corruption, are likely to need all these elements in place in order to reassure the public that everything possible is being doing to minimise misconduct. Other departments might not require the full mix but need to be willing and able to implement specific elements if the need arises. It certainly appears to be the case that a mix of reactive and proactive strategies is essential to both detect and prevent misconduct. Maximum use of information management systems is also required, to ensure that detection and prevention strategies are informed by as much data as can be obtained about levels of compliance with ethical standards and the impacts of different interventions.

SECTION TWO

Courts

Chapter 5

Ethical Issues in Criminal Law

One of the most notorious controversies over lawyers' ethics occurred in
an up-state area of New York in the early 1970s. Francis Belge and Frank
Armani acted as court-appointed attorneys for Robert Garrow, who had
been caught in a police manhunt and charged with the murder of a young
man. (Garrow turned out to be a deranged serial killer who committed
numerous rapes and at least eight murders.) Thinking Garrow might be
able to strike a deal if he informed police of the whereabouts of other
victims, his lawyers quizzed him about missing persons cases. Garrow
revealed he had raped and murdered two girls, and he gave directions to
the locations of their bodies. Belge and Armani investigated the claims
and found the body of one of the girls in an abandoned mine shaft. They
took photos but did not inform the police. The father of the victim travelled from Chicago, met with Belge and begged him to provide any information he had to help locate the girl. Despite a torn conscience and
sleepless nights, Belge stuck to his lawyer's oath to keep the information
confidential. The girl's body was found four months later by two children
playing in the area.

Belge and Armani failed to find the second girl on their first attempt. But
after Garrow drew a map Belge succeeded in locating the body of the
victim. Again, he photographed the body but kept its location a secret. For
two months police and the girl's family desperately searched for her,
thinking she might still be alive, until a university student found her body.

Belge and Armani kept silent for a total of six months. During the trial
Garrow took the stand and was questioned by Belge in an attempt to make
the jury decide he was 'not guilty, by reason of insanity'. After Garrow
admitted to numerous rapes and murders he revealed that he had told the
lawyers about the locations of the bodies. The revelation sparked a furore.
The lawyers became the targets of a hate campaign and their law firms collapsed. A national debate ensued about the legality and ethics of their silence.
A grand jury investigation was launched but the case was eventually
dropped, and a New York State Bar Association investigation found the
lawyers had not violated any professional rules (Australian Broadcasting
Corporation [ABC] Radio National, 2008; Gado, n.d.; 'Slayer's 2 Lawyers
Kept Secret of 2 More Killings', 1974).

The Garrow case illustrates something of the potential difficulty in moral
issues faced by criminal lawyers. This chapter examines the areas of ethical

decision-making faced by practitioners at the second stage of the criminal justice system: the criminal courts. The focus of the chapter is on the three main groups of legal professionals: prosecution lawyers, defence lawyers, and judges and magistrates. Lawyers hold specialist knowledge and skills that give them significant influence over court outcomes, which in turn have different effects on the interests of different stakeholders, including the accused, victims of crime and the public.

The areas of ethical decision-making covered in this chapter are duty to client versus duty to justice and truth, zealousness, plea bargaining, conflicts of interest and bias, graft and gratuities, loyalty and whistleblowing, sentencing and bail decisions, and control of courtroom tactics, as well as some miscellaneous issues. The section on corrections examines broader policy-level issues about sentencing when considering the ethics of punishment. The present chapter also summarises ethical positions as outlined in a number of codes. These are generally protective of client confidentiality, but with some important qualifiers. They also, predictably, emphasise the importance of impartiality, equal protections, serving the public interest and avoiding conflicts of interest.

The Importance of Legal Ethics

From a system perspective, when police arrest a person it is merely a preliminary decision by state representatives about probable culpability. It is not a final decision. A binding determination about the guilt or innocence of that person is made by the courts. One of the fundamental rights held by citizens in modern democracies, in theory, is the requirement on police (or any person making an arrest) to bring the arrested person before a court as quickly as possible so the charges against them can be heard and settled one way or the other. A limbo state where one is charged but not tried is considered to be a major source of stress and a basic unfairness (Prenzler & Sarre, 2009, p. 269).

Being found guilty can have enormous negative effects on a person's reputation, relationships and self-esteem. But what is probably more important for many people is not so much the court's power to determine guilt or innocence but its power to assign penalties to those found guilty. Penalties can range from an admonition and good behaviour bond, to a monetary fine, to a short prison term of several months, to much longer prison terms of between five years and the remainder of a person's life, to loss of life by execution in some jurisdictions. Prison time entails not just loss of liberty but loss of income as well, including difficulties in finding employment on release. Imprisonment means separation from family and other loved ones and exposure to abuses in prisons.

The courts therefore have enormous power over people's lives, and in the process there are a great many things that can go wrong. The worst-case scenario is the conviction of an innocent person, particularly when it leads to execution. But other miscarriages of justice can also occur, including the acquittal of guilty persons and the application of excessive or inadequate penalties. The prosecution of innocent people, even when an acquittal results, is also almost always a very painful process.

The accused person is at the centre of this process, with the most to gain or lose. But there are numerous other stakeholders as well. These include the victims who want to see justice done — including the loved ones of homicide victims. There are also witnesses, who may feel intimidated and threatened. The public also want to see justice done and they bear the financial cost of running the courts. All those who directly participate in the process have different purposes and different things at stake, including reputations, career progression and their conscience.

The gravity of the criminal court process can be underscored by comparing it with the civil courts (Ransley & Prenzler, 2009). With the civil courts the onus for action is normally on a private citizen or company. The state merely acts as an arbiter in the dispute. But with the criminal courts the state acts for the victim and takes on the victim's burden of seeking justice. This is done for the victim but also for the whole community. The civil courts can settle disputes and assign monetary damages and direct certain behaviours. But the criminal courts have the additional power of incarcerating people, and also executing them in some jurisdictions.

We should not underestimate what is at stake in the court process. The lives of accused persons can be ruined with enduring emotional and even physical agony beyond the imagination of many readers. Many victims of crime have a need for the truth to be brought out and to see offenders brought to justice (Home Office, 2003). What happens in the courts occurs in the glare of public observation and media scrutiny like no other criminal justice process. With all this in mind, it is imperative that all participants behave with the greatest possible sense of responsibility and integrity to prevent miscarriages of justice and the other harms that can occur to participants.

Institutional Context

The institutional context in which criminal lawyers operate is particularly important in understanding the ethical dilemmas they face. Here we need to firstly consider the two main types of criminal court systems that operate internationally (Kessler, 2008). There is the continental European system, which is also used in many countries that were once colonised by European powers. This is usually described as an inquisitorial system, in that the emphasis, in theory at least, is on a cooperative inquiry concerned with finding the truth. The process is dominated by professionals. Judges are expected to take an active and questioning role, and the line between an investigation and trial is often blurred so that investigative processes carry forward into the trial. Juries are not used. More serious cases usually require a panel of judges, with a possible layperson on the panel. The second system is an Anglo-Saxon system that evolved in England and is adopted in many former English colonies such as Australia and the United States. This adversarial system involves a strict separation between investigation and trial. The trial is treated essentially as a contest between prosecution and defence, who seek a favourable verdict from a magistrate or jury. In Australia magistrates preside over lower-level cases without a jury. They also have enormous power to dismiss potential jury trials which they vet in a committal hearing.

Scholars who study ethical issues for criminal lawyers tend to the view that the adversarial system magnifies ethical dilemmas and issues (Parker & Evans, 2007, p. 14ff). Like the inquisitorial system, the theoretical ultimate goal of the adversarial system is to find the truth and ensure justice is done. But the method is quite different. The adversarial courtroom requires that the participants adopt roles. The prosecution must make the best case they can against the accused. The defence must make the best case they can in their client's favour. The magistrate or jury must act as impartial arbiters, deciding who has the most convincing case. In theory, the truth will be the product of the contest between two parties equal in skills and resources. Critics, however, allege that this means that extra-legal strategies of rhetoric and persuasion, and even cheating, are adopted by the contestants. According to the 'confidence game' theory, the apparent objectivity of the process hides the fact that the defence and prosecution are working for their own interests (Pollock, 2007, p. 359). Each side will try to hide their strategies and 'ambush' the other side in the courtroom, especially by emotional appeals to the ordinary members of the community who make up the jury. The potential for sudden shifts in the direction of a trial, and surprise revelations from witnesses, is what fuels the drama of the adversarial courtroom. In literature, as in real life, the reader's or viewer's anger is easily stoked by misleading tactics and unfair outcomes. Importantly, the system requires that each participant adopt a role that might be at odds with their personal views about the merits of their case.

Another important contextual factor is the power of lawyers. Legal work requires a licence, and a licence usually requires many years of post-secondary education, followed by vetting by a licensing authority. Accused persons are dependent on lawyers, who hold a virtual monopoly over legal representation. Accused persons can represent themselves and, in some circumstances some jurisdictions will allow applications to the court to permit lay advocacy, but the complexity of the law means self-representation or lay-representation is a very risky strategy (AIJA, 2001). Nonetheless, the fact is that most defence layers 'lose' their cases. The fact is that most defence lawyers 'lose' their cases. In Australia typically only about 9% of defendants are acquitted in the higher courts and 4% in the magistrates courts (ABS, 2008, p. 414). Nonetheless, apart from helping with the acquittal of persons wrongfully charged, defence lawyers also have a crucial role to play in arguing for minimal penalties for convicted persons. On the other hand, victims of crime are dependent on prosecutors. While private criminal prosecutions are possible in some jurisdictions, these are very rare. Victims who wish to see the perpetrator brought to justice are therefore reliant on the knowledge and skills of a prosecutor to obtain a conviction and to obtain the best penalty possible from the victim's perspective.

Like police, lawyers exercise considerable discretion — that is, a legal area of freedom where they can act according to their own judgments about what is right or wrong, or appropriate. This is reflected in the extent to which they commit energy and resources to prosecuting or defending a case. Lawyers also have special privileges, most notably the legal professional privilege of defence lawyers to maintain client confidentiality; in other words, there is usually no legal requirement for them to disclose the full details of their communications with their clients. There are limits to this, as outlined later in this chapter, but it is an area of considerable power that can entail dilemmas and can have profound implications for the outcome of cases.

Another area of privilege is that of professional self-regulation. Historically, lawyers 'got in early' and set up systems by which their professional associations were allowed to grant licences and discipline members, rather than having this done by a government agency. This is changing, but it has traditionally been an area that enlarged the freedom and power of lawyers. It has also served a crucial role in civil liberties in limiting the ability of governments to control who can practise law by giving the public choices about legal representation. It involves a type of separation of powers and provides a check on government abuses by including non-government parties in the criminal justice process (American Bar Association, 2002, preamble).

In the case of criminal law, many of the actors are government employees and therefore public servants. This applies to prosecutors and also to legal aid lawyers. However, the nature of legal practice, even in government bureaucracies, means that these lawyers must still exercise discretionary judgments about what cases to prioritise and how to support them. Defence lawyers in the private sector have much more freedom about what tactics they pursue. They will also be subject to much less scrutiny. For example, outside the unlikely event of a search warrant, they can keep their files completely private. A criminal lawyer in a government job does not have this privilege.

Lawyers as a group also exercise a disproportionate amount of political power. They are over-represented in political parties, parliaments and ministries, and therefore make a key contribution to decisions about what laws apply in any jurisdiction (Pollock, 2007, p. 319). This includes the laws that apply to the regulation of the legal profession. Lawyers also tend to earn above-average incomes and their knowledge of the law facilitates their capacity for wealth creation. Overall then, lawyers exercise extensive political, social, economic and juridical power. How they exercise that power shapes criminal justice outcomes, including stakeholders' experience of the system and public perceptions of the system: whether it be in terms of something professional, fair, just and equitable, or something incompetent, biased, unjust and discriminatory. The independence of lawyers is crucial to the operation of the justice system, but it also limits their accountability, particularly in the case of private sector criminal lawyers who have a greater capacity to keep information confidential. The situation underscores the importance of voluntary compliance with ethical standards.

Lawyers and Ethics

Lawyer jokes have a certain social currency. Many of the jokes relate to the contradiction between the lofty goals of the law and the commercial imperatives of legal work: the so-called 'hired gun' status of many lawyers (Pollock, 2007, pp. 318–319). Serving a client's interests, or an employer's interests (including the public prosecutor), does not necessarily entail serving the interests of justice and the public good. Legal ethics or lawyers' ethics are sometimes described as an oxymoron — two things that are mutually contradictory. As Jocelyn Pollock argues, there is a deep conflict within the profession between the idea of lawyers as 'moral agents' and that of lawyers as 'legal advocates' (2007, p. 323). One can think of the many poorly paid human rights lawyers battling for the rights of oppressed persons and compare their work with that of lawyers for major corporations, such as tobacco companies or major polluters, who seek to use the law to avoid liability for harms done by their company's products. These are members of the same profession, but they are engaged in quite different types of legal practice.

Classic Dilemmas

This section sets out the main areas of ethical challenge and risk for criminal lawyers. The section begins with a brief outline of the main principles guiding legal practice. Then, as with the earlier chapter on police dilemmas, the conflicting principles within dilemmas are described, followed by a 'resolution' of sorts from professional codes. The codes used here are the American Bar Association *Model Rules of Professional Conduct* (2002), the Law Council of

Australia *Model Rules of Professional Conduct and Practice* (2002), the US Courts *Code of Conduct for United States Judges* (2000) and the Council of Chief Justices of Australia *Guide to Judicial Conduct* (2002).

Codes of ethics generally require lawyers to act lawfully, in a diligent and timely manner, ensuring they remain up to date with their knowledge of the law. They are expected to accept all clients, regardless of the lawyer's personal prejudices, so long as the matter is relevant to the law and the lawyer is competent to provide counsel. There is also strong moral pressure to provide free (pro bono) services to the poor. Lawyers are meant to use the law 'only for legitimate purposes and not to harass or intimidate others' (American Bar Association, 2002, preamble). The profession, despite its very large private sector component, is meant to fulfil 'ideals of public service'. These rules are extremely important as a bulwark of civil liberties because they are meant to ensure that even the most repugnant persons are not exposed to false and oppressive prosecutions (Law Council Australia, 2002, p. 12). There are also strict rules about when a lawyer is allowed to abandon a client. At the same time, codes, such as the American Bar Association (2002) model rules, recognise that the practice of law almost inevitably involves 'conflicting responsibilities':

> Virtually all difficult ethical problems arise from conflict between a lawyer's responsibilities to clients, to the legal system and to the lawyer's own interest in remaining an ethical person while earning a satisfactory living. (Preamble)

Duty to Client Versus Duty to Justice and Truth

The most prominent ethical issue in legal work is duty to client versus duty to justice and truth, and is akin to the Dirty Harry or noble cause dilemma in policing. The main structural principle here is that of role taking and role conflict — particularly pronounced in adversarial systems, as we have seen. The dilemma applies to defence lawyers in their role as advocates for accused persons. Their professional duty — indeed their moral duty — is to provide the best legal defence possible. From a system perspective, the role of the defence is to test the state's case. This is necessary as one part of a large machine. The state may be in error — as a result of police corruption, for example, or because of errors in forensic analyses or prosecution bias. Witnesses might be mistaken or lying. The accused might have been framed. The accused might have been responsible for the offence but they might have a defence in provocation or coercion that the prosecution has ignored. If an accused person is found guilty, the prosecution might seek an excessively heavy penalty that pays little regard to the difficult circumstances or personal responsibilities of the guilty person, such as their role as a family breadwinner. Any number of errors or misjudgments can potentially creep into the prosecution case. A competent and conscientious challenge from the defence is therefore vital to justice and to the accountability of the courts. Furthermore, client confidentiality 'serves the public interest' because people will be less inclined to seek legal advice and be informed of the law if they cannot be confident that what they say will remain private (American Bar Association, 2002; Kleinig, 2008, pp. 142–144). Finally, even if a client tells their lawyer they are guilty, they might be deluded or protecting another person or unaware of defences to their actions (Parker & Evans, 2007, p. 103). This is the positive side of the defence lawyer's role.

The negative side is as follows. In the process of preparing a defence the lawyer is obliged to ask questions of the client to ascertain their perspective on the charges, and they may even carry out an investigation using a private investigator. In the process, the lawyer may find evidence of the client's culpability. The client may even volunteer the fact that they are guilty — as occurred in the Garrow case in the introduction to this chapter. What should the lawyer do in this situation where they acquire 'guilty knowledge'? Should they advise the client to plead guilty and take responsibility for their actions? Should they hand over the evidence to the prosecution? Many would argue that by refusing to say 'yes' to these questions the lawyer becomes party to the covering up of a crime and a miscarriage of justice, regardless of whether or not the client is eventually found guilty. Their actions are an insult to justice and a special insult to victims of crime who seek at least some resolution of their pain through the identification and sanctioning of an offender.

Legal codes of practice directly address this dilemma, but something of the difficulty of the issue is embodied in the complex wording and qualifications employed. On the one hand, there are usually strong statements protecting the confidentiality of clients in terms of a general prohibition on disclosures not authorised by the client (American Bar Association, 2002, s.1.6; Law Council of Australia, 2002, p. 5). Lawyers are also required to provide the best defence possible within the law. This is tempered, however, by a number of qualifications. The three most important ones, in the American Bar Association rules, are framed in the following terms (s.1.6):

> (b) A lawyer may reveal information relating to the representation of a client to the extent the lawyer reasonably believes necessary:
>
> (1) to prevent reasonably certain death or substantial bodily harm.
>
> (2) to prevent the client from committing a crime or fraud that is reasonably certain to result in substantial injury to the financial property of another and in furtherance of the client of which the client has used or is using the lawyer's services.
>
> (3) to prevent, mitigate or rectify substantial injury to the financial interests or property of another that is reasonably certain to result or has resulted from the client's commission of a crime or fraud in furtherance of which the client has used the lawyer's services.

Other conditions attached to confidentiality relate to any disputes between the lawyer and the client or in compliance with a court order. This is buttressed by section 3.3(a) that states that 'a lawyer shall not knowingly':

(1) make a false statement of fact or law to a tribunal or fail to correct a false statement of material fact or law previously made to the tribunal by the lawyer …

(3) offer evidence that the lawyer knows to be false.

There is also a duty to report the discovery that evidence given previously was false.

The Law Council of Australia model rules in particular emphasise that lawyers should act 'honestly' and refrain from any practice that is 'calculated to defeat the ends of justice' (2002, p. 5). The strong statements on confidentiality are qualified in similar ways to the American Bar Association rules. Lawyers are permitted to encourage clients to tell the truth. But while lawyers must not in any way advise or encourage anyone to give false evidence, they are permitted to rehearse evidence and discuss inconsistencies or problems (Law Council of Australia, 2002, s.17).

The Law Council of Australia (2002) rules also emphasise the importance of informing clients of alternatives to defending charges and of any possible advantages to them of these alternatives (s.12.3 and s.12.4). This is a clearly implied encouragement for lawyers to make wise use of plea bargaining, which involves at least one plea of guilty by an accused. The rules also state that an advocate must not 'act as the mere mouthpiece of the client' but exercise forensic judgment and refuse to follow the client's instructions where appropriate (s.13.1). While this does not extend to stating the lawyer's personal opinion of the merits of the case in the court, the lawyer is permitted to inform the court of any 'persuasive authority' that might tell against the client (s.13.2.3). As with the American Bar Association rules, 'a practitioner must not knowingly make a misleading statement to a court' and must correct any mistakes that come to light (s.14.1 and s.14.2).

At the same time, in the Law Council's rules there is no obligation on the defence to correct any errors they are aware of in the case made by the other side (s.14.3) or to inform the court if evidence has been wrongly ruled as inadmissible (s.14.9). The sections on 'delinquent or guilty clients' also allow for a good deal of discretion and a generally passive response to the question of guilty knowledge. Section 15 on 'delinquent or guilty clients' covers three main situations where confidentiality might be breached. Section 15.1 concerns a situation where a client admits to their lawyer that they have lied in court in a way that could affect the outcome, or influenced someone else to lie or had another person falsify a document. In this case, the lawyer:

15.1.1   must advise the client that the court should be informed of the lie or falsification and request authority so to inform the court;

15.1.2   must refuse to take any further part in the case unless the client authorises the practitioner to inform the court of the lie or falsification;

15.1.3   must promptly inform the court of the lie or falsification upon the client authorising the practitioner to do so; but

15.1.4   must not otherwise inform the court of the lie or falsification.

Section 15.2 is concerned with a situation where a client confesses they are guilty to the lawyer but elects to continue to plead not guilty. The lawyer:

15.2.1   may cease to act, if there is enough time for another practitioner to take over the case properly before the hearing, and the client does not insist on the practitioner continuing to appear for the client;

If the lawyer continues to act for the client, they (s.15.2.2):

(a) must not falsely suggest that some other person committed the offence charged;

(b) must not set up an affirmative case inconsistent with the confession;

(c) may argue that the evidence as a whole does not prove that the client is guilty of the offence charged;

(d) may argue that for some reason of law the client is not guilty of the offence charged; or

(e) may argue that for any other reason not prohibited by (a) and (b) the client should not be convicted of the offence charged.

Third, in a case where a client tells a lawyer they are intending to disobey a court order, the lawyer 'must':

15.3.1   advise the client against that course and warn the client of its dangers;

15.3.2   not advise the client how to carry out or conceal that course;

15.3.3   not inform the court or the opponent of the client's intention unless:

(a) the client has authorised the practitioner to do so before-hand; or

(b) the practitioner believes on reasonable grounds that the client's conduct constitutes a threat to any person's safety.

Client confidentiality is also something that prosecutors are expected to protect. If prosecutors believe that a defence lawyer is in possession of evidence against their client that the prosecution does not have, there is often an option in law to obtain it by a subpoena or even by a raid on the lawyer's office. However, the American Bar Association rules instruct against this unless the information is 'essential' to complete a case and there is no alternative means of obtaining the information (2002, s.3.8.e).

We have to ask whether or not these provisions are good enough. The American Bar Association rules make many disclosures discretionary. Lawyers 'may reveal information' to the 'extent the lawyer reasonably believes necessary' to prevent serious crimes (2002, s.1.6.b). The Law Council of Australia rules use similar wording. In both codes lawyers are also prohibited from allowing false testimony and must comply with disclosure requests. However, they are not obliged to disclose material that benefits the prosecution or assists with an inquiry. Nor are they are required to disclose confidential communications from their client even if this information could lead to the exoneration of a wrongfully convicted person. The obligation to prevent wrongful convictions lies with the prosecution. The upshot of these differences is that there is potential for the kind of scenario outlined in the introduction to this chapter. There may be serious adverse consequences for interested parties when defence lawyers are not legally obliged to divulge information relevant to a serious crime.

Zealousness

The adversarial system provides plenty of material for courtroom dramas in narrative fiction. For example, one often-used stereotype is the over-zealous defence lawyer who badgers a hapless victim in the witness box. Another is the defence lawyer whose badgering catches out a deceitful witness. Perhaps the most famous example of fictional courtroom drama in an adversarial system is in the 1960 novel *To Kill a Mockingbird* (Lee, 1979; Pope Osborne, Hinton, Handler, & Curtis, 2008). In the story, a black man is falsely accused of raping a white girl. Although the innocent man is convicted, and then shot while trying to escape, the truth is brought to light for all to see in part by the defence lawyer's clever and relentless interrogation of the alleged victim in the witness box. In the process the virtuous lawyer and hero of the book, Atticus Finch, also exposes the institutional racism that dominates the town.

Zealousness involves a dilemma of discretion. In any contest, players will be tempted to break the rules or operate at the limits of the rules. With all the resources of the state behind them, prosecutors have a particular duty to 'assist the court to arrive at the truth' (Law Council of Australia, 2002, s.20.1). However, prosecution lawyers are only human. Once they decide to go with a case they will want to win. They might feel the case is not watertight but that it should, nonetheless, go to trial in the public interest — with a magistrate or jury as the decision-makers. Or they might be 100% satisfied of the guilt of the accused person. Either way, they have to convince a third party, and inevitably they have a personal stake in the outcome in terms of their reputation and career. Consequently, they may be tempted to operate at the margins of permissible practice.

Both prosecution and defence lawyers can push the rules in a number of standard ways — all in the name of the noble cause of justice (Pollock, 2007, p. 334ff). Disclosure rules require the prosecution to share the main elements of their case with the defence in order for the defence to prepare a response.

However, witnesses or evidence can be withheld and brought in at the last minute — as part of an 'ambush' strategy — by claiming they were only discovered after the trial got underway. Another strategy used by both sides is 'jury nullification' — diverting the jury's attention from the law and the facts of the case by playing on their emotions and prejudices (Parker & Evans, 2007, p. 105). Another tactic, often featured in fictional courtroom dramas, is to present inadmissible evidence, which is struck out by the judge but remains in the minds of jurors. A classic example would be to introduce a rape victim's previous sexual history as a way of making the jury think she might have been a willing participant in the sexual act or that she led on the accused.

Another example concerns the selective use of questions in the courtroom. Witnesses are normally only allowed to answer questions put to them. When interviewing a scientific witness the prosecutor might avoid any questions that would allow the witness to express doubts about the scientific evidence or present alternative explanations. Although the defence should pick up on this, a sloppy or ill-prepared defence lawyer might miss the chance. The overall result of these tactics is that the case is not presented in a fully truthful way that permits a fair trial.

The American Bar Association rules prohibit prosecutors from pursuing a charge against a person when they know there is insufficient evidence of 'probable cause' (2002, s.3.8.a). Prosecutors are also required to ensure that the accused has had an opportunity to access legal advice and support. As noted previously, they are also required to disclose to the defence counsel any information that might assist in the defence of the accused and assist in any plea of mitigation (s.3.8.d). And they are required to disclose any evidence that comes to light after a trial that might support an acquittal (s.3.8.h). Both sides are prohibited from obstructing investigations or falsifying or destroying evidence (s.3.4). Importantly, they are instructed, in trial, not to

> allude to any matter that the lawyer does not reasonably believe is relevant or that will not be supported by admissible evidence [or] assert personal knowledge of facts in issue except when testifying as a witness. (s.3.4.e).

Similar rules apply to prosecutors under the Law Council of Australia rules, with an additional prohibition on language or behaviour in court designed to 'inflame or bias the court against the accused' (2002, s.20.3). The Law Council of Australia disclosure rules for prosecutors are qualified by a duty to withhold information that could adversely affect the 'integrity of the administration of justice … or jeopardise the safety of any persons' (s.20.5.1). Prosecutors are also prohibited from communicating with the accused (except via their counsel) and must alert the defence if any evidence they have presented may have been obtained illegally (s.20.9 and s.20.8). They are barred from seeking a sentence that is 'vindictive' (s.20.12).

Plea Bargaining

Plea bargaining involves a negotiation between the prosecution and defence, prior to the trial, regarding a possible trade-off between a plea of guilty for one or more charges in return for the dropping of one or more other charges. Plea bargaining is an example of 'bureaucratic justice' (Pollock, 2007, p. 360) because efficiency — through sidestepping a trial — is the main goal. For prosecutors, the dilemma is that there is a reduction in the quantum of justice in exchange for greater certainty about the outcome. For the accused, there is the likelihood of a reduced sentence but in exchange for foregoing a trial and the chance of an acquittal. An innocent person might be tempted to plead guilty if they feel the court is biased.

Conflicts of Interest and Bias

Lawyers may have personal, political or other biases against defendants and need to guard against these or even step aside if they feel their prejudices will influence their decisions. At the same time, they might avoid stepping aside because of the difficulty in explaining why, or because they might be tempted to exercise these prejudices, especially when it is felt that they have social validity. Financial conflicts of interest are also possible in criminal law in cases where corporate misconduct results in criminal charges. Codes of conduct make it clear that lawyers need to avoid conflicts of interest, including conflicts involving more than one client or conflicts involving the lawyer's own business or personal interests. A case involving a friend or relative of a judge or prosecutor obviously presents a conflict of interest. In all such cases they should step aside. The American Bar Association model rules allow a lawyer to represent more than one party involved in the same matter if they provide written consent, but not when the parties' interests are clearly at odds (2002, s.1.7.a.1). An example would be a lawyer representing co-accused who decide to testify against each other.

When it comes to judges and magistrates there is a recognition that independence and the appearance of independence are at their most important. In the words of the *Code of Conduct for United States Judges* (US Courts, 2000):

> Deference to the judgments and ruling of courts depends on public confidence in the integrity and independence of judges. The integrity and independence of judges depend in turn upon their acting without fear or favour. (p. 2)

Generally, judicial officers are expected to 'recuse' themselves from a conflict of interest — that is, step out of the role. More generally, judicial integrity depends on compliance with the following rules, in summary (Council of Chief Justices of Australia, 2002; US Courts, 2000):

- Judges themselves need to show respect for the law and comply with the law.
- They need to remain up to date in their knowledge of the law.

- They must not be swayed by 'partisan interests, public clamour, or fear of criticism' (US Courts, 2000, p. 4).
- They must maintain order and a dignified atmosphere in the courtroom.
- They must be efficient and prompt but also patient and courteous to all participants in the process.
- They cannot allow any real or apparent conflicts of interest. This means they cannot use their office to advance their own financial interests or those of their families, relatives or friends; and they must avoid any appearance of bias.
- They need to avoid holding investments, owning companies, sitting on committees or holding office in any organisations where a conflict of interest might arise.
- They should not grant any special treatment to any party.
- They should not communicate with any party in a case outside the presence of opposing counsel.
- They should not join any organisations that practice any kind of racial, sexual, religious, ethnic or other discrimination.
- They cannot work as lawyers, except to give legal advice in a private capacity.
- Judges may give lectures and speeches and engage in a variety of activities related to the legal profession as long as these do not reflect adversely on the appearance of their capacity to act impartially.
- They may also be involved in activities related to 'the improvement of the law' (US courts, 2000, p. 9), but again with regard to the appearance of impartiality.
- Judges are also prohibited from political activity while in office.

See also *The Bangalore Principles of Judicial Conduct* (2002).

Graft and Gratuities

As with police, judges may be offered bribes, such as cash, for providing defendants with a favourable judgment. While this might not be a classic dilemma in that the right thing to do should be obvious, a judge who is under financial pressure may feel that the benefit to them and their family outweighs any harm done. Prosecutors can be similarly tempted. The codes used here do not directly address the issue of bribery, presumably because it is illegal anyway, and there is an implied prohibition in all statements about impartiality and influence. The *Guide to Judicial Conduct* emphasises the importance of rejecting any gratuities other than the most minor gifts, such as a bottle of wine or a book, which might be handed over after a speech or presentation (Council of Chief Justices of Australia, 2002, p. 24). The *Code of Conduct for United States Judges* generally prohibits judges, or close family members, from soliciting or accepting any gifts or payments from anyone with might be 'substantially affected' by a judge's official duties (US Courts, 2000, p. 11). Others sections also prohibit gratuities where an impression might be created of favouritism or potential favouritism. However, there are some fairly wide guidelines on other gifts such as attendance at cocktail parties and dinners and payments to attend conferences paid for by professional legal associations. Functions are to be avoided when paid for by a lawyer or law firm that has a stake in current cases (US Courts, 1998).

Loyalty and Whistleblowing

Under the heading 'Maintaining the Integrity of the Profession' the American Bar Association rules require lawyers to inform 'the appropriate authority' if they know or suspect that a lawyer or judge has engaged in any violations of relevant rules or may be unfit for duty in any way (2002, s.8.3). As with police, this requirement does not necessarily make a decision to inform on a colleague any easier, but it does provide a clear standard and help lawyers in that situation justify their actions in breaking any codes of loyalty and silence. Oddly perhaps, this is not something explicitly addressed in the codes for judges used in this chapter.

Sentencing and Bail Decisions

Sentencing of convicted persons can involve dilemmas for judges and magistrates where they have discretion. It may be difficult for a judge to completely ignore a large group of protesters outside a courthouse lobbying for or against a harsh or light sentence. There can also be intense, if silent, pressure from interested parties inside the courtroom. While judges are expected to follow precedent this is not always binding and the particular circumstances of a case — the mitigating and aggravating factors — may not fit with precedents. The judge might also disagree with the precedents. How much weight to give to mitigating and aggravating factors can be difficult and controversial. Furthermore, sentencing has different and potentially contradictory goals. A judge may have to choose between emphasising punishment or rehabilitation, and between punishing a specific offender and sending a message to deter others. Pollock (2007, pp. 163–166) notes that in ideological and political terms judges' sentencing options divide across a spectrum between 'liberal' views that emphasise social and biological pressures on offenders and reduced responsibility, and 'conservative' views that emphasise free will, personal responsibility and the need for punishment.

In some jurisdictions judges are now faced with the additional conundrum of an indefinite detention option. This is invoked when the state feels an offender has such a bad history that they represent an ongoing high risk to society and should be held in custody indefinitely. A person is 'punished' by ongoing incarceration for crimes they have not committed but might commit, and their release would appear to pose a grave risk. Judges may be personally blamed if they release defendants who then reoffend.

Similar issues apply with bail decisions where a judge must weigh the risk of the accused not appearing at the trial or committing another crime on bail against the cost to the state of remand, the fact the defendant might be found not guilty after a long period on remand, and harms to the defendant's employment and family.

Control of Courtroom Tactics

This is an issue for judges and magistrates. As noted earlier, in lower-level courts, presided over by magistrates, the magistrate hears the evidence, makes the finding on guilt or innocence and also applies the penalty. In a jury trial the judgment on the allegations is made by a jury with the judge managing the hearing and then, normally, separately deciding on the penalty. Dilemmas here relate primarily to the degree to which the 'judge' allows the prosecution and defence free reign to pursue zealous tactics. A key area concerns the admissibility of evidence. Judges are required to ensure rules of evidence are followed. For example, evidence obtained illegally should be excluded, as should hearsay evidence or speculation. Judges can be accused of being too detached or too involved. If they suppress submissions they may be accused of suppressing the truth. If they allow too much to be admitted in evidence they may be accused of allowing biased testimony.

Personal Conduct

As with police, lawyers are expected to maintain high standards of personal conduct to contribute to the image of the profession as one of integrity and responsibility. Disciplinary rules usually require a lawyer to be disbarred for offences such as fraud or serious assault even if the offences were unrelated to their work (American Bar Association, 2002, s. 8.4).

Miscellaneous Issues

There are a number of other areas of ethical challenge for criminal lawyers. While accused persons have a right to a quality legal defence it is possible that the money to fund the defence comes from the proceeds of crime. Should lawyers refuse to accept fees suspected or known to have come from crime or does this mean denying an accused person a right to a quality defence?

In some countries, like Australia, lawyers were barred from advertising their services. This was seen as encouraging unwarranted contesting of charges or litigation — the latter sometimes referred to as 'ambulance chasing'. (This is less relevant to criminal law practice.)

Also, some countries — again Australia is an example — have a traditional strong divide between solicitors and barristers. The latter are specialists and in criminal law a defendant on serious charges who engages a solicitor is likely to also end up with a barrister and have to pay their costs as well. This is sometimes seen as necessary for an expert defence and sometimes seen as unnecessarily doubling up and exploitation of defendants.

Conclusion

This chapter has discussed the main ethical issues and dilemmas facing criminal law practitioners. The choices and behaviour of lawyers and judges have significant and long-term effects on the lives of many people. While we should expect all legal professionals to act competently and without bias, adherence to a code does not mean they will escape difficult dilemmas. Codes of conduct for lawyers provide important guidance and official expectations about how to act and how to resolve dilemmas. The following chapter looks in depth at types of unethical practices indulged in by judges and lawyers, and some key consequences of those actions.

Chapter 6

Misconduct and Miscarriages of Justice in the Criminal Courts

This chapter focuses on types of bad behaviour by practitioners of criminal law and the effects of that behaviour. Here there are some similarities with police misconduct, especially in the areas of graft and bias, while direct brutality is obviously a lesser problem. In many countries judicial misconduct appears to be much less extensive than police misconduct, although it remains a major problem in many developing nations. The chapter focuses on miscarriages of justice, particularly wrongful convictions, as a specific problem area for criminal justice related to unethical conduct. In many of the cases examined there is a direct overlap between police corruption and complicity or incompetence by legal professionals. The adversarial system is also often seen as a major influence on miscarriages of justice. A culture of denial and defensiveness has contributed to resistance to reform and failure to remedy mistakes.

Types of Misconduct by Criminal Law Professionals

This section sets out the main types of misconduct in which criminal lawyers and judges might engage (Pollock, 2007, chap. 10 and 11; Transparency International, 2007, pp. xxii–xxiv). The following section outlines some examples of attempts to measure the extent of these problems.

Graft

Graft here involves similar processes to those in police corruption, but, obviously, at the next stage of the criminal justice system. Accused persons will offer money to have charges dropped or reduced or sentences minimised, either through prosecutors or judges. Some people will also attempt to use the criminal courts to harm their enemies by paying prosecutors or judges to pursue trumped-up charges. Prosecutors, the defence and court employees (such as clerks of the court) can extort additional 'fees' from defendants or victims to speed up or slow down cases, lose evidence or provide access to witnesses (Transparency International, 2007, p. xxvii). Indefinite adjournments can also be used to force payments.

Bias

A related area of misconduct is that of bias. Bias is a type of corruption of process in that it represents a deviation from an impartial judgment, but the motive is not a direct financial or material reward. Prosecutors may be biased by political or other motives in the exercise of their discretion in regard to laying charges, the number of charges they lay and the severity of the penalties they recommend. The defence can also be biased against providing an adequate defence. Discrimination also occurs internally and systemically, in the historical prohibition on women lawyers for example (Australian Law Reform Commission, 1994, chap. 9).

Politicisation

Political bias occurs primarily when ruling parties install judges and prosecutors who are personally or ideologically aligned with the government. This can result in a failure to prosecute government members or favourable court outcomes for them, as well as selective prosecutions and adverse judgments against political enemies.

Misleading the Court

Misleading the court is one type of tactic by which bias and corruption are exercised. It can also result from an excess of zeal or a lack of zeal by both prosecutors and defence (Pollock, 2007, pp. 334ff, 348ff). The withholding of evidence that might favour the other side is a key tactic here. This can be done by asking selective questions of witnesses that do not elicit the whole truth. 'Shopping' for experts with selective testimony is another questionable tactic. Another, mentioned in the previous chapter, is that of broaching inadmissible evidence. This can be done in part to prejudice a jury for or against a defendant and to inflame the jurors' emotions.

Intimidation and Manipulation of Witnesses

Witnesses can be made to alter or withdraw their testimony, either by threats made outside the court or by shouting, insinuations, character assassination and other histrionics in the courtroom.

Exploiting Cases

Prosecutors and defence lawyers are sometimes accused of 'milking cases' for personal benefit. With private sector defence lawyers there is a strong financial incentive to keep a case going as long as possible by using delaying tactics in the court. Prosecutors can be motivated to exploit cases for career purposes, especially when they are elected officials. 'Piling up charges' is one way to add to the gravity and profile of a case and help characterise the prosecutor as a crime fighter. 'Over-charging' can also be used to intimidate a defendant into plea bargaining.

Exploiting Proceeds of Crime

Defence lawyers may be tempted to exploit cases where they know or suspect that the defendant's funds are the proceeds of crime. Drug traffickers in particular often have access to large quantities of cash.

Regressive Sentencing

Courts can easily become sentencing factories where discretion is exercised regressively. Sanctions are assigned in a robotic and punitive fashion with little regard to progressive alternatives that include rehabilitation programs, compensation to victims, community work programs and periodic detention (see discussion on punishment in chapters 8 and 10). Particularly mindless and ethically questionable sentences include fines for people who have no money and full-time imprisonment for non-violent offences when the offender has family responsibilities and a capacity to work and repay victims.

The Extent of Misconduct and Unethical Practices

Measuring misconduct in the criminal courts is extremely difficult (Transparency International, 2007, pp. 318–323). It is likely to be hidden, and suspicions are usually difficult to prove. Convictions of lawyers for corrupt activities or other forms of misconduct are a strong measure where there is a robust judicial system with high standards of evidence and quality prosecution and defence services. But even then conviction rates are difficult to interpret. They may represent only the tip of the iceberg and the more obvious cases that prosecutors could not ignore.

In most countries it could be said that this is an under-researched area, and there is little apparent in the way of proactive regulation that might identify misconduct that does not come to light through complaints or disclosures (Transparency International, 2007, Pt. 3). As with police misconduct, however, there have been attempts to get beyond surface appearances. Methods employed include surveys of court participants and the public, case study analyses, and complaints data.

One example of research in this area is the use of quantitative studies of sentencing outcomes with a view to detecting judicial bias. As many variables as possible, such as aggravating and mitigating factors, are controlled for in these studies. Results vary with methods and jurisdictions, but many show 'dramatic differences' between judges that appear to follow primarily from different ideologies about offender culpability and punishment (Hofer, Blackwell, & Ruback, 1999, p. 3). One Australian study that attempted to control for types of cases found enormous differences between judges in the use of imprisonment as a sentencing option. In a sample of 51 judges, the most severe five judges handed out jail terms twice as often as the most lenient five judges (Weatherburn, 1994, p. 7ff).

Another method is to examine the number of cases overturned where misconduct by lawyers has been identified. For example, journalists from the *Chicago Tribune* analysed a national sample of 381 homicide convictions that had been overturned because of prosecutorial misconduct (with retrials in some cases) in the United States (Armstrong & Possley, 1999). The cases occurred between 1963, following a Supreme Court ruling aimed at reducing errors caused by unethical practices, and 1998. The sample included 67 defendants on death row who served between five and 26 years before their convictions were overturned. None of the prosecutors involved suffered any serious consequences. Examples of tactics that led to unsafe convictions included:

- Concealing evidence that a witness or other person had committed the crime.
- Hiding a knife, gun or other weapon used against a defendant who claimed self-defence.
- In one case, not disclosing expert testimony that a blood spatter pattern indicated suicide not murder.
- In another case, concealing the fact a key witness saw white men when the defendants were black.

Despite findings like these, we do not see major inquiries into judicial corruption of the type we have seen with police — although one criticism of such inquiries is that they fail to follow through properly from police to lawyers. Detective Robert Leuci, one of the main internal witnesses for the Knapp Commission, repeatedly railed against the Commission's failure, in his view, to investigate lawyers and judges on the take (Daley, 1978; e.g., pp. 19–21). According to Leuci:

> There was also massive corruption at every stage of the criminal justice system, starting with the assistant district attorneys who helped detectives prepare wiretap orders, and routinely told them to perjure themselves, to lawyers who met them in hallways wearing three- and four-hundred dollar suits, and came over and whispered that this case didn't mean anything, here's $50, $100, $500, $1,500, let's forget it. (p. 17)

Trevor Haken, the most important 'roll over' witness in the New South Wales Wood Commission inquiry, was similarly embittered by the focus on police at the expense of lawyers. According to Haken, defence and prosecution lawyers, and judges and magistrates, were complicit in police corruption at least by guilty knowledge and inaction (Padraic, 2005).

From a longer-term historical perspective the situation is arguably even more clouded. An Australian high court judge, Michael Kirby, made the following observation:

> In the days of the British Empire, the spectre of a corrupt judge or magistrate was so horrible that it could be largely dismissed as impossible. The judicial traditions had a strong ethos of honesty and integrity. A judge on the take was unthinkable. The problems of the judiciary were different: laziness, bad temper, dilatoriness, ignorance of the law, prejudice … Financial corruption was out of the question; although it was not unknown for judges sometimes to be corrupted intellectually by ambition, the hope of promotion or the prayer for a title. (Kirby, 2005, p. 2)

We can contrast this view with that of Critchley (1976) in his history of policing in England and Wales. He cites sources indicating that the criminal court system for many centuries up to at least the early 19th century was deeply corrupt, with rampant bribery, favouritism and a trade in appointments. The availability of graft, and close associations between justices and criminals, allowed 'ingenious criminals … to exploit the state of affairs in such a way as to enjoy virtual immunity from prosecution' (p. 19).

Case Studies

Case studies demonstrate the potential for unethical and corrupt behaviour. Australian lawyers have predictably been accused of many unethical behaviours. The following subsections provide a small number of cases.

Murray Farquhar

There are two particularly infamous cases of judicial corruption in Australia that centre on Sydney. The first of these involved a New South Wales Chief Stipendiary Magistrate Murray Farquhar, who was widely suspected of being a major figure in a racket with corrupt police to fix cases in the 1970s. After retiring he was convicted and then jailed in 1985 for having perverted the course of justice by trying to influence a junior magistrate to discharge a famous Sydney sporting identity in a fraud-related committal proceeding. Farquhar was also notorious for consorting with major organised crime figures (Sutton & Warnock, 1993).

High Court Judge Lionel Murphy

Also in 1985 High Court Judge Lionel Murphy was sentenced to 18 months imprisonment for attempting to pervert the course of justice by influencing a committal proceeding in favour of a friend charged with fraud and conspiracy. The New South Wales Court of Appeal set aside his conviction in the same year and ordered a new trial at which he was found not guilty. The not guilty verdict was in part ascribed to the fact he refused to give testimony in the second trial. The federal government ordered a commission of inquiry into the matter after the Stewart Royal Commission authenticated the secret tape recordings that had been a source of evidence against Murphy. The inquiry was closed down in 1987 after it emerged that Murphy was dying of cancer (Whitton, 1987).

'Lawyers, Drugs and Money'

In Queensland a *4 Corners* television report, 'Lawyers, Drugs and Money' (ABC Television, 1993), made multiple imputations of unethical practices. The case began in 1987 when Australian Federal Police in Brisbane arrested a group of Americans for importing 1.3 kilograms of hash — only 87 kilograms of which was recovered. Lawyers for five members of the group, including the ringleaders Richard Leeth and Paul Donovan, immediately secured an amount of over $1.1 million held in an offshore account by Leeth in Vanuatu. Leeth later stated it was obvious the money was from trafficking drugs. The prosecution and defence then fought in the courts for control of the money, with 17 applications from the prosecution before it was able to sequester the funds — subject to costs to the defence.

Leeth reported that initially the main communications with the defence were about the money. The case progressed to a 16-week committal hearing. During the committal the accused realised they had no answer to the prosecution's phone taps and 263 witnesses. They claimed they informed the defence they wanted to plead guilty. But the lawyers ploughed on with defending the committal, pitting solicitors, and seven barristers on AU$1,500 a day, against the prosecution's three barristers, 'two juniors, and a phalanx of solicitors and Australian Federal Police'.

It took a further 10 months before the accused were able to stand up in court and plead guilty. From their prison cells they were dependent on their lawyers to communicate with the prosecution. The defence and the prosecution each blamed the other for intransigence over pleas. The pleas did little good. The judge handed Donovan a 20-year sentence and Leeth 25 years. *4 Corners* pointed out that these were among the harshest sentences ever handed out for a non-violent crime, involving the importation of a relatively mild recreational drug. According to one of the defence barristers, 'There was so much money spent on the prosecution that there just had to be the maximum venom extracted from the penalty'. The defence bill ended up at $1.3 million, cleaning out the $1.1 million in the restrained fund. Leeth told *4 Corners*: 'I had no idea that it would cost that kind of money to plead guilty'. He elaborated on his experience:

> When I think of the case, what I think of is an old movie I saw once where they piled a bunch of money in the middle of the floor and everybody was scrambling to get it — pushing grandmothers out of the way, kicking babies. I mean, that's

the impression I get of the whole case. Who can get the money? That's the prosecution, the defence, everybody — let's get the money in any way we can …

Chis Masters: Did you believe that you had a sensible, workable defence?

Richard Leeth: Oh, no. I don't think there was ever any question of actually taking it to trial to defend it and actually get found not guilty.

Chis Masters: So it's hard to understand why it could have gone on for so long if you believed, pretty much from the beginning, that you didn't have much of a defence yourself.

Richard Leeth: Yes … it was like a snowball, you know, and there's nothing you can do about it. You're just sitting in gaol and the lawyers are going to court. You don't even hear what happens most of the time. I mean, as long as there was money there, I don't believe it would have ended. If there was another million to be spent, we would probably still be in court … I mean, how hard is it to negotiate a plea?

Defence Counsel in the 'Pinkenba Six' Case

Also in Queensland, there was considerable criticism of defence tactics in the 'Pinkenba Six' case, a committal in which six police officers were charged with deprivation of liberty. The drama began late on a cold night in 1994 in Brisbane's Fortitude Valley when three Aboriginal boys were ordered into police vehicles by six officers. The boys — aged 12, 13 and 14 — were driven separately in three vehicles 14 kilometres to a swampy area of wasteland at Pinkenba. The officers threatened to throw the boys into a creek and referred to a place where people's fingers were cut off. Police ordered the boys to remove their shoes and threw the shoes into bushes. They then drove away. The boys retrieved their shoes and began to walk back to the Valley. They took part of the journey in a taxi paid for by a security guard they met along the way.

When the story came out, police admitted the boys were not suspected of any crimes. But because they were loose on the street, and had previously committed offences, police removed them to Pinkenba to deter them from committing crimes and being a public nuisance. This was not consistent with any official policy. The officers left the area without authority and left it understaffed during their absence. Following an investigation the officers were charged with the criminal offence of deprivation of liberty. The Police Union used its large fighting fund to hire two of the state's most expensive barristers to fight the committal before a single magistrate. The defence case was that the boys voluntarily got in the car.

In her book, *Courtroom Talk and Neo-Colonial Control* (2008), Diana Eades, a socio-linguist, made a close analysis of the three days of cross-examination of the Aboriginal boys. Her complex analysis highlights the disjunction between the formal intimidating environment and arcane language of the courtroom — packed with uniformed police — and the traditional cultural values and language of the boys. In particular, Eades asserts that the barristers exploited the boys' habit of responding to questions by way of 'gratuitous concurrence'. This is a pervasive linguistic device in many traditional cultures for showing respect, modesty and deference by replying 'yes' to questions. This is regardless of the respondent's true opinion or whether or not they even understand the question. Where respondents do not say 'yes' they may still avoid saying 'no'. The tendency is particularly marked when talking to authority figures.

In the Pinkenba Six case, the defence lawyers ruthlessly and relentlessly interrogated the children on the stand. They bombarded them with accusations and confusing double negatives that eventually gave them the answers they sought. In the following two very short extracts, two of the boys can be observed to be struggling either to avoid the questions or to state their view that they felt forced into the police vehicles (Eades, 2008, pp. 101–102, 105–106). Eades cautions that the typed transcripts cannot properly show the rhetorical aspects of the spoken language, with its meaning-laden intonations, anger and indignation, dramatic pauses and emphases. (Note: small capitals indicate shouting, numbers in parenthesis indicate the length of the pauses in seconds, and italics indicate emphasis.)

> DC2: David — let me just try to summarise if I can — what you — what you've told us (3.1) you told us yesterday that the *real* problem wasn't anything that happened getting into the car or *in* the car — but the fact that you were left at Pinkenba — that right?
>
> David: (1.5) Mm.
>
> DC2: Mm — that's the truth isn't it?
>
> DC2: (4.3) You see — you weren't *deprived* of your liberty at all — uh in going out there — it was the fact that you were *left* there that you thought was wrong?
>
> David: (1.2) Yeh [softly].
>
> (in Eades, 2008, pp. 101–102, slightly edited)
>
> * * *
>
> DC1: And you *knew* (1.4) when you spoke to these six police in the Valley that you didn't have to go with them if you didn't want to, didn't you?
>
> Barry: (1.3) No.
>
> DC1: You *knew* that Mr (1.2) Coley I'd suggest to you — PLEASE DO NOT LIE YOU KNEW THAT YOU DIDN'T HAVE TO GO ANYWHERE if you didn't want to, didn't you? (2.2) DIDN'T YOU? (2.2) DIDN'T YOU, MR COLEY?
>
> Barry: (1.3) Yeh.
>
> DC1: WHY DID YOU JUST LIE TO ME? WHY DID YOU JUST SAY NO, MR COLEY? (4.4) YOU WANT ME TO SUGGEST A REASON TO YOU, MR COLEY? THE REASON WAS THIS — THAT YOU WANTED THIS COURT TO *BELIEVE* (2.1) THAT YOU THOUGHT THAT YOU HAD TO GO WITH THE POLICE, ISN'T THAT SO?

Barry: (1.2) Yeh.

DC1: AND YOU *LIED* TO THE COURT TRYING TO (1.2) YOU *LIED* TO THE COURT TRYING TO PUT ONE *OVER* THE COURT, DIDN'T YOU?

Barry: (1.8) No [Softly].

DC1: THAT WAS YOUR REASON, MR COLEY, WASN'T IT? (3.1) WASN'T IT? (3.2) WASN'T IT, MR COLEY?

Barry: (1.9) Yeh.

DC1: YES (2.9) BECAUSE YOU WANTED THE *COURT* TO *THINK* THAT *YOU* DIDN'T KNOW THAT YOU COULD TELL THESE POLICE YOU WEREN'T GOING *ANYWHERE* WITH THEM — THAT WAS THE REASON, WASN'T IT? (1.5) WASN'T IT?

Barry: (0.6) Yes.

DC1: Yes.

(in Eades, 2008, pp. 105–106, slightly edited)

The magistrate's finding was that the boys voluntarily got into the car without coercion and he dismissed the case. In a subsequent disciplinary hearing the deputy police commissioner dismissed three of the officers and demoted four (including their supervisor). He then suspended the sentences, effectively absolving all seven officers involved (Prenzler, 2000, pp. 669–670).

Transparency International

Transparency International has maintained a strong program of global research into corruption in government and business using a variety of sources. The 2007 *Global Corruption Report* focused on judicial corruption. The report includes accounts of the convictions for corruption of various judicial officers in different countries. Another tool used by Transparency International was the Global Corruption Barometer — a public opinion and experience survey conducted by a reputable private sector research firm. The 2006 survey asked respondents in 62 countries if they 'had contact with the judiciary in the past year'. Of seven global zones, responses varied between a high of 23% in North America and a low of 5% in the Asia-Pacific. These

Table 6.1 Respondents Who Interacted With the Judiciary in the Past Year and Paid a Bribe

Region	Per cent
Africa	21%
Latin America	18%
Newly independent states	15%
South East Europe	9%
Asia-Pacific	15%
EU/Other Western European countries	1%
North America	2%

Note: Adapted from the Global Corruption Barometer in the *Global Corruption Report* (Transparency International, 2007, p. 11).

groups were then asked if they had 'paid a bribe'. The results, by average per region, are shown in Table 6.1.

The results report experiences of corruption. Perceptions of corruption were much worse. In 33 of the 62 countries, 50% or more of respondents described their legal system as 'corrupt' or 'very corrupt' (Transparency International, 2007, p. 13). The following are some snapshots of findings from specific country studies in Transparency International reports. The cases include criminal courts within the total court system.

- In 2000 the Zimbabwean government of Robert Mugabe began a process of replacing independent judges with judges who were loyal to the ruling ZANU PF Party. Independent judges were forced to resign by physical intimidation and threats, including death threats. The process was designed to pave the way for the government's circumvention of legal processes for removing ex-colonial farmers and replacing them with government loyalists. When farmers challenged the legality of the forced acquisitions and associated violence they lost their cases in the courts. (Transparency International, 2007, p. 35ff)

- In Mexico drug trafficking is a federal offence. This means that adjudication of drug cases is monopolised by a relatively small group of federal judges. Some of these are known as 'the traffickers judges'. In a variety of notorious cases they have been responsible for dismissing charges, allegedly for lack of evidence, or downgrading custodial sentences to monetary fines that are easily paid by drug barons. (Transparency International, 2007, p. 77ff)

- In the United States the widespread use of elections for judicial appointments causes a problem of perceptions of biased courtrooms, especially when judges supervise trials involving major donors to their political campaigns. Some donations amount to many millions of dollars, and cases have been identified where judges have refused to recuse themselves when donors were before their courts and then ruled in favour of the donor. (Transparency International, p. 26ff)

- In Guatemala public trust in the courts reached a low point in the 1990s as a result of constant delays and low conviction rates. A survey revealed that 70% of people thought the system was untrustworthy and was only applied against the poor. One response was an upsurge in vigilante justice, with 480 lynchings recorded between 1996 and 2002. (Transparency International, p. 211ff)

- In Bangladesh a survey revealed that 42% of households who were involved with the courts claimed they were obliged to pay bribes. Court officials were the main recipients, but payments were also made to the prosecution and defence and some judges. (Transparency International, 2008, p. xiii)

Miscarriages of Justice

One of the worst outcomes of incompetent and unethical legal practices is a miscarriage of justice. The prime miscarriage of justice is the conviction and punishment of an innocent person. Miscarriages of justice also include the acquittal of guilty parties, the refusal to prosecute guilty persons, excessively lenient or excessively harsh penalties and excessive time on remand awaiting trial. The most extreme aspect of false convictions is the execution of innocent people. Revelations of miscarriages of justice generate a loss of public confidence in the criminal justice system (Royal Commission, 1993, p. 6).

There have been famous cases where persons responsible for serious crimes were not prosecuted or convicted, and they either went on to commit further crimes or were later discovered to have committed multiple murders. A notorious example from recent times is that of an English doctor, John Bodkin Adams. In 1957 Adams was tried on a charge of murdering a patient by an overdose of drugs. He was acquitted after irregularities in the trial and there was controversy after the Attorney-General discontinued a second prosecution. It is now widely accepted that Adams was a serial killer who may have killed up to 400 patients in his career, many of whom left him money and property in their wills (Devlin, 1986; Kinnell, 2000).

Exonerations provide some evidence of wrongful convictions. One study in the United States of America asked a sample of judges and other key officials on the prosecution side to estimate the percentage of felony cases that were overturned without successful retrials. The average was approximately 0.5%, which sounds rather small. However, the authors estimated this meant that nationally a total of 7,500 people in one year were wrongfully arrested and convicted for serious criminal offences (Huff, 2008). Research in the United States has also shown that between 1973, when executions were resumed in some states, and the end of 2008, 130 people on death row were exonerated and freed (Death Penalty Information Center, 2009). An obvious implication of this is that many more innocent people — probably thousands in the United States alone — have been executed in the past.

The English Miscarriages of Justice Cases

Arguably the most famous miscarriages of justice occurred in England in the 1970s and 1980s. The events occurred in the context of the mainland terrorist bombing campaign by the Provisional Irish Republican Army (IRA) in the mid-1970s as part of its struggle to free Northern Ireland from English rule. (There were also several major cases that were not related to terrorism.) The terrorism cases revealed extensive process corruption by police, although the officers responsible escaped convictions in the adversarial courts. Judicial corruption was less obvious. However, highly educated and well-paid government lawyers — including prosecutors, judges and magis-trates — lied, misled the courts or failed to intervene to protect innocent people. They displayed 'official incompetence, narrow-mindedness and — occasionally — malice' (Rozenberg, 1992, p. 92). Forensic scientists were also culpable. In the terrorism cases, innocent people were incarcerated for a combined total of just under 200 years. The trials and appeals cost many millions of pounds, paid for by taxpayers. Subsequent inquiries and reviews also cost millions of pounds, and many millions of taxpayers' money was eventually paid in compensation to the victims — although the amounts were widely seen as inadequate, provided grudgingly and without punitive damages. The four main cases are described here (see Conlon, 1993; Rozenberg, 1992; Woffinden, 1987).

The Guildford Four

In 1975 four young people — Gerry Conlon (see also Chapter 3), Patrick Armstrong, Carole Richardson (aged 17) and Paul Hill — were sentenced to life imprisonment for multiple murders in the 1974 bombing of a pub in Guildford, south of London. Armstrong and Hill were also convicted of murder in relation to a second pub bombing in Woolwich. The only real evidence was typed signed confessions, produced while in police custody, which all four retracted at the trial. The Four had argued they signed the confessions while being held without charge in police custody after being beaten, tortured, starved, deprived of sleep and after threats were made against their loved ones. There were 153 factual inconsistencies in the con-fessions and there was no external corroboration. In 1977 members of an IRA bombing unit — 'the Balcombe Street gang' — captured in a siege in London stated at their trial that they were responsible for the Guildford and Woolwich bombings and that their lawyers had informed the Director of Public Prosecutions of this in 1975. Despite all this a 1977 appeal of the Guildford Four failed.

In 1989 the Guildford Four managed to again reach the Court of Appeal following a concerted national campaign. The Home Secretary was forced to concede that Richardson was withdrawing from barbiturates when she made the confession and that there were alibi witnesses for Richardson and Hill. A Home Office report also conceded that the Four were dropouts and hippies who were unlikely terrorists, and that there was no evidence of any connec-tion with the IRA. To prepare for the appeal, police assigned Detective Inspector Doreen Bryant to review the evidence contained in an archive. Bryant reported that there were different versions of the notes and typed confessions. It looked as though the hand-written notes may have been made after the confessions were typed. It also emerged that a bundle of documents — marked 'not to be shown to the defence' — contained an alibi witness statement for Conlon. Sir Michael Havers, the Chief Prosecutor, had taunted Conlon in the dock about the lack of an alibi. The Public Prosecutor decided the material rendered the verdicts unsafe and decided not to oppose the appeal. The Chief Justice, Lord Lane, quashed the convictions — 14 years after the four had been found guilty.

The Maguire Seven

In 1976 the 'Maguire Seven' were convicted of possessing nitroglycerine for an unlawful purpose — an offence under the *Explosive Substances Act*. In lay terms this meant the group operated a kitchen 'bomb factory' that supplied the Guildford bombing and other London bombings. Anne Maguire and her husband 'Paddy' were sentenced to 14 years' prison. Anne's brother, Shaun Smyth, and Paddy's brother-in-law, 'Guiseppe' Conlon (Gerry Conlon's father) were sentenced to 12 years. A family friend, Patrick O'Neill, received eight years on appeal. The Maguire's 17-year-old son, Vincent, received a five-year sentence. Their 14-year-old son, Patrick, was given four years.

Police raided the Maguire home after Gerry Conlon told them in jest that his aunt Anne Maguire had taught him how to make bombs. There was no evidence of any connection between the family and the IRA. The case hinged on the evidence of government scientists, who testified that all the defendants had traces of nitroglycerine on their hands and under their fingernails — with the exception of Anne Maguire, who allegedly had traces on her gloves. The scientists argued that the traces could only have been obtained by close handling of the explosives. During the incarceration of the Maguire Seven, government scientists repeatedly refused to concede that the traces might have been innocently acquired. (It was argued, for example, that a visitor may have left traces on a bathroom towel.) They also categorically ruled out laboratory contamination despite the fact the tests for traces of explosives were not repeated and no independent tests were undertaken. A Court of Appeal was convened after the acquittals of the Guildford Four, and the convictions of the Maguire Seven were overturned. However, six of the Maguire Seven had already completed their sentences, and the seventh — Guiseppe Conlon — had died in custody in 1980.

The Birmingham Six

In 1975 six men were found guilty and sentenced to life in prison over the murders of 21 people in the bombings of two pubs in Birmingham in 1974. Hugh Callaghan, Patrick Hill, Gerry Hunter, Richard McIlkenny, Billy Power and John Walker were convicted on the basis of alleged confessions and alleged evidence that two of them had handled nitroglycerine. The loose social connections with IRA members also told against the men. In 1988 three Justices rejected an appeal prompted by allegations from a former police officer of brutality against the men when they were in police custody. A third appeal in 1991 proved successful and the men were released after 16 years of imprisonment. The Court accepted that there were similar discrepancies in the police interview notes as occurred in the Guildford Four case. This was supported by a new forensic technique of electrostatic document analysis, which examines indentations in paper to see if tampering has occurred. The court also heard from the May Inquiry into the Maguire Seven case that the Greiss test that was used did not show the presence of nitroglycerine but was a preliminary test for the possible presence of nitrates. The government forensic scientist Dr Frank Skuse argued that nitrates from the test evidenced nitroglycerine. But subsequent research and testimony from scientists revealed that positive results for nitrates could also be obtained from detergents and even from smoking cigarettes. One plausible explanation therefore was that the traces in the Maguire Seven and Birmingham Six cases came from the process of cleaning the forensic laboratory equipment.

Judith Ward

The revelations of unreliable scientific evidence in the Maguire Seven case prompted the Home Office to step outside its traditionally passive role and review questionable cases. There was a particular focus on cases involving Dr Skuse. One involved Judith Ward, who was convicted of three IRA bombings that occurred between 1973 and 1974 — including an attack on a bus in which 12 soldiers and their family members were killed. She was convicted on the basis of a confession and forensic evidence of nitroglycerine on her hands and in the caravan where she lived. Her conviction was quashed by the Court of Appeal in 1992 after she served 18 years in prison. The prosecution had hidden her history of mental illness. It also hid the fact that she had changed her testimony several times so that the prosecution had to present an edited version that removed implausible and inconsistent elements. The Court also heard that the alleged traces of nitrogylcerine could have been obtained from shoe polish. The Justices accused three senior scientists of hiding forensic evidence and exaggerating the value of other evidence.

Australian Miscarriages of Justice Cases

Australia has not been immune from the problem of wrongful convictions. In one study Paul Wilson identified 20 serious criminal cases, involving 23 people in Australia between 1947 and 1983, where verdicts were overturned or where there was a high probability of error (Wilson, 1991). The following summarises just three of the more prominent cases.

Lindy Chamberlain

Lindy Chamberlain's baby daughter Azaria disappeared from an Uluru camp ground in 1980. The body was never found. The mother alleged she saw a dingo take the baby from the family's tent. In 1982 Chamberlain was convicted of the murder of Azaria on the basis of forensic testimony regarding foetal blood in the family car and the discovery of Azaria's ripped jumpsuit. The prosecution alleged Chamberlain slit her baby's throat in the car and then hid the body. Lindy Chamberlain was widely vilified in the Australian media. She was released in 1986 and her conviction overturned in 1988 after new tests falsified the earlier blood test results and Azaria's jacket was discovered near a dingo lair (Bryson, 2000).

The Sydney Hilton Bombing

In 1989 Tim Anderson was convicted over the murders of a police officer and two council garbage collectors, and the attempted murder of the Indian Prime Minister, in relation to the 1978 bombing of the Sydney Hilton Hotel. Seven people were also seriously injured in the blast. The attack was presumed to be a terrorist bombing aimed at the Indian Prime Minister who was attending a meeting inside the hotel. Anderson had been the public relations officer for the Australian arm of the Indian-based Ananda Marga sect whose leader was imprisoned in India. The charges derived from a confession first made to a priest in Brisbane by Evan Pederick, a former member of Ananda Marga. Pederick claimed he planted the bomb after being recruited by Anderson who supplied him with explosives and drove him to the hotel where Pederick placed the bomb in a rubbish bin. The sceptical priest took Pederick to Queensland Police who passed his statement to New South Wales Police. He was extradited to Sydney where he was convicted of murder and sentenced to 20 years' imprisonment, mitigated by the assumption he had been manipulated by Anderson. At Anderson's trial the court passed over a barrage of inconsistencies in Pederick's account. For example, he had insisted he had 50 sticks of gelignite but changed the number to 20 after police told him that 50 would not have fitted in the bin. He also claimed he used a remote detonator, but expert witnesses asserted that the device he described did not exist. As Anderson's trial developed it became clear that the police and prosecution had coached Pederick to alter his testimony to align with facts about the bombing and information about Anderson. The conviction was overturned two years later in 1991. The Chief Justice of the Appeal Court was scathing of the prosecution's manipulation of information and its manipulation of the jury (Academics for Justice, 1991; Freeman, 1995, 'How Fair is the Legal System?', 1991).

James Finch
In 1973 James Finch was convicted of multiple murders in one of Australia's worst mass killings: the Whiskey-Au-Go-Go nightclub firebombing in Brisbane in which 15 people died. Finch and his co-accused, John Andrew Stuart, were convicted largely on the strength of an unsigned record of inter-view allegedly made shortly after their arrest. Both men accused police of brutality and Finch denied making the confession. Stuart died in prison. Finch was paroled in 1988 after a police officer in the case came forward to state the confession was fabricated and an international authority on speech pattern analysis testified that the confession was probably not authentic. After he left the country Finch claimed responsibility for the murders. Finch, it seems, was convicted on false evidence, but he was also wrongfully released (Prenzler, 2002).

Causes of Misconduct and Miscarriages of Justice

Two factors that discourage corruption in the criminal courts are openness to public scrutiny and the separation of personnel by functions (the latter can limit the chain of corruption). Nonetheless, corruption does occur, and a primary cause of graft in the criminal courts is the same as for policing: the demand and supply equation related to a trade in benefits. With so much at stake, accused persons are willing to offer money and other benefits for charges to be dropped or mishandled by the prosecution, or for judges to throw out a case or manage the case in such a way that an acquittal is assured. Prosecutors and judges will be tempted by money, especially in jurisdictions where they are poorly paid or if they have developed debts. More generally, corruption will flourish if there are weak systems for the accreditation and licensing of legal professionals; if prosecutors and judges are not properly vetted; if the appointment of judges is politically biased; if there are weak systems for the reception, investigation and adjudication of complaints; and if there is a lack of political will to stop corruption in the courts (Transparency International, 2007, pp. 3–7).

When it comes to miscarriages of justice, there is a range of other con-tributing factors. There is now a sizeable body of knowledge from academic research and judicial inquiries, based primarily on case study analyses, that have identified the following factors (Brants, 2008; Carrington, Dever, Hogg, Bargen, & Lohrey, 1991; Huff & Killias, 2008; Kessler, 2008; Royal Commission, 1993; Rozenberg, 1992; Transparency International, 2007; Woffinden, 1987).

Wrongful convictions usually begin with the type of police process cor-ruption described in chapter 3. They can also begin with investigative incompetence, primarily through a process in which detectives develop tunnel vision. This happens when initial inquiries bring one or a small number of suspects to the fore. The investigation then shifts from a process of open-minded inquiry and a wide collection of evidence to one focused on building a case against the prime suspects. Police discard or undervalue exculpatory evidence, and place particular interpretations on evidence that favours their assumptions.

Police incompetence or corruption then combines with unethical or incompetent practices by prosecutors, judges and the defence. When any of these players are bribed or when they fail to properly scrutinise the police case, then a miscarriage of justice can result.

It has also been proposed that the adversarial system contributes to the risk of miscarriages of justice. Although inquisitorial systems are by no means immune from the problem, and although the system is often highly politicised and corrupt in post-colonial societies, continental criminal courts do not appear to have been plagued by miscarriages of justice to the same extent as Anglo-Saxon systems. As we have seen, the way in which the adversarial system generates a contest creates pressures and temptations to cheat on both sides, and the idea of a detached judge does not necessarily contribute to an appropriate process of open inquiry.

Excessive trust in the adversarial system as a reliable determinant of truth and justice also involves wishful thinking about the self-regulatory capabilities of the system. Key participants, especially prosecutors and judges, are unwilling to question the system that nourishes them. There may be a grudging admission that mistakes occur, but they are depicted as rare and an unfortunate casualty of a system that is basically sound. Thus miscarriages of justice are a product of a culture of excessive trust, and also a culture of professional arrogance and belief in the god-like status of lawyers. Blind faith always produces defensiveness. This was evidenced graphically in the self-serving reasons given by one of England's most notable justices, Lord Denning, for refusing leave to the Birmingham Six to sue police over their treatment:

> If the six men win, it will mean that the police were guilty of perjury, that they were guilty of violence and threats, that the confessions were involuntary and were improperly admitted in evidence, and that the convictions were erroneous. That would mean that the Home Secretary would have either to recommend they be pardoned or he would have to remit the case to the Court of Appeal … This is such an appalling vista that every sensible person in the land would say: 'It cannot be right that these actions should go any further' (in Krone, 2007, p. 3).

Excessive faith in the system includes unjustified faith in police probity. The naive view that police will not lie in the witness box can carry through from the judiciary to jury prejudices that favour police testimony.

The lopsided resourcing of the prosecution and the defence is another factor. Unless a defendant is very wealthy they cannot afford a defence capable of conducting a counter-investigation to match that of the prosecution. This was evident in the English miscarriages of justice cases outlined earlier, when the release of prosecution documents many years after the trial revealed a variety of alibi witnesses and contrary information that the defence failed to unearth.

Once a convicted person is locked away it is easy to ignore them and to repress any doubts about the validity of their conviction. Traditional adversarial systems strongly militate against rectifying mistakes. Convicted persons, especially if they are in prison, usually have little or no access to the necessary resources to have a case reopened. The bar is also usually set very high for any review of a case. The defendant must produce fresh evidence or demonstrate errors by the prosecution or errors in the interpretation of law, or gross incompetence by the defence. Appeal courts are often considered to be reluctant to find fault with their colleagues; and a traditional system has limited institutional capacity for launching a fresh investigation funded by the state.

Public hysteria about terrorism or major crimes can also be key catalysts for errors in justice when police and the courts come under intense pressure for quick results. Often the media contributes to the lynch mob mentality by demonising suspects. This happened notoriously in the Lindy Chamberlain case when her apparent lack of emotion over her baby's disappearance was taken by the press and many members of the public as a sure sign of guilt. In the English cases, the IRA bombings, which killed and wounded many scores of innocent people, evoked natural outrage and fear that turned to blind hate focused on the wrong suspects — most of whom were Irish.

The capacity for police to hold people without charge is also a major factor. People's defences quickly break down when they are isolated in a cell, denied food and sleep, and subjected to constant badgering by police. In their desperation to escape these conditions they will sign false confessions. The torture is hidden from the courts, where lawyers and judges fail to properly inquire into the sources of confessions. With the English cases, the then-new *Prevention of Terrorism Act* allowed police to hold suspects without charge for 48 hours, with a five-day extension permitted by the Home Secretary. This allowed ample time for the victims to collapse under torture and sign false confessions.

An over-reliance on confessional statements without corroborating evidence is part of a traditional adversarial system that adopts a 'rational man' view of the accused. There is incredulity about the capacity of people to sign self-incriminating statements. Research now shows that people will make false confessions for a variety of reasons apart from torture, such as mental illness and self-aggrandisement.

Another factor is perjury by police informants. Again, this involves excessive trust in the integrity of police who manage the informants. 'Jailhouse snitches' who claim a cellmate confessed to them feature prominently in miscarriage of justice cases, such as in the Sydney Hilton bombing case. It often turns out that these people are serial informants who trade testimony for reduced charges.

Excessive trust has also been placed in witness testimony. Research on witnesses in the last few decades has provided a more realistic picture of their very limited capacity to accurately recall what they observed and their suggestibility to promptings from police.

Plea bargaining can also lead to suspects being pressured to plead guilty to obtain a reduction in charges, especially when the prosecution pile up charges or defence lawyers encourage a quick turnaround of cases.

Sloppy forensics and an excessive faith in science and scientific witnesses has been another feature of miscarriages of justice cases. This problem emerged most significantly from the 1970s with questionable scientific assertions about trace evidence of explosives and blood, and questionable blood splatter analyses.

Bias by judges and prosecutors has also been a feature of miscarriages of justice cases. Within the adversarial system judges usually have scope to influence juries through their summing of the case or their control of courtroom tactics. A more general system bias is especially evident in wrongful death penalty cases. Research in the United States has shown that racial bias operates in 'like' cases so that black defendants are much more likely to receive the death penalty (Miller-Potter, 2005, pp. 330–332).

Conclusion

The criminal courts represent an area of high risk for corruption and misconduct. There is certainly an urgent need for reforms in many countries where citizens have very little faith in lawyers and judges because of extensive problems of graft, bias and politicisation. In more advanced countries with more sophisticated checks and balances, and a strong tradition of legal professionalism, there have still been significant problems with miscarriages of justice, even in very recent times. The inevitable conclusion is that there needs to be closer scrutiny of the conduct of legal professionals; with more robust systems for ensuring ethical conduct and for preventing, detecting and remedying miscarriages of justice.

Chapter 7

Integrity Management and Accountability in the Criminal Courts

This chapter examines the question of how to ensure democratic accountability of the criminal court system and how to maximise ethical conduct by criminal law professionals, primarily judicial officers (judges and magistrates), prosecutors and defence lawyers. In the previous section on the police we noted that a 'traditional model' of police accountability is highly inadequate. When it comes to the courts in many democratic countries we cannot be as dismissive of traditional safeguards. There are many established rules and procedures in the criminal courts that have contributed to greater integrity — such as open court and the appeals system. Nonetheless, the problem of miscarriages of justice and associated conduct issues illustrate the need to implement a more advanced model of integrity management.

This chapter elaborates on both models, with a focus on advanced strategies to enhance traditional protections. There are a number of more contemporary innovations that are now considered essential to a more finely tuned criminal justice system, with built-in counterweights to deliberate or accidental errors. These include downgrading confessional evidence and instituting an independent agency for examining suspected miscarriages of justice. The additions are particularly vital given pressure on police and courts to produce 'results' in the post-9/11 counter-terrorism environment. As with police, corruption prevention for the courts should involve a process of matching interventions to risk indicators. If there are indicators, from complaints or surveys, for example, that corruption is an extensive problem, then aggressive techniques like integrity tests and phone taps might be required. In many other cases, however, it is probable that these sorts of techniques will not be needed as regular integrity tools.

Accountability for What?

'Justice' is the obvious answer to a question about the purpose of accountability in the criminal courts. Unfortunately, opinions vary about justice, although in theory most people would probably expect justice to entail, at a minimum, finding the right culprit, and consistency in sentencing, with consideration of mitigating and aggravating factors. We could also formulate these goals in terms of the prevention of miscarriages of justice. Here, there is a problem of opinion as well, especially in relation to excessively harsh or lenient sentences, although a consensus view of sentences is a goal worth pursuing. The prevention of wrongful convictions might be an area where there is greater unanimity. To this list of aspirations we can add some others: mainly protection of the dignity, welfare and rights of all participants; public confidence; and efficient processing of cases and efficient use of public finances.

Traditional English-based Model of Accountability

As we have seen, many advanced democratic countries, like Australia, have a criminal court system that follows an English model. A variety of guidelines and due process rights designed to limit opportunities for corruption and to minimise miscarriages of justice have been developed over time within these systems. These make for a fairly long list, and include the following in abbreviated form (see, e.g., White & Perrone, 1997, pp. 81–88):

- Criminal law should be an expression of the consensus view of the people formed through an open democratic process of law making.
- The guiding principles of neutrality and equality are central to the administration of justice in a fair and equitable manner.
- The separation of powers should be in operation. The people who make the laws do not adjudicate the law. Arresting officers do not adjudicate the case. Jurors do not defend or accuse a defendant.
- Accused persons should be tried as quickly as is reasonably possible because 'justice delayed is justice denied'.
- Accused persons are 'presumed innocent' in that the obligation is on the state to prove charges — rather than the obligation being on the accused to defend charges.
- 'Judges' rules' must apply to the pre-trial process of police investigations, interviews and case preparation. This includes informing suspects of their legal rights and providing access to a lawyer.
- Accused persons have a right to silence to protect against inadvertent or false self-incrimination.
- Under the principle of habeas corpus accused persons have a right to be present at their trial and reply to the charges against them.
- The open court system allows members of the public, including the media, to observe court proceedings and report on them outside the court.
- The presentation of evidence is controlled by rules of evidence. Some types of evidence, such as hearsay or evidence obtained illegally, are usually not admissible.

- Judgments about guilt or innocence are guided by standards of proof. In criminal cases, given the greater penalties involved, this is usually 'beyond reasonable doubt'.

- Defendants are entitled to legal representation at their trial and in the pre-trial preparation of their defence. Low-income defendants should have access to a publicly funded defence.

- More serious cases are judged by a jury of citizens.

- More serious cases are taken over from police by lawyers in a public prosecutors office. This provides an intermediate set of checks and balances on police process corruption and the quality of the police case.

- There is a jury selection process in which the prosecutor and the defendant (or their representative) have the right to veto a number of potential jurors who they might consider to be biased.

- Once a person has been found guilty the sentence for that offence is either fixed or set within a maximum and minimum range. Judges should follow precedents exercising discretion to ensure equality.

- In recognition of the fact that mistakes can be made, convicted persons should have access to an appeal system. Appeals should be heard by judicial officers who were not involved in the original hearing.

- Judges are usually given tenure in their employment and are paid above-average salaries so they are independent from political influences and financial temptation.

- Judicial independence is buttressed by rules about the removal of judges, such as a requirement for a two-thirds majority in parliament to remove a judge.

- Judicial officers are also subject to the rule of law. They are not immune from being charged with criminal offences, such as corruption.

- Professional codes of conduct govern the behaviour of all legal officers participating in the criminal court process. Breaches of codes are investigated by professional associations and punishable by a range of sanctions, including loss of licence.

- Parliaments should have the capacity to establish commissions of inquiry with sufficient powers and resources to properly inquire into any suspected misconduct in the courts and make recommendations for improvements.

- Standing law reform commissions should conduct research on all aspects of the criminal law and operations of the criminal courts to contribute to democratic legitimacy, relevance and efficiency.

How Effective Are These Guidelines?

The previous chapter on miscarriages of justice and associated forms of unethical conduct in the criminal courts showed that traditional mechanisms on their own are not sufficient to prevent abuses. The first chapter of the book showed how democratic law making is deeply flawed. Most electoral systems do not provide for one-vote-one-value in electing representatives, and there are usually no accurate mechanisms for ensuring that laws reflect the will of the people. Readers can ask themselves when it was that they last had the opportunity to vote directly on anything to do with criminal law or even had an opportunity to express an opinion about it as part of a systematic government-run study.

We have also seen that miscarriages of justice, including wrongful convictions, are recurring features of many criminal court systems. Traditional criminal courts are also characterised by long delays in processing matters (Prenzler & Sarre, 2009). They generate high levels of participant dissatisfaction and lack of public confidence — although public knowledge about the courts, especially factors taken into account in sentencing, can by ill informed (Sarre & O'Connell, 2009, p. 300). Traditional criminal courts tend to compound the problem of miscarriages of justice through a culture of denial and covering up of misconduct and error. The system also lacks proper mechanisms for reviewing questionable cases. A traditional system is characterised by a wide potential gap between the quality of legal defence available to those with the capacity to pay in the private sector and those dependent on state provision. Finally, the traditional model tends to be reactionary in sentencing, with limited use of creative and more constructive alternatives to imprisonment and fines.

An Advanced Model?

Is it possible to devise an accountability system for the criminal courts that preserves the best elements of the traditional system, counters its weaknesses and minimises miscarriages of justice without any unintended negative consequences? This section lists some reforms that critics argue are necessary to ensure the best available criminal court system in terms of fairness, efficiency, utility and accountability.

Inquisitorial Elements

The build up of miscarriage of justice cases in countries with adversarial systems stimulated an interest in importing inquisitorial elements to reduce the risks of misconduct and errors. Although there is disagreement among scholars about particular elements, and despite the fact that inquisitorial systems are highly variable, there are areas of potential change that are broadly supported (Huff & Killias, 2008; Kessler, 2008; Zalman, 2008). Generally there is little support for dispensing with juries, which are seen as an important form of citizen participation and an important check on any potential for judicial despotism. At the same time, judge-only trials may have a place where there is considerable public controversy and impartial juries might be hard to find and/or when the parties agree to dispense with a jury. But there is considerable interest in several areas where the inquisitorial aspects of court processes can be enlarged. For example, the role of the judge (and magistrate) could be enlarged along the lines of the continental system. In inquisitorial systems judges are much more interventionist. The judge takes less of a detached umpire's role and is more involved in an ongoing inquiry. For example, they may more willingly adjourn proceedings to order investigators to follow other lines of inquiry. The defence may ask for an adjournment in order for the police to conduct investigations on behalf of their client, and judges may support this. The judge can also be more active in questioning witnesses, to the point in some cases where prosecution or defence cross-examination becomes almost redundant.

In an inquisitorial system the investigation involves building up a shared dossier around a case. There are more pre-trial meetings and negotiations involving the judge. The prosecution is expected to be even more open with information than is the case with disclosure requirements in the adversarial system, including presenting evidence they have discovered but planned not to use that could be seen as assisting the defence in some way. The prosecution holds a more explicit mission to be impartial, test the police case, order more inquires where necessary and also act to find evidence supporting the defence. The defence still has a central role in challenging the case made by the state, but it is also expected to be more open and to cooperate with the investigation. For example, there is less concern with prejudice and the whole background of the defendant can be admissible.

The inquisitorial system involves more give and take between prosecution and defence. It was perhaps not surprising then that the Runciman Commission on criminal justice in the United Kingdom recommended enlarged requirements on the defence to disclose the main substance of their strategy, with rights for the prosecution to apply for an order from the court if they felt that adequate disclosure had not occurred (1993, p. 200). Lack of disclosure could also be interpreted adversely by a jury. One of the Commission's more controversial conclusions (by a majority) was that juries should be entitled to make adverse inferences from the refusal of an accused person to answer questions, subject to directions from the judge that this is not a ground for conviction and that the prosecution must prove its case (pp. 55–56).

Introducing changes like this to the adversarial system would require changes to rules and statements about roles. But it would also require cultural change. Some retraining of parties would also be required.

More Accessible Appeals and a Case Review Commission

To remedy miscarriages of justice it is also essential for convicted persons to have access to a well-resourced and expert standing body whose sole task is to review questionable cases without the high threshold tests applied by traditional appeal courts. However, for the review body to be effective, appeal courts need to be more alive to the possibility of miscarriages of justice and be more willing to hear cases where there are any suspicions of errors. Strict conditions about what constitutes fresh evidence, and references to 'flagrantly incompetent advocacy', need to be moderated. The terms should be much more open by way of the possibility that a conviction 'is or may be unsafe' (Royal Commission, 1993, p. 215). Appeal court judges should also be less passive — not simply listening to both sides — and familiarise themselves with the original case, suggest lines of inquiry, and question witnesses and the defendant. There also needs to be scope for convicted persons to apply for legal aid to assist them develop an application for review (Royal Commission, 1993, pp. 214–215).

A key recommendation of the Runciman Commission, and an important innovation, was the creation of a permanent agency to independently review questionable cases and recommend or launch appeals. The Criminal Cases Review Commission (CCRC) was established in the United Kingdom in 1997. An agency of this type would analyse case records for inconsistencies and omissions, and also conduct fresh inquiries by means such as new tests, re-interviewing witnesses, and locating and interviewing other witnesses. Its main workload will come from responding to applications, but it should also have own motion powers to initiate a review without an application from a convicted person.

The CCRC has shown itself to be an agency with teeth. Despite the many limitations under which it operates, one study found that about 65% of the convictions it challenged have been quashed (Scher & Weathered, 2004). More recent figures show a slightly higher rate of 68%, although they also show the extremely high attrition of applications. The outcomes of a decade of its work, from 1997 to 2006, are shown in Table 7.1.

Despite the enormous workload and high attrition of applications, the CCRC's successes in overturning wrongful convictions is now largely unquestioned and it is an accepted institution:

> Not only is it an independent body, separate from both the executive and the judiciary, but it has enhanced resources, staffing and even, arguably, expertise. Most important, its receptive approach and attitude are in complete

Table 7.1 Criminal Cases Review Commission, Case Outcomes 1997–2006

Outcome	Placeholders	
Total applications	9,044	
Open	278	
Actively being worked on	424	
Completed	8,342	(including ineligible)
Referrals (to Court of Appeal)	341	
Heard by Court of Appeal	291	
Quashed	199	
Reversed	3	

Note: Adapted from Campbell (2008, p. 131).

contrast to the reluctance, endemic in the governmental departments, to reinvestigate cases with thoroughness. (Walker & McCartney, 2008, p. 197)

'Fieldwork' is crucial. The CCRC does not simply conduct paper reviews. It can deploy a range of investigators and experts, and makes use of forensic laboratories. One criticism has been that it is overly dependent on police investigators and, by implication, needs to develop a pool of non-police investigators to demonstrate greater independence. There is also an enormous backlog of cases, and one of the implications of the successes to date is that there are probably cases of innocence sitting in the long waiting list. There are also accusations that the backlog puts pressure on staff to reject applications without adequate review (Walker & McCartney, 2008).

The absence of such bodies in countries like Australia can only serve as testimony to the continuation of a culture of excessive trust in the existing system.

Training

Pre-service and in-service training curricula for judges and criminal lawyers should include in-depth studies of miscarriages of justice, and the chains of events that produce wrongful convictions and other miscarriages of justice, in a case study approach. International comparative studies of different criminal court systems should also make lawyers more sceptical of the system they work in. All lawyers must have extensive training in ethical issues and professional responsibilities. This should not be just a perfunctory tour of codes of conduct, but involve understanding the rationales for code positions and include studies of real professional misconduct cases.

Downgrading Confessional Evidence

One highly significant lesson from the analysis of wrongful conviction cases is the need to downgrade confessional evidence (Langdon & Wilson, 2005; Stevens, 2008). There must be a recognition that people will make false confessions, sometimes even under what appears to be relatively light duress or because of the presence of mental illness or other motives. Confessions must be shown to be voluntary, corroborating evidence should always be sought and retractions should generally nullify the standing of confessions (although a recorded confession may still be admitted to the court for consideration). The Runciman Commission left the door open for juries to consider confessions when no other evidence was presented, but with the proviso that corroborating evidence had been sought and with a 'strong warning' from the judge (1993, p. 196).

Recording Interviews

The tape recording of interviews for presentation in court has been another major innovation aimed at reducing the risk of false confessions and addressing the general problem of loss of confidence in confessions and interview notes presented by police. This was a requirement of the *Police and Criminal Evidence Act 1984* (PACE) in England and Wales that predated the Runciman Commission. The Commission considered tape recording 'a strikingly successful innovation' in protecting both suspects and police from false allegations (Royal Commission, 1993, p. 26). It did, however, emphasise that the requirement for recording was not meant to work alone. Due process rights were to be enhanced by placing restrictions on recording when it was likely that suspects were affected by alcohol or drugs, by prioritising treatment for mentally ill persons over recording their interview, and by ensuring extra protections for young people such as the presence of a suitable adult other than a lawyer during the recording. The Commission did not suggest that video-recording was necessarily better, but video-recording has slowly taken over from tape recording in many locations. In Australia research has been conducted into the effectiveness of audiovisual recording of interviews by analysing the content of tapes, and surveying police, prosecutors, defence lawyers and judges. The study (Dixon, 2006) found that recording of police interviews did not provide complete protection against manipulation of suspects. However, overall, it:

> has been successful in putting an end to the long dispute about verballing, and is perceived by many criminal justice professionals to have increased guilty pleas, reduced trial length, reduced challenges to the admission of confessional evidence and increased public confidence in the justice process. (Dixon, 2006, p. 330)

Downgrading Witness Evidence

Evidence from witnesses should also be accorded much less value than in the past. The testimony of one witness should not be sufficient on its own to convict a person. Police should not only admit evidence from eyewitnesses who made a positive identification of the accused, but they should also inform the court of witnesses who did not identify the accused (Royal Commission, 1993, p. 188). Evidence from criminals and from prison cellmates should also be considered highly questionable. The motives of witnesses, especially persons in prison or facing charges or investigation, should always be considered highly suspect.

Forensic Procedures

Since many of the more notorious miscarriages of justice came to light in the 1980s much stricter forensic procedures have been introduced in regard to the preservation and analysis of crime scene data. Forensic laboratories must meet strict standards and be subject to frequent inspections by an independent agency. It is also essential that, wherever possible, the defence be allowed to carry out independent tests on samples and observe tests conducted in government forensic laboratories. A more inquisitorial process should also entail more comprehensive statements from scientists about the limits of their tests and alternative explanations for prosecutorial hypotheses about cause and effect relationships. Forensic scientists should also be subject to a professional code of conduct that includes duties of disclosure. Preservation of evidence is also essential to allow for access during reviews and appeals (see Huff & Killias, 2008, pp. 296–298; Royal Commission, 1993, pp. 211–213).

Pre-Charge Detention

Legislation about pre-charge detention by police in many countries recognises that there are justifications for allowing police to hold a person without charge, subject to strict controls. Police must be able to show evidence for their suspicions that the person has committed a serious offence or is likely to commit an offence, and that police need more time to preserve evidence or obtain evidence that will meet the criminal standard of proof. Many countries find that periods of 24 to 48 hours strike a good balance in giving police some scope for follow-up inquiries while preventing abuse. Up to three days is also a fairly common standard for terrorism-related offences (Russell, 2007; see also Royal Commission, 1993, pp. 29–30).

A number of protections must be in place within these time frames (Human Rights Watch, 2008). Prompt access to a lawyer is absolutely essential. The suspect must be informed of the grounds for detention. The suspect must also be provided with adequate sustenance and there must be strict rules and monitoring procedures to prevent oppressive questioning, coercion or torture. A senior officer must authorise the initial detention, and extensions beyond 24 hours should be approved by a judge who must be shown the evidence for the detention. Next of kin must also be informed of the detention.

Lengthy pre-charge detention periods allowed in many countries under counter-terrorism laws — even where they rely on judicial approval for extension — fail to account for the high risks of coercion and torture, psychological deterioration and false confessions. In any case, according to the United Kingdom's National Council for Civil Liberties there is no evidence that long detention periods assist in preventing terrorist attacks or bringing terrorists to justice (Russell, 2007).

Sentencing Guidelines

In an effort to reduce bias in sentencing, sentencing guidelines or sentencing Acts have been developed that are supplemental to the specific penalties, including maximum and minimum penalties, listed in criminal law (Tonry, 2002). Guidelines may make clearer the purposes of sentencing and set priorities, such as restitution to victims or public safety. They will identify factors to be taken into account when deciding between maximum and minimum penalties and other options. Typical factors to be considered include the offender's age, if the offender was on bail or had committed previous offences, the amount of physical or emotional harm inflicted, mental health issues, the offender's ability to support themselves on release, evidence of remorse and evidence of character, cooperation with police, and if the offender pleaded guilty.

How effective these are is somewhat open to question. One study in the United States, following the introduction in late-1987 of federal sentencing guidelines, found a reduction in disparities in sentences as far as the study was able to control for case variables. The difference in average length of sentences between judges fell from 4.9 months before the guidelines were operationalised to 3.9 months over the following five years (Anderson, Kling, & Stith, 1999, p. 2).

Internal and External Regulation

Concerns about unethical conduct by lawyers have driven a trend away from self-regulation of the legal profession to greater external involvement (see Ross, 2005, pp. 110–123). Proponents of internal processes argue the profession should be encouraged to keep its own house in order and that only lawyers really understand the issues. They also warn that an external government-run regulatory body would threaten the traditional independence of lawyers and their role in defending civil liberties. A government regulatory body could be used to exclude and remove lawyers who challenge government decisions or expose government abuses. Advocates of external regulation point to the fact that self-regulation has been unique to the legal profession in many countries and is no longer tenable in an age of greater accountability. Analyses of miscarriages of justice often demonstrate an abject failure of in-house bodies or the courts to discipline and remove members for unethical conduct and to properly deter misconduct.

Scholars like Ross (2005) argue that the profession has had too much freedom to regulate itself for too long and that more of a balance is required. Certainly it would seem that strictly in-house systems by professional associations for processing complaints lack the amount of independence necessary to support public confidence and satisfy objective tests of independence. Government regulation, in any case, would not be carried out by a line department like a licensing authority. Regulation would be through an independent statutory commission or ombudsman-like body that has independence written into its governing legislation. Its main role would be to receive and investigate complaints and to act against suspected misconduct (Ross, 2005, pp. 208–209).

Possibly the best balance would be achieved through a co-regulatory arrangement. In fact, a four-part model is conceivable in the following terms:

1. Professional associations deal with initial licensing and routine renewals, and can act to discipline and disbar members.

2. The justice department and courts deal with disciplinary matters related to employees, including prosecutors, judges and magistrates.

3. A legal services commission investigates and adjudicates complaints and has own motion powers to investigate matters it thinks may be important, and reviews the work of the internal agencies in parts 1 and 2.

4. A public sector integrity commission investigates more serious cases of corruption, including through the use of undercover operations where appropriate.

There is also normally a fifth tier of accountability through the capacity of parliament to remove judicial officers for gross misconduct. And the courts themselves provide a parallel institution to hear appeals and criminal cases. A potential criticism here is that the model involves too much overlap and double handling. However, some cross-over is arguably a good thing in providing comprehensive coverage and opportunities for a fall-back response. For example, if an external body fails to properly respond to misconduct there is still the chance of positive action at the in-house level. An in-house body might discipline a member or employee and also refer the case to an external body for further investigations within their terms of reference.

Affirmative Action and Appointment by Merit?

As noted, historically in most countries employment and power in the criminal court system has been monopolised by males and the dominant ethnic group. To break this monopoly and create a more representative judiciary, and a more diverse range of prosecutors and defence lawyers, it is probably necessary for some kind of affirmative action program. One option is preferential selection. This works by prioritising the equity target group candidate when two candidates are ranked equally. However, preferential selection can be seen to conflict with the principle of appointment by merit when equally ranked candidates are examined more closely. And, naturally enough, it can provoke resentment. However, conflict can be reduced by focusing affirmative action initiatives on the feeder channels for careers in law. In other words, the focus can be placed on making target groups more competitive. Scholarships and mentoring programs for law students from equity target groups are two examples. Mentoring and support groups can also operate within the courts, justice departments and private practice. There is also a case for a more open system of advertising of judicial vacancies and selection by politically independent panels.

Conclusion

Criminal courts are at risk for a variety of harmful and demoralising errors of judgment or deliberate corruption of the system. Consequently, greater checks and balances are required than are provided for by the traditional adversarial system. While many legal systems have traditional elements that need to be preserved, there appears to be scope for improvements to provide a greater level of protection against abuses of procedure and associated due process rights to prevent miscarriages of justice. Reforms that need to be considered include the importation of more inquisitorial elements into the criminal trial process, greater responsibilities imposed on both sides to cooperate in a process of finding the truth, greater external regulation of the legal profession, and the establishment of case review commissions in each jurisdiction as a permanent counter to the potential for wrongful convictions.

Corrections

Chapter 8

Ethical Issues in Corrections

This is the first chapter in the section of chapters on corrections. It begins by examining macro-level ethical issues in correctional policy. These big picture issues revolve around a central question of what to do with offenders. There is some overlap here with the sentencing issues discussed in Chapter 5 on legal ethics, but there the focus was on the personal dilemmas judges and magistrates face in making sentencing decisions within their field of discretion. Here the concern is with government policy on sentencing. The issue of the right to punish is discussed, along with issues of mandatory sentencing, truth in sentencing and discretionary sentencing, selective incapacitation, coercive treatment, capital punishment, prison conditions and the treatment of special needs groups.

The discussion then moves to the more familiar ground of micro-level ethical issues for practitioners. On this topic the chapter examines issues of discretion, security versus treatment, personal relationships, loyalty and whistleblowing, use of force, confidentiality, internal discipline and in-house justice, use of isolation and prisoners as control agents. Each subsection concludes with an outline and explanation of a code position. In this case a combination of three codes is used. Standard public service principles of impartiality and public interest are applied in the correctional context.

Background

Corrections is the final main stage of the criminal justice system. Corrective services departments administer sentences, including custodial sentences. This entails administering probation and other non-custodial orders, preventing escapes from custody, maintaining order in prisons, administering rehabilitation and training programs, and making decisions about early release. Correctional services is usually thought of in terms of a two-part structure:

1. Custodial corrections maintains prisoners in secure facilities.
2. Community corrections is mainly concerned with managing offenders on orders undertaken outside prisons — such as community service, probation and parole — but can include quasi-prison environments such as halfway houses with night-time or weekend lock-in.

As we have seen previously, the authority of the state to punish and to attempt to correct behaviour is justified by contract theory (Pollock, 2007, p.

132). People agree to live by rules to avoid competition that produces constant conflict and violence. The rules are determined by the will of the majority expressed through democratic government. This process, in theory, grants the state the right to punish those who refuse to comply with the rules.

'Punishment' here can be misconstrued as the mere infliction of pain — as retribution in ethical formalist terms. But while punishment can be viewed as something that is morally required to right a wrong it can also be seen as a tool of behavioural change. In modern criminal justice systems punishment overlaps with a wider concept of 'penalties' or 'sanctions' intended to compel or generate compliance. This can entail a broad spectrum of techniques including compulsory rehabilitation programs. In pursuing these goals of punishment and correction, criminal justice systems are challenged by the mystery of free will. A major function of the courts is to assess degrees of responsibility for criminal acts, but this is a highly speculative process. Punishment and coerced treatment are also deeply challenged by the highly unequal nature of society. The law seeks to treat people equally but people's backgrounds and formative experiences are vastly different and frequently unequal (Kappeler & Potter, 2005, pp. 269–272).

The specific goals of correctional systems are normally formulated in the following terms (Prenzler & Sarre, 2009, p. 261):

- *Retribution* is punishment in its purest form. 'Justice' requires an approximate form of proportional harm to the offender for the offence.
- *Restitution* involves an offender paying compensation to a victim, or to society as a proxy victim.
- *Deterrence* involves any measure that prevents a person committing a crime because of fear of being identified and punished. 'Specific deterrence' relates to an individual's desistance as a consequence of having been punished before. Under 'general deterrence', people decide against crime because of the perceived probability of punishment.
- *Incapacitation* prevents crime by restricting potential offenders' access to victims. This is usually through imprisonment but can include home detention or security 'bracelets'.
- *Rehabilitation* entails behavioural change through therapeutic programs and employment skills programs.

These goals represent both formalist and utilitarian principles. Retribution is a pure form of formalism in that it is only concerned with righting a wrong through a transfer of loss to an offender approximately equal to the loss to the victim (tempered in modern times by the loss of liberty in lieu of corporal punishments). Strictly speaking, the consequences in terms of future behaviour are irrelevant to the imperatives of justice. In that regard, symbolism is particularly important in showing society that justice has been done, but without the need for brutality. On the other hand, deterrence, incapacitation and rehabilitation are all utilitarian in only being concerned with changing behaviour for the future benefit of society. Any pain inflicted on offenders in the process is not related to retribution but measured out, in theory, for the desired behavioural response. It is simply a tool. Restitution can be seen to straddle both principles. It is probably more in the formalist camp, in emphasising the need to right a wrong through a payment, but it can also be part of a behavioural change process — especially through victim–offender mediation where offenders are expected to appreciate the harm inflicted on victims as part of a negotiated agreement on reparation.

Macro-Level Policy Issues

Macro-level policy issues concern social and government responses to the problem of finding productive and fair responses to offending behaviour. These policies are developed in a highly charged political environment. The multiple aims of correctional systems listed at the start of this chapter can result in competition for priority or they can also be seen as inherently contradictory. For example, in theory, the infliction of various forms of pain as punishment might undermine attempts to improve offenders' attitudes, values and self-discipline with a view to their future integration into mainstream society. Even within the utilitarian framework there can be contradictions. A focus on incapacitation can conflict with rehabilitation and the need to move offenders out of an institutional setting into the community. This means that policymakers may be faced with difficult choices about which correctional goals to prioritise, with the inevitable effect that those not selected will suffer.

Mandatory Sentencing

A major issue in correctional policy that has arisen, especially from the 1980s in many countries, is that of mandatory sentencing. A key influence was the rapidly rising crime rates from the 1970s (Makkai & Prenzler, 2009). This set off alarm bells in many jurisdictions. Victims groups were formed and lobbied governments for tougher sentences. A desperate search ensued for a solution to the problem, and light sentences were often condemned as a major cause of a lack of deterrence. The exercise of judicial discretion was also seen as a major factor. Many judges were characterised as 'liberal' and soft on offenders. To counter this, parliaments increased sentences, but some also reduced judges' discretion or took it away completely through the introduction of mandatory sentencing (Pratt, Brown, Brown, Hallsworth, & Morrison, 2005). Once a person was found guilty, the magistrate or judge was obliged to hand down the prescribed sentence, without regard to mitigating or aggravating factors or rehabilitative objectives. Some jurisdictions added 'three strikes and you're out' provisions to sentencing policy. This meant that a person found guilty of a third offence would automatically receive a much longer sentence than would be given for that offence alone.

Mandatory sentencing and three strikes laws provoked enormous controversy. Both sides claimed the moral high ground. Conservatives claimed they were appropriately punishing serious crimes and protecting potential victims of crime. Liberal opponents claimed the laws were ineffectual, unfair in failing to address the nuances of crime events and motivations, and discriminatory in disproportionately locking up impoverished racial minorities. The academic research on the topic has produced mixed results. It seems that the deterrent effect of long prison terms is limited because most offenders simply miscalculate the risks of apprehension and punishment and are generally ignorant of sentencing regimes. However, the extended imprisonment of repeat offenders has probably contributed to reductions in crime through incapacitation (Weatherburn, 2004, p. 123ff). At the same time, this has come at a very high cost both to taxpayers and to minority communities that have lost many of their young men to long prison terms (Kappeler & Potter, 2005, p. 272).

Truth in Sentencing

There is also controversy over a related policy referred to as 'truth in sentencing', where the initial stated sentence must be served. This approach contrasts with some aspects of discretionary sentencing, which involves giving judicial officers choices about the type and length of sentences — usually with minimum and maximum periods. Additional elements are also usually available, such as allowing two or more sentences to be served concurrently. Discretionary sentencing and other associated sentencing categories are designed to allow judges to match sentences to circumstances. However, they attract a lot of criticism, including media reports that generate outrage about sentencing 'discounts'. The following is a list of types of sentencing options that tend to attract the most criticism (Prenzler & Sarre, 2009, p. 268):

- probation (a type of good behaviour bond in lieu of prison)
- parole (release of a prisoner, under supervision, after they have served a stipulated non-parole period)
- early release (release from prison for good behaviour)
- concurrent sentences (when multiple sentences are combined to the length of the longest sentence)
- suspended sentences (similar to probation but a person will be required to serve the full term of the original sentence if they breach the conditions of the suspension)
- statutes of limitations (periods after which a person cannot be charged)

- unrecorded convictions (a person is found guilty but they usually cannot be discriminated against on the basis of the conviction)
- life sentences which do not mean imprisonment for life but for a significant portion of a person's life — which can mean as little as 10 years with parole.

Many of these options cause consternation among victims of crime and the general public. For example, following a conviction, a sentence of imprisonment is read out — perhaps 'five months' — and then it is 'suspended'! Many ordinary people see this as a type of fraud — a bureaucratic doublespeak or doublethink of the type described in George Orwell's *Big Brother* (2002).

Truth in sentencing is designed to sweep away these subversions and remove the cloud of confusing language that surrounds sentencing. There would seem to be a case for more accurate and honest terminology. Parole and suspended sentences could be removed as options offensive to justice and victims of crime. This does not mean that parole, for example, has to be dispensed with, but simply utilised under a better name. In theory, prison discipline should be managed by in-house sanctions, not the threat of the denial of parole, and post-release behaviour should be managed by behaviour bonds. Instead of a sentence reading as '12 months … with a non-parole period of six months', it could read as 'six months imprisonment plus six months supervised good behaviour bond'. Furthermore, it should be noted that a 'parole deal', where inmates must admit guilt to obtain parole, can result in a miscarriage of justice when prisoners who genuinely believe they are innocent are put in a difficult bind. Making a stand and refusing to admit guilt can result in many years of extra jail time (Walker & McCartney, 2008, p. 205).

Concurrent sentences represent a particular conundrum (Tonry, 2002). For example, aggregating multiple sentences could mean that a person spends many years in prison for a large number of relatively minor crimes such as household burglary. This might seem a waste of a significant portion of a person's life and an excessive cost to the community. However, simply combining all the sentences into the longest sentence also seems to detract unfairly from the totality of the offences and from the victims of all the other offences. Some better compromise needs to be found. Community consultation by sentencing commissions or law reform research units is one way forward to achieve greater consensus and more public acceptance of responses to multiple offences.

Coercive Treatment

Coercive treatment is another difficult issue. Should offenders be forced to participate in therapy? For utilitarians, the answer depends largely on the consequences. There is certainly research that indicates that treatment programs can reduce reoffending — or reconvictions to be exact — although a 30% reduction in recidivism appears as a very high result for treatment effects (Gendreau & Andrews, 1990; Gornik, 2001). It seems logical to insist that offenders participate in rehabilitative efforts with a view to their own welfare and that of society. However, some civil libertarians will argue that this is also a violation of an offender's right to simply serve out their sentence in peace without the state intruding into their minds — consistent with a 'justice model' of sentencing (Pollock, 2007, p. 393). The basic argument is formalist: 'do the crime and do the time' … but no more than that. It is unfair for the state to assume an offender will offend again and subject them to intrusive interventions, especially given that predicting reoffending is very inexact (Hayes & Geerken, 1997). People should be punished for crimes they have committed, not 'punished' for crimes they might commit. Furthermore, therapies often involve a requirement for participants to admit guilt, and talk frankly about personal experiences and thoughts. Some will maintain their innocence and many may find therapies embarrassing or distressful.

A related issue, involving medical officers, concerns chemical interventions. Inmates and other sentenced persons can agree to take a range of prescribed drugs, or they might refuse. In the latter case, correctional authorities might deem there is an overriding case for institutional order or public safety that necessitates forced administration of drugs, many of which can have highly soporific effects. The UN guide to *International Human Rights Standards for Prison Officials* (2005) emphasises that medical decisions should be made by persons with medical qualifications and that prisoners should be allowed to request a second medical option.

Selective Incapacitation

Another issue concerns the selective incapacitation of seriously violent repeat offenders through indefinite detention. This is now an option for sentencing in some Australian jurisdictions for offenders deemed 'dangerous' (McSherry, Keyzer, & Freiberg, 2006). The number detained so far under this legislation is very small and these people have shocking histories of violent crime. However, civil libertarians point out that imprisoning someone for a crime they *might* commit is contrary to the most basic principles of procedural justice.

One alternative to indeterminate sentencing of repeat offenders is very close supervision in the community (Paparozzi & Gendreau, 2005; Roberts, 2005), which can be extended to include curfews and night-time lock-ins in community correctional facilities. However, it may be that some persons have such a large number of horrific crimes on their record that it is highly probable they will reoffend and that it would be grossly irresponsible to release them until old age sets in.

Capital Punishment

There is probably no issue in sentencing that attracts more fierce controversy than capital punishment. For many, the death penalty is the logical conclusion of a formalist eye-for-an-eye philosophy. Why should a person who deliberately or callously takes another person's life not be required to lose their life in return? This is the 'forfeiture principle' used to defend capital punishment. There are also strong utilitarian arguments in support of capital punishment. Execution is the ultimate form of incapacitation to prevent future victimisation. In theory, the possibility of losing one's life should also act as a powerful deterrent to serious crimes. Against these positions there is a range of philosophical and scientific arguments (Miller-Potter, 2005):

- Critics argue that capital punishment is murder by the State, which sets a poor precedent for killing as a way of settling scores (this is also arguably a formalist position).
- There is no evidence that the death penalty has a deterrent effect on crime, including murder.
- There is some evidence that murders can increase in a jurisdiction leading up to and after an execution.
- An offender who loses their life is unable to repay victims or society in tangible ways such as compensation from work.
- 'Life imprisonment' involves a kind of social and spiritual death that provides a very rough equivalence to execution.

The death penalty almost invariably entails the most extreme type of miscarriage of justice: the killing of an innocent person by the state justice system. Even cases that appear to be watertight at the time of trial have later been seen to involve serious errors. We have already seen that in the United States a large number of people have been freed from death row after a convoluted appeals process (Death Penalty Information Centre, 2009). These represent 'near misses'. Presumably thousands of others have lost their lives in the United States alone in the preceding centuries. With executions there is no way of reversing the judgment to the benefit of the wrongfully convicted person.

Prison Conditions

Prison conditions present another major ethical challenge for policymakers. Prisons cost very large amounts of money. In Australia it costs almost AU$200 a day to keep a prisoner (Prenzler & Sarre, 2009, p. 266). While politicians might agree on minimum standards for humane and secure prisons, funding this entails taking money from other more attractive programs such as medical research. Added to this is the fact that there is little public support for prison conditions as a progressive issue. Opposition politicians will often take opportunities to paint prison reforms as something 'soft on crims'. So even where governments are committed to adequate standards they have to watch that this does not reduce their popularity.

Special Needs Groups

A final issue concerns special treatment issues for young people, women, disabled persons, ethnic minorities and foreign nationals. How far should sentencing policies and corrective services go in accommodating people outside the main male prison population? For example, should children be allowed to live in prisons with their mothers? Progressive prisons now allow babies and toddlers to stay in prisons with their mothers, primarily for the child's sake, subject to the availability of adequate facilities. UN guidelines now set out guidelines for the treatment of equity target groups (UN, 2005, pp. 13–16). The guidelines are premised on the recognition that equal treatment of people who are unequal results in inequality. Women, for example, require separate facilities to men and to be searched only be women officers. Young inmates should also be accommodated separately to adults for their safety and to protect them from inappropriate influences. It is also particularly important that juveniles have access to education, are free from oppressive discipline and have greater access to their families than normal. Special efforts need to be made to communicate effectively with inmates who do not speak the main language, and modern prison design can fairly easily take into account the needs of disabled persons, with general wheelchair access, for example. Arguably, there should even be scope for inmates to practise their religion where feasible.

Micro-Level Ethical Dilemmas: The Working Environment

The correctional environment entails a relationship between two groups: the powerful (correctional officers) and the powerless (offenders). The situation is particularly acute in prisons, where guards control and monitor every aspect of an inmate's life. The imbalance creates intrinsic conflict and an opportunity structure for corruption and abuse. Prisons constitute closed societies, largely cut off from the outside world and mainstream society, where the lives of prisoners and guards are marked by often-acute boredom and considerable danger (Kleinig, 2008, chap. 12). Working in a prison can be like serving a prison term. Added to this mix is the discretion exercised by correctional officers over many aspects of the ways in which offenders are treated (ABC, 1985).

Conflict between offenders and correctional staff can be exacerbated by the type of negative informal organisational culture we have already seen in relation to police (Pollock, 2007, pp. 424–428). Stress, danger, boredom and isolation pull staff together, with the development of group attitudes and values that involve disparaging views of inmates, a code of silence and solidarity that covers up misconduct, and opposition to improved accountability and progressive correctional policies. Misconduct by correctional officers is also unlikely to attract the same kind of public outrage that many other forms of professional misconduct will attract, such as abuses of children in state care. Prison escapes frequently generate more fear and loathing than revelations of mistreatment of prisoners.

Practitioner Dilemmas

The following subsections introduce the main ethical dilemmas faced by correctional staff, including management, when on the job. As with previous chapters, each dilemma is followed by an outline of common code positions. In this case, the sources are the American Probation and Parole Association (APPA) summary *Code of Ethics* (2008), the UN publication *Human Rights and Prisons: A Pocketbook of International Human Rights Standards for Prison Officials* (2005; also used again in chapter 10 in regard to prison conditions), and the New South Wales Department of Corrective Services *Guide to Conduct and Ethics* (2005). The APPA code, copied in full below, sets out basic principles that should apply to custodial as much as community corrections (APPA, 2008; see also Probation and Community Corrections Officers' Association, 2009, p. 1):

1. I will render professional service to the justice system and the community at large in effecting the social adjustment of the offender.
2. I will uphold the law with dignity, displaying an awareness of my responsibility to offenders while recognizing the right of the public to be safeguarded from criminal activity.
3. I will strive to be objective in the performance of my duties, recognizing the inalienable right of all persons, appreciating the inherent worth of the individual, and respecting those confidences which can be reposed in me.
4. I will conduct my personal life with decorum, neither accepting nor granting favours in connection with my office.
5. I will cooperate with my co-workers and related agencies and will continually strive to improve my professional competence through the seeking and sharing of knowledge and understanding.
6. I will distinguish clearly, in public, between my statements and actions as an individual and as a representative of my profession.
7. I will encourage policy, procedures and personnel practices, which will enable others to conduct themselves in accordance with the values, goals and objectives of the American Probation and Parole Association.

8. I recognize my office as a symbol of public faith and I accept it as a public trust to be held as long as I am true to the ethics of the American Probation and Parole Association.

9. I will constantly strive to achieve these objectives and ideals, dedicating myself to my chosen profession.

This is obviously a very brief code. It reiterates a number of basic public service principles we have seen before in this book, including commitment to professionalism, an (implied) rejection of gratuities and bribes, and acting for the public benefit with impartiality. Other public service principles developed in more complex codes cover issues in much the same terms as we have seen previously. The issues include politicisation, public comment on internal matters, reporting misconduct, whistleblower protection, resolving conflicts of interest and secondary employment.

The New South Wales Department of Corrective Services guide is a useful example of a more detailed code. It begins with a utilitarian statement of corporate mission that prioritises 'reducing re-offending through secure, safe and humane management of offenders' (2005, p. 8), and includes a statement of values, as follows (p. 8):

- Commitment to the safety and welfare of offenders supervised in custody and/or in the community
- Commitment to rehabilitation and re-settlement of offenders
- Commitment to the dignity and worth of the individual
- Promotion of reparation to the community and to victims of crime
- Commitment to professionalism and quality service delivery
- Commitment to staff welfare
- Commitment to employment equity, cultural and ethnic diversity and family and community friendly workplaces
- Commitment to accountability, fairness and transparency in using public assets and resources
- Engagement with the community, interest groups and relevant research and teaching institutions.

A particularly commendable aspect of this guide is its emphasis on ethical leadership through the consistent enforcement of rules, communication and personal role modelling. Managers are strongly encouraged to (2005, p. 12):

- Show respect when communicating with staff. Threatening or abusive language is the sign of a poor and insecure manager and should not be used. Communicate clearly and empathetically and keep your staff informed of issues that relate to their work practices and welfare.
- Deal promptly with problems brought to you. This gives staff confidence in your professionalism and stops the problem from escalating.

- Provide advice without 'fear or favour'. This means you should provide information to staff, including your superiors, according to the facts of the situation, not with regard to your own best interests ...
- Bring ethical issues to the attention of your staff and advise them of the relevant sections of this Guide or other procedural documentation.
- Develop a firm, fair and equitable management style and not bully, harass or discriminate against staff or others.
- Not be afraid to make decisions. Staff will value your leadership if you act reasonably and fairly.

The guide also provides a set of questions to help staff focus on the issues at stake in ethical dilemmas and to comply with departmental standards. Examples include the following (2005, p. 11):

- Is the conduct or decision lawful?
- Does the outcome raise a potential conflict of interest or lead to private gain at public expense?
- How would this decision be perceived by the public?

Discretion

As we have seen, correctional officers have numerous opportunities to behave in ways that show favouritism or discrimination. Bias can have mild to serious consequences for the welfare of inmates and for general perceptions of fairness. The APPA code stresses the importance of being 'objective' and 'neither accepting nor granting favours in connection with my office'. The New South Wales Department of Corrective Services guide enlarges on these points, requiring staff to 'follow the letter and spirit of policies and procedures ... being fair to all [and] giving reasons for decisions, where appropriate' (p. 9). It also addresses the exercise of discretion in regard to relations between staff, and between staff and management (2005, p. 21):

> Staff appreciate the importance of dealing with issues consistently, promptly and fairly. This involves dealing with matters in accordance with approved procedures, in a non-discriminatory manner, and consistent with the rules of natural justice.
>
> Acts of unfairness involving favouritism, inconsistency or discrimination adversely affect morale and good working relationships and should not occur in the workplace.

Correctional officer discretion is particularly important for offenders in regard to assessments of their compliance with probation and parole orders. These assessments can present dilemmas for correctional professionals. Officers who wish to support an offender may be tempted to understate bad behaviour — and vice versa. While there is a formalist challenge here concerning truth telling and fairness, important consequences can flow from these decisions. New crime victimisations can occur at the hands of offenders who should not have been released. Or families can lose income and family bonds can be broken as a result of fathers or mothers committing minor violations and ending up in prison. Third parties, including potential crime victims and offenders' families, have a great deal at stake in these decisions. Pollock (2007, p. 478) summarises one aspect of this dilemma in the following scenario:

> You are a parole officer who has a single mother with three hyperactive, attention-deficit-disordered young children on your caseload. She receives no support from her ex-husband. Her mother wants nothing to do with her or the children, believing that 'God is punishing her'. The mother works as a topless dancer but hates it. She continues dancing because it pays the bills so well. You know that she smokes marijuana on a regular basis in an effort to deal with stress. Obviously, this is a violation of probation. However, if you file a violation report on her, she will go back to prison. You know she is doing the best she can with her kids, she is very involved with their school, and they are strongly bonded to her. You worry about what will happen to the kids. What would you do?

The codes of conduct for correctional officers reported here do not directly address this issue. It is arguably covered by general statements about impartiality and compliance with rules. The dilemma is framed in a way that probably appeals to most readers' sense of sympathy. However, even a utilitarian view that argues that the welfare of the children and the mother should come first must take into account the precedent set by ignoring rules and the potential harm from marijuana use. The scenario also does not say that the parole officer has proof of the marijuana use. Arguably the best course of action is for the officer to be honest to the parole board and let it take the nuances of the case into account.

Security Versus Treatment

Prisons policy can involve a dilemma between security and treatment. This conflict also has implications for the operational side of prison management, depending on how much control managers have over security standards and treatment programs under their command. Basically, the more non-custodial treatment-oriented staff — such as therapists and counsellors — are allowed into prisons, the more the risk of security breaches increases (Pollock, 2007, p. 445) A fixed budget also has to be divided between security and treatment. Improvements in one will probably entail losses in the other.

Modern codes emphasise the responsibility to ensure security. Escapes, riots or violence of any kind are contrary to the purposes of sentencing. They undermine public confidence in the prison system and the public's sense of safety. Prisoners and staff also need to be protected. However, codes temper a legitimate concern for security with restrictions on oppressive forms of restraints, such as handcuffs. Codes tend to restrict the use of such devices to transfers or for medical reasons (UN, 2005, p. 8). And, while keeping a keen eye on security, managers are also expected to retain a focus on the social goal of rehabilitation. In fact, these goals should be brought into harmony, in part because rehabilitation programs require a stable, safe environment.

Personal Relationships

When guards and prisoners are locked together, especially for long periods, there are opportunities for the development of personal relationships. This can also happen with offenders and community correctional officers. Should officers make friends with offenders? On the one hand, it seems unreasonable and oppressive to prohibit relationships. They may even help with rehabilitation. On the other, relationships present a range of risks, including real or perceived favouritism, and sexual exploitation — to the extent that a total ban seems the only appropriate policy. Officers can enjoy the company of offenders and engage in social chat with them, but they need to guard against any potential perception of 'a relationship'. The New South Wales Department of Corrective Services guide recognises the risks of such relationships and prohibits contact without authorisation; however, the grounds for authorisation are not spelt out (2005, p. 2).

Bribery, Gratuities and Corruption

As we have seen already in this book, criminal justice professionals, even when they are essentially honest and well-meaning, can be tempted to engage in various forms of corruption for personal gain — including stealing stationery or getting personal work done in the prison workshop. Rationalisations can be made for bending the rules, and a cynical attitude towards one's employer is often an ingredient. However, any gratuities that create a sense of obligation or appearance of favouritism are prohibited under codes of conduct. The APPA position on discretion also covers illegal transactions in 'neither accepting nor granting favours in connection with my office'. Similarly, any form of corruption is prohibited under the New South Wales Department of Corrective Services principles, which enjoin officers to 'place public interest and integrity above private interest' (2005, pp. 10–11). The guide also emphasises the fact that 'any form of bribery is illegal' (p. 15).

Loyalty and Whistleblowing

Correctional officers face many of the same dilemmas related to whistleblowing as those experienced by police. Making disclosures about observed or suspected misconduct can involve ostracism from a close-knit group, and even threats and physical danger. Nonetheless, the need to stop misconduct and ensure department-wide compliance with rules informs the imperative of whistleblowing in modern statements of ethics. The New South Wales Department of Correctional Services guide does, however, warn against false accusations, and also lists a number of different authorities with whom disclosures can be made (2005, p. 15). The guide also notes the availability of protection for whistleblowers but does not enlarge on what this might entail. Nor does it address the question of whether or not anonymous disclosers are acceptable.

Use of Force

Again, correctional officers face similar dilemmas to police in the use of force. Force can be required in self-defence by officers against physical threats from prisoners, in the defence of other officers, and in the defence of prisoners threatened by other prisoners. These threats can occur in confined spaces and in situations where officers are outnumbered. Threats from inmates can be calculated or occur when inmates are having psychotic episodes with limited capacity for self-control. Force can also be required to move prisoners in and out of cells or different sections of a prison. Community correctional officers can also be faced with aggression from the offenders they are managing, and they may need to make decisions about self-defence or about coming to the aid of a colleague while risking injury to themselves. As with police, too little force can result in a variety of harms to innocent people, with adverse career repercussions. Too much force can also have negative consequences, including fatal consequences. Force can also be required to enforce disciplinary orders. As with policing, correctional codes recognise the need for force while emphasising the imperative of minimum force and using force 'only when it is strictly necessary' (UN, 2005, p. 3). The UN code also addresses the issue of firearms in prisons:

> Firearms shall not be used against persons in custody or detention except in the following circumstances:
> – In self-defence or defence of others against imminent threat of death or serious injury;
> – When strictly necessary to prevent the escape of a person presenting a grave threat to life. (UN, 2005, p. 25)

Confidentiality

Correctional officers also face many of the same dilemmas of confidentiality faced by police and lawyers. This is an area that needs development in some codes. The APPA code refers to 'respecting those confidences which can be reposed in me'. This is regrettably vague, and while it may be appropriate in regard to some personal matters disclosed by offenders, it needs to deal with the issue of disclosures about rule violations or threats. The UN code makes a similar statement but adds a qualifier of sorts: 'Law enforcement officials shall respect the confidentiality of information in their possession unless the performance of duty or the needs of justice strictly require otherwise' (2005, p. 24). More examples about what these qualifiers relate to are needed. We should expect that correctional officers preface their communications with offenders in terms that make it clear that confidentiality is not guaranteed and that imperatives of justice and security take precedence.

Internal Discipline and In-house Justice

Internal discipline and control of prisons also presents dilemmas. Chapter 10 of this book, on correctional accountability, sets out some important principles in this area, including the need to involve police and the courts in criminal matters. For lower-level breaches of rules a system is needed that facilitates natural justice while continuing to allow the prison to run efficiently and maintain the authority of prison officials. A mini-court system with high evidentiary standards, rights to legal support and appeals can be resource-intensive and open to abuse by inmates. However, too much summary justice meted out by officers and managers can involve unfairness and provoke resentment. Finding appropriate punishments within a prison can also be difficult and involve privations in an environment that is already deficient in most of the basic requirements of civilisation. Consequently, punishments in prison can seem harsh and also counter-productive; for example, in removing prisoners from work programs or therapies.

The UN code asserts that 'discipline and order shall be maintained with firmness, but with no more restriction than is necessary for safe custody and well-ordered community life' (2005, p. 10). However, it emphasises the importance of prisoners being fully informed of rules and knowing their rights. It qualifies the statement on discipline and order with the principles on use of force — outlined earlier in this chapter — and the principles on procedural justice and complaints procedures developed in chapter 10.

Isolation

In an effort to maintain order and prevent offences occurring within prisons, managers have often resorted to the use of isolation. Isolation can be used both as a deterrent and for incapacitation, and can be employed for long periods beyond a few days. On the one hand, the need for isolation must be appreciated as a last resort device for protecting other prisoners and officers from assaults and harassment. At the same time, isolation can be abused, and prolonged isolation can have destructive psychological effects on top of those already inflicted by prolonged imprisonment (see Haney, 2001). The codes used here do not address this important point.

Prisoners as Control Agents

Prison managers, especially when understaffed, can also be tempted to trade privileges with some prisoners in return for them serving as a first level of informal discipline. This is an ends–means dilemma where the good end of prison order is achieved through an unethical means, but where failure to adopt the means may mean the end is not achieved. These prisoners are usually more aggressive and intimidating and willing to use standover tactics and minor assaults to ensure basic good order in the prison. This is an issue that needs to be addressed in codes, with clear prohibitions on the practice.

Conclusion

Several key themes emerge from this discussion of ethical issues in corrections. The first is that sentencing policy often involves a conflict between sentiment and social science. What people might feel is the right thing to do often simply does not work in the way expected. Examples include the deterrent effect of harsh sentences and the death penalty in reducing crime rates. This is not to say that imprisonment, even very long prison terms in some cases, do not have their place in a fair and productive sentencing policy. But it is very important to take the criminology into account along with the sentiment to find the best mix of sentencing options that meet society's demand for justice and need for security.

Another major theme concerns the conflict between a justice model and a treatment model of responses to crime. This is a difficult area that pits the idea of the rights of convicted persons, which theoretically could be anyone, against social engineering in society's interests — 'the greater good'. The final chapter of this book, on integrity management and accountability in corrections, revisits these issues and proposes several policy resolutions around the issues of punishment and imprisonment.

Corrections also generates day-to-day ethical dilemmas for correctional officers and managers in keeping order in prisons and ensuring offenders complete the sentences without harm to themselves, other offenders and other staff. Codes emphasise the need to balance security and treatment goals, while acting without discrimination. Codes vary widely in detail and in coverage of key topics. Certainly there would seem to be a case for the development of a more sophisticated international code that is both comprehensive and practical.

Chapter 9

Abuses in Corrections

Neddy Smith is one of Australia's most notorious criminals. He was an extremely violent man who treated pub fights as a sport. He trafficked heroin, and received convictions for theft, armed robbery, rape and murder. He is suspected of committing eight murders. In Sydney in the 1970s and 1980s he had the 'green light' from Australia's most notorious corrupt police officer, Roger Rogerson, to sell drugs and commit brazen armed robberies. Smith has spent more than half his life in prison. He was brought up by his grandmother who neglected him, and he turned to a life on the streets committing petty theft to survive. He was one of a generation of violent criminals who emerged in the 1970s who spent much of their formative years in boys' homes and youth detention facilities. He learnt how to fight to survive at Gosford Boys home where he was sent at the age of 15. The sentence included hard labour, which mainly consisted of shovelling dirt between dirt heaps. At 16 he was sent to a 'Boys' Shelter' in Surry Hills where 'standovers and bashing were a daily occurrence' (Smith, 1993, p. 25). At the age of 17 he ended up at 'the lowest place on this earth':

> Tamworth Boys' Home was a real concentration camp. They treated the young boys like animals, with daily bashings and starvation. People treated their dogs better than they treated us at Tamworth. I've been to the notorious Grafton jail twice for a period of more than four years all told: I was systematically bashed daily, flogged into unconsciousness several times but, believe me, that was nothing compared with the treatment I got at Tamworth. (Smith, 1993, pp. 25–26)

Smith recalls a particularly large guard who liked to bounce boys off walls. The 'rest of the screws … had other ways to make your life a misery':

> There was the non-stop screaming at us all day long; they made us do exercises all day without a rest; they would starve us for minor things like sniffing, a loose button or a loose shoelace. We were not allowed within two metres of another boy; we couldn't talk to anyone *at all*; we weren't allowed to look at another boy. If we did, they put us in solitary confinement on one slice of bread per day. If we wanted to ask a screw for something we had to stand at attention and hold our hand in the air for 15 to 20 minutes at a time and, if you put your hand down, you were bounced — and that meant no meal for you.
>
> That was their favourite go. They would drive you all day long, nagging you and yelling at you. Then when you were at your lowest they would smile and say: 'you're bounced'.
>
> It drove me insane. (p. 26)

Unfortunately, Smith's experience has been more the norm than the exception for many children and adults who have found themselves in prison. This chapter examines abuses, corruption, maladministration and misconduct in what is now called corrective services or corrections. Both custodial and community corrections are subject to 'corruption' in the form of discrimination and favouritism by correctional officers towards offenders. However, it is in prisons and other secure facilities where problems are at their most intense, including graft, denial of due process, assault and cruelty. Prisons are also extremely prone to a general problem of physical and mental neglect of basic human needs.

This chapter begins by elaborating upon the social and political context in which corrections functions, developing key points made in the previous chapter. This sets the scene for understanding the peculiar vulnerabilities of prisoners to abuse. It then examines the types of misconduct that occur across corrective services, relating these back to the contextual section. The final section of the chapter introduces case studies in abuses from Australia and overseas that illustrate the extent of problems that can occur in the correctional environment.

Contexts

An essential point to be taken into account when considering accountability in corrections is the vulnerability of prisoners. They do not necessarily 'lose all their rights' when they cross the threshold into prison, but their rights are extremely constrained. They obviously cannot move outside the prison grounds and, even in fairly liberal prisons, are often confined to their cells for 12 hours per day. Visits with family and others is usually very limited, once a month, for example, and even this can be difficult to achieve if family live far away from the facility. Prisoners must eat, sleep, work and exercise to a strict routine, not of their own making, which can itself be tightened even further at any time by lockdowns. Prisoners have little or no choice about food and work. They usually have very little or no money, and very little on which to spend their money. Alcohol and other drugs are prohibited and, increasingly, facilities are banning smoking. Normally prisoners cannot access the Internet, and television viewing is limited and controlled. They must obtain permission to see a doctor or a lawyer or to make phone calls and post letters, and all phone calls and letters are likely to be monitored. If, as is often the case, they do not have a cell to themselves, they lose almost all privacy. In higher security facilities they are unlikely to be able to shower or go to the toilet without being monitored.

Prisoners are highly vulnerable to the discretionary decisions of staff in relation to requests for all the things mentioned above, such as phone calls, contact with a lawyer, health visits and work assignments. Correctional officers can respond to these requests in ways that are fair and unbiased, with the prisoner's legitimate interests in the forefront; or they can be slow, difficult, rude, uncooperative and biased. Prisoners are also highly vulnerable to the more malign intentions of guards in relation to behaviours that are normally prohibited, such as harassment, verbal abuse, assault and sexual assault.

In many jurisdictions prisoners are given a parole option that can considerably shorten their time in jail. The criteria for parole usually relate to good behaviour in jail and participation in programs. Custodial officers provide reports that are used by parole boards when considering applications. It can be very difficult or impossible for inmates to provide any supportive evidence if they want to challenge an adverse parole decision. There is wide scope for community corrections officers to act in discriminatory and vindictive ways against offenders when making assessments about compliance with parole conditions or other orders, such as work orders (Pollock, 2007, pp. 460–462). There is a great deal at stake here for offenders on orders — primarily the risk of a return to prison and all the losses and deprivation that entails.

Prisoners are also highly vulnerable to other prisoners. They can be subject to various levels of overt and covert harassment, threats, assault, sexual assault and murder, depending on the levels of surveillance and control in the prison. This can make prison life a living hell for prisoners who are less able to defend themselves or find protection, and this nightmare can go on for years. The design of many older prisons often left spaces where it was difficult for guards to exercise surveillance, although prisoner-on-prisoner abuses have often occurred with the knowledge or even encouragement of staff. One of the risks with prison work is access to manufactured weapons, from kitchens and workshops, which can be used against other prisoners. Prisoners can be extraordinarily inventive in making weapons, mainly knives, and keeping them hidden. Vulnerability between prisoners is of course greatly enlarged when prisoners are unable to live in single cells. While some prisoners may prefer the company of a shared cell, being locked down each night with a malicious or psychopathic roommate can also make life a living hell.

In poorly managed prisons prisoners usually form gangs that serve in part to protect members, but they can also be used to launch campaigns of terror and control over other prisoners, including monopolising any illicit trade within the prison. Gangs can easily become organised crime groups within prisons (Gaes, Wallace, Gilman, Klein-Saffran, & Suppa, 2001).

A common characteristic of a poorly managed prison is the use of selected prisoners as enforcers of prison rules (see chapter 8). Prison managers will trade privileges with these people in return for them using strongarm tactics to keep order. While this can be a very attractive efficiency measure for managers, it essentially leaves prisoners at the mercy of other prisoners and departs from basic principles of due process rights and the rule of law.

Prisoners are also vulnerable to self-harm. The stresses of prison life can produce despair and chronic depression that can tempt prisoners to attempt suicide or engage in self-harm behaviours, including cutting their skin or ingesting wires or toxins (insideprison, 2006).

The many restrictions on prisoners can add up to massive frustration, feelings of complete impotence and hopelessness (Haney, 2001). Prisoners are already usually deemed to have low levels of self-control and high irritability. Prison is not only a closed society but it is also a pressure-cooker environment where minor altercations and frictions can trigger rampages and brutal fights. Frustration can be greatly exacerbated by the powerlessness of prisoners when faced with problems occurring outside the prison that they can do nothing about, such as financial problems, child rearing issues or spousal infidelity.

As with policing, there are intense demand pressures for corruption in corrective services. Persons serving prison sentences and community-based orders have a range of needs and aspirations that they are willing to satisfy by any means available to them. They can offer money, often in the form of proceeds of crime held by compatriots outside prison. They can offer drugs smuggled into prison and they can offer their bodies for sexual purposes. On the other side of the equation, correctional officers have a great deal to offer in return — in the form of smuggled contraband (including drugs and pornography), assistance with escape plans, favourable reports, access to 'privileges' such as phone calls, mail, better accommodation, work and easy assignments; and sex as well. The motivations of correctional officers to engage in corruption can be enlarged by poor pay and conditions, and resentment against their employer.

As with police, correctional services is often described as displaying a wide divide between management and rank-and-file cultures (Pollock, 2007, p. 421ff). While modern managers espouse progressive policies of prisoner reform, front-line staff can develop a highly oppositional and confrontational relationship with prisoners. The origin of this conflict is something of a chicken-and-egg situation. Staff accuse prisoners of being ungrateful, disrespectful, uncooperative, threatening and violent. Prisoners accuse staff of being petty tyrants, insensitive and unfair. Certainly many inmates bring to prison a culture of aggression and foul language. At the same time, guards in traditional prisons were usually drawn from the lower working class, were poorly educated, and often had highly conservative views on law and order that made them naturally antagonistic toward prisoners (ABC, 1985).

Another factor that affects accountability in corrections is the alleged 'punitive public' (Pratt et al., 2005) — or apathetic public. Most prisoners are there for serious crimes, and issues of privations or abuses in prisons are unlikely to arouse public sympathy. This situation is exacerbated by law and order politics, where politicians, usually in opposition, will try to exploit any appearance of the government running prisons like 'a holiday camp'. Breaches of parole are particularly risky because when a parolee commits a serious crime, such as rape, the resulting media frenzy and politicisation throws the whole parole system into doubt. The situation is further exacerbated by the multi-million-dollar cost of prisons. The insult of crime is compounded by the cost to taxpayers of housing prisoners and any improvements in prison conditions impose an additional burden.

Types of Misconduct

The following briefly sets out the main types of misconduct risks in corrective services (Pollock, 2007, chap. 13 and 14). The descriptions are kept short because the majority overlap closely with categories we have already considered in some depth in relation to police and the courts, and the primary elements of misconduct transactions and actions remain the same.

Bribery

As noted earlier in this chapter, offenders serving sentences are highly motivated to offer bribes in the form of cash, sex, drugs and other benefits to correctional officers for assistance with access to privileges, favourable reports for early release, other benefits that can be acquired within the system or assistance with escape plans. Graft can also occur in commercial areas of the correctional system such as through bribery for preferential treatment by firms tendering for business.

Workplace Crime and Deviance

Internal corruption can also occur through forms of workplace crime and deviance including theft of property belonging to correctional services or inmates; embezzlement; use of telecommunications, stationery or other equipment for personal benefit; time wasting; workers' compensation fraud; and being intoxicated or drug affected while on duty.

Bias

Inmates and offenders can benefit or suffer from favouritism or discrimination not directly related to bribes, in areas such as access to privileges, favourable reports and other benefits. Motivations for bias might include personal likes and dislikes, or political, religious or racial prejudices.

Harassment and Brutality

Prison inmates are highly vulnerable to persecution or harassment by prison officials in the form of derogatory comments, including racist or homophobic comments or ethnic slurs, as well as low-level physical harassment such as poking or pushing. Prison officials can also fail to intervene to protect prisoners from the same behaviour from other prisoners.

Brutality involves more serious levels of excessive force, including routine beatings of prisoners on reception, corporal punishment for rule violations or ad hoc assaults. It can include excessive isolation, punishment in cramped 'black holes' with sensory deprivation, and tacit permission for guards to act brutally without consequences.

Sexual Exploitation

Sexual exploitation can be perpetrated by correctional officers or occur between prisoners without intervention by guards. This category can include unjustified observation of prisoners bathing or changing, unwanted touching or physical contact, as well as rape.

Neglect

Prison systems are vulnerable to malign neglect. Conditions may be deliberately allowed to run down to substandard levels, such as lack of hygiene, allowance of pests and diseases, lack of health services, unhealthy or unpalatable food, excessive heat and cold, lack of fresh air and overcrowding of cells.

Denial of Due Process

Denial of due process occurs when the whole correctional system operates on summary justice so that decisions by correctional officers about rule violations do not require written reasons or presentation of evidence, where decisions cannot be challenged by the accused and where there are no appeal mechanisms.

Collective Punishment

Collective punishment is another form of abuse where all prisoners are punished, by lockdowns or denial of privileges, for example, because of breaches committed by other prisoners. Collective punishment can be used to make a guilty person confess to relieve the suffering and potential hostility of their fellows.

Inaction on Misconduct

The code of silence and non-disclosure of problems and the failure to report misconduct are now recognised as ethically unacceptable within corrective services because they contribute to the perpetuation of abuses. Cover-ups involve more deliberate and culpable attempts to avoid accountability and protect guilty staff. Persecution of whistleblowers is part of the problem of protection of corrupt conduct and systemic abuses and is particularly onerous in that it involves suffering, stress and threats to people who are trying to do the right thing.

Inaction on staff misconduct is a middle and upper-middle management problem. It includes the absence of penalties or remedial interventions for substantiated offences, as well as inadequate responses or the general failure to thoroughly investigate misconduct allegations and indicators and attempt to stop abuses.

Historically, corrective services management has also suffered from a lack of will to professionalise, and deliberate ignorance about standards that should apply in prisons. There was little effort to apply scientific and humanitarian principles to prisoner treatment programs, to understand the psychological effects of imprisonment or the impacts of imprisonment on future offending and social wellbeing.

A Very Short History of Prisons

The practice of physically confining people goes back to the earliest human records (Peters, 1998). People were restrained behind bars, walls or other devices as punishment for crimes; as a temporary measure before trial, exile, enslavement or execution; or in association with punishments such as starvation and mutilation. Confinement often extended to public displays such as stocks and pillories. It is likely that up until the 19th century, outside some European and colonial settings, most prisoners were kept under appalling physical conditions: in overcrowded cells infested with vermin; with no proper food, exercise, sanitation or lighting; and subject to all manner of physical abuses by guards and fellow inmates. Still, many convicted persons probably preferred prison over popular punishments such as floggings, crucifixion, hanging, beheading or other cruel public executions.

The Enlightenment period in Europe — centred on the 18th century — saw the development of ideas of justice that were opposed to corporal punishment. Loss of liberty was increasingly seen as a fundamental sanction in itself, and there was also growing interest in using prisons to reform offenders. Unreformed prisons were characterised by 'disorder and neglect', as opposed to the new 'well-ordered prisons' (McGowen, 1998, p. 71) planned and run along rational lines. However, the new more orderly and purposeful prisons, built with religious or humanist zeal, were typically inadequate to the task and quickly deteriorated under pressures of overcrowding and insufficient resources.

The establishment of Australia as a penal colony was in part to relieve the chronic overcrowding of English prisons in the late 18th century. In the 19th century the colony of New South Wales also adopted for a period aspects of the 'separation system' developed in 18th-century puritan America and later in England. This involved keeping prisoners in isolation for long periods to allow them to ponder on the need for personal moral and spiritual transformation and to protect them from the contaminating influence of other prisoners. Isolation 'remained in vogue for more than 100 years, despite the fact that many prisoners who were subjected to it were driven insane' (Nagle, 1978, p. 33).

The period between the 1960s and 1980s saw the exposure of abuses in modern prisons, sometimes through judicial inquiries. This was associated with a more general critique of repressive and inhumane conditions in 'total institutions' like insane asylums (Goffman, 1968). This mini-Enlightenment saw many reform initiatives, although pre-reform conditions have been seen nostalgically by some authorities on the inside as a time of proper discipline and appropriate treatment of prisoners. Pollock (2007, p. 432) summarises an account of a Texas prison warden reminiscing about disciplinary methods the early 1960s:

> The 'rail' was a two-by-four turned on its side. An inmate found guilty of a minor offence was required to stand on the rail for a period of four hours; if he fell off, the same time would start again. If an inmate didn't pick enough cotton, he would be made to stand on a barrel for four or five hours. Up to four inmates might be placed on a single barrel, and if one fell off, the time would start again for them all. Other inmates would have their hands raised above their head and handcuffed to the bars in the inmate mess hall; their feet would be cuffed as well. They might be hanging all night.

Case Studies

The following subsections go into more detail on a small number of cases that provide insights into the types of abuses that can develop in prisons without proper management and oversight, and one case that concerns classic financial corruption. Some cases of individual or small group corruption are also included.

The Arkansas Prison Scandal

In 1968 Tom Murton, an academic penologist, was hired by the Governor of Arkansas to reform Arkansas' two infamous prison farms. The new Governor, Winthrop Rockefeller, had released a report on the condition of the prison system that had been suppressed by his predecessor. The report catalogued extreme abuses on the prison farms, including frequent rapes, horrific beatings, and a thriving trade in alcohol and drugs. The farms were known for the significant profits they returned from the forced labour of inmates. Profits were enlarged by substandard food and conditions, and the use of unpaid prisoners as guards. These guards, known as Trusties, terrorised the inmates, extorted money from them, ran contraband operations, and inflicted cruel corporal punishments. One of their favourite tools of discipline was 'the Tucker Telephone', which was used to electrocute inmates' genitals. Early into his program Murton was informed that the bodies of up to 200 prisoners, who had been killed by Trusties and their deaths covered up, were buried on the prison grounds. Murton ordered excavations, and the resulting publicity and political embarrassment led to the Governor terminating his contract. Murton's account of the events, *Accomplices to the Crime: The Arkansas Prison Scandal* (Murton & Hyams, 1969), was adapted into a movie, *Brubaker*, starring Robert Redford.

The Nagle Inquiry

The Nagle Inquiry in New South Wales, from 1976 to 1978, was the most thorough examination of correctional processes in Australia's history and its 511-page report exposed a system of gross mismanagement and systematic abuses (Nagle, 1978). The Inquiry was stimulated by a series of riots in the early 1970s. The worst riot at Bathurst in 1973 resulted in the almost complete destruction of the prison. Nagle was damning in his assessment of the policies and management practices of the New South Wales Department of Corrective Services. He described it as 'inefficient, disorganized and badly administered' (Nagle, 1978, p. 378). Despite some reforms in the years prior to the inquiry:

> There still remained an inefficient Department administering antiquated and disgraceful goals; untrained and sometimes ignorant prison officers, resentful, intransigent and incapable of performing their tasks; and a high proportion of restive and rebellious prisoners. Disturbances and industrial strife abound as never before. (p. 378)

The report was particularly scathing of the role of Commissioner Walter McGeechan in ignoring or encouraging abuses. He was replaced after Nagle recommended his dismissal. Senior managers were also characterised as defensive, insular and deceitful. The prison officers union was characterised as intransigent and opposed to reform. Nagle pessimistically observed that there had been a pattern of crises and inquiries over the last two centuries that had led to numerous reform recommendations, almost all of which had been ignored. The report found evidence of the same problems of brutality, oppressive regimentation, excessive discipline, lack of purpose, inadequate programs and activities, and appalling conditions across the system. At the same time, the Commission singled out three prisons as particularly problematic in different ways. The following subsections elaborate on these findings.

The Bathurst Riots

On October 1970 approximately 150 prisoners at the Bathurst Jail staged a sit-in over a range of grievances including rancid food, inadequate medical services, and limited time with lights and radios at night. Some negotiations ensued and prisoners ended the protest following reassurances there would be no reprisals. Three days later prison officers, directed by the prison superintendent, bashed many of the prisoners, leaving them bloody and bruised. The following year an anonymous document was circulated that included testimony from prisoners and departmental psychologists about the bashings. The psychologists were shuffled out of the department, as was a prison officer and union official who called for a royal commission.

Another sit-in in 1973 followed a particularly cold winter, in which inmates were exposed to the elements, and was triggered by the sacking of prisoners working in the carpentry shop. The sit-in ended peacefully with more reassurances there would be no repercussions. However, seven of the prisoners were transferred and there was a tightening of discipline. A third sit-in occurred in early-1974 over the cancellation of mid-week sports. Despite further reassurances, the prisoners involved were punished by being locked in their cells for three days.

Then in February 1974 a large group of prisoners were watching a movie in the prison chapel when a petrol bomb was thrown inside the venue. The fire was doused and the suspected arsonist was assaulted by guards. The prisoner's screams triggered an overnight rampage in which most of the prison was destroyed by fire and vandalism as prisoners took over the complex. About 20 prisoners were shot and injured as guards struggled to regain control. After order was restored guards systematically beat prisoners. Some received severe injuries.

Failure to address the underlying problems at Bathurst led inevitably to the destructive riot of February 1974. Following the riot, calls for an inquiry increased from many quarters, but despite commitments from the state government two years elapsed before the Nagle Commission began its work. Apart from documenting the sequence of events that led to the riot, the Nagle report analysed the institutional context that underlay the events. Major factors included the lack of activities for prisoners, a system of 'petty restrictions', erratic discipline, and 'unsuitable and badly trained' management and staff (1976, p. 17).

Grafton and the 'Intractables'

In 1943 a section of Grafton Jail was established as a special prison within a prison, designed to house 'recalcitrant intractable prisoners' who were deemed unmanageable elsewhere (Nagle, 1978, p. 14). The men were shipped to Grafton after repeated breaches of prison rules. The average number of inmates was 15 but the number went as high as 25. The Nagle report devoted a full chapter to documenting 'the regime of terror' that persisted up until the section's closure in 1976 (p. 108). Evidence included accounts by ex-prisoners and a damning statement made by staff to the Commission. From its beginning the policy at the section was one of pre-emptive violence. Prisoners were bashed on arrival in what was known as the 'reception biff'. The purpose was to intimidate them into future compliance. They were told to strip naked in a prison yard where they were set upon by between two and five officers who would hit them repeatedly with hard rubber batons causing extensive bruising, cuts and internal injuries. They were verbally abused, and hit across the back, legs, arms, shoulders, buttocks and head. Many were rendered semiconscious. They were then left in their cells for several days to recover on their own, although they were often assaulted a second time.

The violence continued for the whole of the prisoners' stay. A bashing could occur arbitrarily but usually in response to any violation of the many petty and complex rules that applied in the institution. Inmates learnt the rules by being bashed when they broke them. Having a toothbrush in the wrong place, or a spec of dust in the cell, could provoke an assault. Many prisoners lived in a state of constant nervous tension and anxiety because they could be bashed at any time. Rules included a complex form of making a bed, standing to attention in specified ways when guards were in attendance and detailed step-by-step procedures for showering. Inmates were isolated in their cells for more than 17 hours each day. Toilets were only added to cells in the 1960s. Highly monotonous work was performed for a short period each day. There was a 20-minute exercise routine that entailed marching in a line back and forth across a space of four metres. There was virtually no communication between inmates and fellow inmates, guards or the outside world. Family visits were usually limited to 20 minutes per month, but even this was difficult for most families because of the distance they lived from Grafton. There were several suicides and cases of self-mutilation. Although the Commission could not prove that the regime at Grafton made prisoners worse, it did report anecdotal evidence that some prisoners originally convicted for minor offences went on to commit extremely violent crimes.

Nagle described an organised system of 'brutal, savage and sometimes sadistic physical violence' that operated without interruption for 33 years

(1978, p. 108). All levels of management were complicit in the secret world of abuse. It was 'one of the most sordid and shameful episodes in NSW penal history ... contrary to all concepts of humanity' (pp. 108, 119).

Katingal

Katingal was opened in 1975 as a high-tech modern alternative to Grafton. It was referred to as a Special Security Unit and was located adjacent to Malabar prison. The unit, designed to accommodate 40 prisoners, was built at great expense for the time at AU$1.5 million, and its running costs were three times those of other prisons. It was fully air conditioned, artificially lit, and had doors that opened electronically by remote control. The intention was to completely separate guards and inmates. Despite the absence of violence, Katingal created an impersonal nightmare environment with no access to the outside world and virtually no human contact. It was described as an 'electronic zoo' marked by almost perpetual solitary confinement, extreme boredom and sensory deprivation (Nagle, 1978, p. 122). Nagle considered it could not be improved and should be shut down.

The Rex Jackson Release on Licence Scandal

In 1982 the Corrective Services Department of New South Wales initiated a new program for the early release of prisoners. The scheme was explained as a progressive policy of 'decarceration', as a measure to relieve chronic prison overcrowding, and as an incentive for prisoners to behave and demonstrate reform. It operated outside the sentences applied by the courts and cut into the non-parole period. It was made possible by the fact that the Minister for Corrective Services held a discretionary authority under the law to release prisoners from jail 'on licence'. The authority was normally used for 'extreme compassionate cases' (Chan, 1992, p. xi). The Minister at the time, Rex Jackson, became a vocal supporter of the release scheme. It was originally limited to low tariff prisoners on a sentence with a non-parole period of 12 months or less. The licence entailed a number of conditions including not committing any offences. Breaches of licence conditions would mean a return to jail. In the first three months 206 prisoners were released, but the system had a number of problems. It was short staffed, and probation and parole officers were overwhelmed with applications. Prisoners who were rejected or experienced delays became frustrated. Prison staff felt too many prisoners were getting out too early.

The program was enlarged in 1983, and by the end of 15 months of operation 640 prisoners had been released. At the same time it came under increasing attack from correctional staff, the media, and judges and magistrates as undermining the justice system. One story that attracted attention was the premature release of three corrupt police involved with organised crime. Then in mid-June the *Sun Herald* headlined allegations that prisoners were paying amounts between AU$2,500 and AU$15,000 to have their applications approved or fast tracked. A jailed former police officer was identified as a go-between for prisoners and corrupt correctional staff. A police task force was formed to investigate the claims.

The scheme had become a liability and it was soon shut down by the state government. In the meantime, covert tape recordings of conversations from a federal police investigation into drug smuggling implicated Jackson in illicit payments to release three prisoners on licence. The prisoners had been convicted for growing marijuana. A judicial inquiry was established to investigate the specific case. The inquiry revealed a scam in which a solicitor supplied a businessman with the names of eligible prisoners willing to pay for early release. The names were passed to another man, who passed them to Jackson. Jackson was convicted of conspiracy in relation to accepting AU$12,000 for the release of the three men from the Broken Hill prison. It was alleged Jackson used the money to pay a gambling debt. The three other men, and a fourth, were found guilty of conspiracy to bribe Jackson — who received a sentence of 10 years with a non-parole period of five years. A subsequent police inquiry found that corruption of the release on licence scheme probably only extended to 12 or so additional cases, and that no correctional staff were involved (Chan, 1992).

The Kennedy Review

The 1988 Kennedy Review into Queensland Corrective Services was established in response to recurring prisoner and officer unrest and escapes. The review was oriented to administrative and management issues, but Kennedy also identified a problem with piecemeal corruption. He noted reports of the smuggling into prisons of contraband, including weapons and drugs, with the assistance of staff; and the possible involvement of some staff in escapes. He observed that staff who were known to be corrupt were tolerated.

The overall focus of the review's assessment was the backward orientation of the department and the substandard nature of prisons. The system had been neglected and under-resourced for decades. There was a general lack of professionalism and mission, and no policy-oriented research. Management was parochial and ill-informed of developments in corrections internationally. Prisoners were warehoused for the duration of their sentences, with little in the way of rehabilitation programs or meaningful work. 'Corrections' was a misnomer. Kennedy asserted that, 'Many prisoners are released worse than when they went in' (1988, p. xxii). Staff received 'hardly any training and little support and recognition of their role' (p. xxii). There was a significant morale problem. Prisons were overcrowded, primitive and harsh. Some sections were in the same basic condition as when they were built in the 19th century, with no temperature control, no running water and buckets for toilets. There were no power outlets for radios and reading lamps. Stained and blackened walls, covered in graffiti, created 'an atmosphere of hopelessness' (p. 64). The design and layout of prisons also facilitated disorder. In the case of Boggo Road Jail, there was one large open area where prisoners congregated in large numbers and caused trouble.

Kennedy did not identify the kinds of systematic and extreme brutality found by Justice Nagle in some parts of the New South Wales prison systems. But he did identify excesses in discipline and lack of due process, and some apparent cases of assault. There was also a significant problem with prisoners being assaulted by other prisoners. The review described a range of administrative and procedural problems, with prisoners spending excessive amounts of time in remand before their trials, and inequalities and inefficiencies in parole. Prisoners were not properly classified and segregated. For example, there were up to 50 people under 18 in adult prisons. Security was poor. Security technology and procedures were not up to date and there was a growing problem with illicit drugs coming unchecked into prisons. Disturbances were allowed to grow into riots. At a higher policy level there was a general over-reliance on prison as a sanction for non-violent offences and an under-utilisation of community correctional options. In short, Queensland, near the end of the 20th century, had a second-rate 19th century prison system, and Kennedy recommended a suite of improvements — discussed in the next chapter.

Miscellaneous

The following are some snapshots of cases of corruption in Australian correctional services from the last few decades to illustrate the types of small group or individual corruption that can occur.

- In 1998 the New South Wales ICAC found that two female employees of the Department of Corrective Services had engaged in corruption by forming inappropriate relationships with male inmates. One counsellor developed an emotional and physical relationship with a prisoner she was counselling and assisted him to inject himself with heroin during one counselling session. The other woman had sexual contact with two inmates. She also signed a misleading reference written by an inmate whom she had previously treated on a methadone program. (ICAC, 1998)

- In Queensland in 1996 a male former prison psychologist was jailed for having sex with three male prisoners in return for writing favourable reports. He also threatened inmates in a bid to have sex with them. The psychologist was the head of the sex offender treatment program. He had been the subject of complaints for several years and was moved around prisons in response. He was eventually caught on a hidden camera installed in his office. (Doneman, 1996; 'Jail Psychologist on Inmate Sex Charges', 1996)

- Also in Queensland, in 2000 the state's anti-corruption watchdog exposed scams spanning several years in which prison officers, inmates, ex-inmates and others conspired to have work done for free or arranged fraudulent payments. Vehicles were repaired and re-sprayed for free in a workshop, and a prison printery was used to pay false invoices. (Griffiths, 2000)

Conclusion

As with policing, corrective services entails a high opportunity structure for corruption, abuses and neglect. Prisons present a particular challenge for accountability in that security considerations, separation from the community and the concentration of serious offenders in one location, make for a pressure cooker environment where fights, harassment, crime and disorder readily take hold. Prisoners are highly vulnerable to forms of physical and mental abuse by guards, and lack of protection from other prisoners. Prison systems are also prone to the entrenchment of inefficiencies and unproductive practices that can become inter-generational. These problems include the warehousing of prisoners and lack of opportunity for exercise, work, therapy, and education and training. Prisoners are released back into the community with no indicators of any positive improvement in the aspects of their lives that contributed to their offending behaviour. Many, it would seem, come out worse than when they went in.

As we have seen with policing and the criminal court system, system maintenance and improvement strategies are essential to reverse this constant tendency to regression. Strategies to prevent corruption and misconduct, and to maximise the social mission of corrections, are the subject of the next chapter.

Chapter 10

Integrity Management and Accountability in Corrections

This final chapter elaborates on strategies to ensure ethical conduct in corrective services. Many of the strategies already examined in relation to police and the courts also apply here. There are, however, some important permutations that apply to the specific environment of corrections, especially the peculiar problems of accountability that occur in prisons. Again, as we have seen previously, a mix of strategies is essential to cover the variety of corruption opportunities that occur in both community and custodial corrections and to break through the walls of silence. These strategies and standards need to be set out as clear requirements for any correctional system anywhere in the world.

Substandard and violent prisons, and underdeveloped community corrections options, are not inevitable and something with which we just have to live. It is possible to establish and maintain good prisons. Pollock (2007, p. 434) observes that in countries like the United States much of the officially sanctioned violence and abuse of the past has been 'drastically reduced or even eliminated entirely'. She cautions, nonetheless, that 'less pervasive violence continues' and that more sophisticated and effective accountability mechanisms are needed. The author of this book has visited prisons and community corrections facilities that appear to strike an excellent balance between security, amenity and rehabilitation. Prisons can employ positive, professional staff. They can provide facilities that are clean, airy and bright, with open spaces and more personal accommodation in apartment-style groupings of cells. They can provide a range of educational and therapeutic programs and work options for inmates. And they can create a safe and civilised environment.

Accountability for What?

As with previous chapters on this topic, we can ask ourselves what accountability in corrections is specifically intended to achieve. The answer, in the context of accountability for integrity, is primarily 'corruption and misconduct prevention'. The previous chapter demonstrated that corrections is a high-risk occupation for corruption and for abuses directed towards inmates and other persons serving sentences. To this we must add a special concern with adequate conditions in prisons and associated places of custody. Again, as we saw in the previous chapter, prisons are extremely vulnerable to deteriorations in the physical environment within which offenders serve out their time. The protection and maintenance of due process legal and procedural rights for prisoners is also a closely associated challenge.

In the correctional environment there is a particularly difficult balancing act to be performed between adequate security, on the one hand, and adequate 'humane' conditions, on the other hand. As we have seen throughout this book, 'openness' and 'transparency' are foundation principles of accountability. But prisons, by their very nature, are closed and opaque environments. Security is paramount, and all the procedures and devices for keeping prisoners in also serve to restrict access to outsiders. The more a prison is open to social visitors, official visitors, and therapy and training staff, the more it is vulnerable to corruption of these persons, and therefore problems such as information corruption, the smuggling of drugs, and the smuggling of equipment for escapes or for running crime operations from inside. Any attempts at prison reform will be quickly undermined if escapes occur or if assaults or murders or any other insider crimes occur. Security shutdowns and crackdowns inevitably result in reduced conditions through reduced movement; long periods in cells; punishment in isolation; and restricted access to therapies, work and training. All accountability mechanisms will therefore need to be evaluated from a security perspective, but, equally, all security measures need to be evaluated for their impacts on prisoner conditions and rights.

Accountability Contexts

The accountability contexts already discussed in relation to police and the criminal courts apply in very much the same terms to corrections. Under a system of 'responsible government' corrections is likely to be a line department with an elected member of parliament at its head: the minister for corrective services. The minister is the vital driver or interface in the democratic system of delegated authority. It is the duty of the minister to implement government policy on corrections, and to ensure the whole system is running effectively, efficiently and lawfully. The minister is expected to resign or be removed if major breakdowns occur in the system, including corruption or abuses, or if the minister can in any way be considered negligent or deficient in their duty. Below the minister is an appointed head of department — a secretary or director-general — who is responsible for the day-to-day operations of the department. Similarly, this person should resign or be removed if any adverse events occur 'on their watch' in a way that involved any foreknowledge or lack of action on their part.

Another essential tool in the toolkit of democratic accountability is the capacity for parliaments to initiate ad hoc inquiries or reviews. Inquiries are oriented towards finding evidence of misconduct, while reviews are more oriented to issues of administrative efficiency, policy effectiveness and prison conditions. It is essential that inquiries in particular are properly resourced and empowered to follow all leads, require testimony, turn corrupt officers where necessary, and conduct covert operations — in order to assure the public that the nature and extent of any possible problems have been fully assessed.

Establishing Purposes and Institutions: Macro-Level Policy

The first chapter in this section on corrections examined macro-level policy issues for corrective services. There are a number of framing positions that all governments need to adopt in relation to these big-picture issues concerning punishment and prison conditions. As we have seen, cost is always a major challenge for corrections because prisons are often at the bottom of the government's shopping list. However, there are some potential win-win outcomes to be had from some of the better reform initiatives of the last few decades. A system that has a fail rate of 50%+ is not efficient and effective, and any reductions in reoffending through inmate programs should produce cost savings. A shift from a punitive focus and warehousing of offenders to scientifically based active rehabilitation and supervision programs should yield positive outcomes in crime reduction and reductions in re-convictions (Gendreau & Andrews, 1990; Gornik, 2001; Paparozzi & Gendreau, 2005; Roberts, 2005).

One key principle that has emerged from the prison reform movement of the last 200 years is the idea that offenders should 'come to prison as a punishment, not for punishment'. This maxim was popularised by Sir Alexander Paterson, a pioneer in improving prisons and developing alternatives to prison (Paterson, 1951, p. 23). However, it is not a new idea. The ancient Roman jurist Ulpian similarly wrote that 'Prison indeed ought to be employed for confining men, not for punishing them' (in Peters, 1998, p. 20). This position recognises the suffering entailed in simply losing one's liberty, especially in modern liberal democracies that place a high value on personal freedom and self-determination. Imprisonment entails separation from loved ones, loss of income, and damage to work and career prospects and reputation. Thus, losing one's freedom is potentially a sufficient punishment in itself for more serious offences. There is no need, in other words, to pile on further suffering through additional punishments within prison, including deprivation, illness, beatings and torture. This philosophy then informs a set of very practical standards for determining decent prison conditions (see following).

Another fundamental principle of modern sentencing policy that has also been put forward in part to counter prison abuses is that of 'imprisonment as a last resort' (Nagle, 1978, p. 392; UN, 2005, pp. 21–22). Where imprisonment is used, according to UN standards, 'any form of release from an institution to a non-custodial program shall be considered at the earliest possible stage' (p. 21). Again, the argument here is that loss of liberty in itself is a severe punishment, especially for periods of years. Additionally, the financial costs of incarceration, the limited efficacy of prison in reducing crime and the intrinsic potential for abuses in prison all mean that alternatives to prison should be the first consideration in sentencing policy, not the last. Alternatives to prison are also generally much cheaper. The average cost of keeping an offender in an Australian jail is 15 times the cost of community corrections (Prenzler & Sarre, 2009, p. 266).

A policy of decarceration need not entail a weak response to crime. Alternatives to prison can be more onerous than sitting in prison, especially if they involve work requirements. Nor is incarceration necessary for therapy. Compulsory or conditional programs can operate outside prisons. Alternatives such as weekend detention, home detention or curfews all entail degrees of loss of liberty while allowing for participation in programs, maintenance of family relationships and maintenance of work — either normal work that allows the offender to bring home money and to remain financially independent or work that involves direct reparation for crime. Another alternative or supplement to imprisonment is victim–offender conferences, which can attract very high levels of satisfaction from all participants. In fact, public opinion supports many of these alternatives to a simple model of justice through harsh prison terms (Palk, Hayes, & Prenzler, 1998; see also Nagle, 1978, p. 358ff on productive alternatives to prison).

The final macro-level core accountability principle that needs to be articulated is that of openness to scrutiny. As noted, a juggling act is required between security and openness, but we should be cautious about security being used as an excuse to escape scrutiny. Even maximum security prisons can manage to accommodate inspections from government officials and from a variety of independent non-government organisations given sufficient time to arrange escorts and security clearances. Transparency is also essential in information about complaints, incidents, investigations, programs, escapes and recidivism.

Integrity Management and Accountability in Operation

The following sub-sections describe more specific integrity management strategies that should work within the accountability framework set out in the previous section to operationalise misconduct prevention and the development of an ethical culture within corrective services departments.

Internal and External Integrity Institutions

Any modern advanced integrity system will require a mix of internal and external operational units and agencies with responsibilities for integrity management. An internal professional standards unit will ensure department-wide coverage of ethical issues, corruption prevention strategies, and complaints investigation and resolution processes. While the exact division of labour here is debatable, some type of external oversight by a public sector anti-corruption commission is also essential to ensure independent scrutiny of integrity management and complaints investigations and adjudication. Certainly, more serious matters should automatically be dealt with by an external agency, including deaths in custody, serious assaults and allegations of corruption. The old adage that 'police cannot investigate police' applies equally to corrections. Internal investigations will always be viewed with suspicion even where the investigators are personally independent and highly professional.

It is also essential that both internal and external agencies are proactive in going beyond complaints investigation to gathering intelligence, conducting risk assessments and implementing early intervention systems (as described in relation to police in chapter 4). The armoury should include a capacity to use undercover agents, covert physical and electronic surveillance, and integrity tests (Kennedy, 1988, pp. 48–49).

Prisoner Discipline

Another essential principle of operational integrity management designed for accountability is the preservation of due process rights for sentenced persons (UN, 2005). Prisoners should not have to leave their rights at the prison gate or the door of the community corrections office. As we saw in chapter 8 on correctional ethics, prisons require their own internal justice system to deal with alleged infringements of prison rules. An important point here is that more serious breaches of the wider criminal law, such as assault, sexual assault, serious thefts, extortion and murder, that occur inside prisons all need to be dealt with in the same way as any alleged offence — through a police investigation and a possible appearance in a criminal court, with prisoners enjoying the same rights to legal representation and habeas corpus as any citizen. Lower-level and intermediate criminal charges can be dealt with by visiting magistrates so the prisoner does not need to be transported to a court (Nagle, 1978, pp. 388–389).

That still leaves a great number of potential breaches to be dealt with internally, including in areas such as harassment, threats, insubordination, minor assaults and contraband offences. A degree of summary decision-making is essential here so that action can be taken quickly and so that the prison administration is not ground down by endless mini-court cases over relatively petty offences. At the same time, there needs to be an avenue for prisoners to appeal decisions, including through access to external review for more serious cases. Internal discipline is an area that needs to be closely monitored as a risk area for abuses.

Standard Guidelines for Prison Conditions

An extremely valuable innovation in the area of prison conditions is that of standard guidelines. The UN *Standard Minimum Rules for the Treatment of Prisoners* includes 95 elements in plain language. These can be used as a checklist in any walk-around inspection of an adult prison and examination of prison records and policies. The rules draw a clear line. Below this line any prison can be considered to be operating without reasonable humane standards. The preamble recognises that some jurisdictions might not be able to fulfil all the rules at once, but that they should be committed and actively engaged in working towards fulfilling them over time. The following extracts give a flavour of the language and approach taken (UN, 1977):

6. (1) The following rules shall be applied impartially. There shall be no discrimination on grounds of race, colour, sex, language, religion, political or other opinion, national or social origin, property, birth or other status ...

7. (1) In every place where persons are imprisoned there shall be kept a bound registration book with numbered pages in which shall be entered in respect of each prisoner received:

(a) Information concerning his identity;

(b) The reasons for his commitment and the authority therefore;

(c) The day and hour of his admission and release ...

9. (1) Where sleeping accommodation is in individual cells or rooms, each prisoner shall occupy by night a cell or room by himself ...

11. In all places where prisoners are required to live or work,

(a) The windows shall be large enough to enable the prisoners to read or work by natural light, and shall be so constructed that they can allow the entrance of fresh air whether or not there is artificial ventilation;

(b) Artificial light shall be provided sufficient for the prisoners to read or work without injury to eyesight.

12. The sanitary installations shall be adequate to enable every prisoner to comply with the needs of nature when necessary and in a clean and decent manner.

13. Adequate bathing and shower installations shall be provided so that every prisoner may be enabled and required to have a bath or shower, at a temperature suitable to the climate, as frequently as necessary for general hygiene according to season and geographical region, but at least once a week in a temperate climate ...

17. (1) Every prisoner who is not allowed to wear his own clothing shall be provided with an outfit of clothing suitable for the climate and adequate to keep him in good health. Such clothing shall in no manner be degrading or humiliating ...

20. (1) Every prisoner shall be provided by the administration at the usual hours with food of nutritional value adequate for health and strength, of wholesome quality and well prepared and served.

(2) Drinking water shall be available to every prisoner whenever he needs it ...

Other rules include the following (subject to a variety of qualifiers related to specific circumstances):

- Prisons should be governed by a progressive philosophy that emphasises public safety, crime reduction and the restoration of prisoners as responsible members of society.
- Close attention should be made to preparing prisoners for release through tailor-made transition programs, maintenance of family relations, assurance of post-release accommodation and financial means, work search assistance, and arrangements for contact with supportive agencies.
- Prisoners should be graded and organised according to security classifications and/or special needs.
- Prisoners deemed dangerous should be separated from mainstream prisoners.
- Security classifications should entail degrees of privileges with a view to supporting good conduct.
- All prisoners should be assessed for treatment needs, and treatment supplied where deemed appropriate to support post-release social integration.
- While the issue of compulsory therapy is not addressed, the availability of therapies is deemed fundamental to inmates' personal improvement and the goal of protecting society.
- All prison staff should receive specialist training.
- Training should include the use of physical restraint techniques and self-defence tactics.
- In-service training should be provided to maintain and advance skills.
- Prison staff should include a mix of social workers, psychologists and teachers.
- Prison staff should be physically fit and healthy.
- Prison staff should, in general, be provided with secure full-time employment with salaries and conditions adequate to attract committed and conscientious persons.
- Prisons must provide basic medical services and qualified medical personnel.

- Medical staff have special responsibilities in relation to prisoner health and welfare. They must report any inadequacies in medical services, and they must be deferred to by prison officials in most instances.
- A disciplinary system should be established with clear authorities, rules and sanctions that are communicated to all prisoners and consistently enforced.
- Prisoners should be allowed to provide a defence to charges, and the designated authority in the case must make a systematic examination of the facts.
- No prisoners are to be used in a disciplinary role.
- There should be no corporal or degrading punishments, and no incarceration in a cell without light or with poor light.
- While close confinement is permissible it should only be used in extreme cases. The prisoner should be monitored by a medical officer and the confinement stopped if there is any evidence of physical or mental harm.
- Restraint devices, such as handcuffs, should only be used where there is a threat of physical harm or while a prisoner is being transported.
- Prisoners should be informed of their right to make complaints, and they should have opportunities to make complaints anonymously and to make confidential complaints to independent prison inspectors or external authorities.
- Opportunities should be provided on a regular basis for communication with family and loved ones by correspondence and in person.
- Family and close friends must be informed of any prisoner transfers or health issues or death.
- Foreigners should be allowed access to consular officials.
- Translators should be made available where necessary for effective communication.
- Prisoners' personal property should be stored and returned to them upon release.
- Prisoners should be allowed at least one hour of outdoor exercise per day.
- Male and female inmates must be separated, with strict limits on male staff in female prisons.
- Prisoners awaiting trial should be separated from sentenced prisoners.
- The legal defence of untried prisoners should be facilitated by ease of communications with legal counsel.
- All capable prisoners should be engaged in useful work — with remuneration, an ability to make small purchases and compulsory savings for a post-release fund.

- Wherever possible work should be oriented towards post-release employment.
- Work should be directly owned and controlled by the institution to avoid conflicts of interest.
- Prisoners should have access to educational, recreational and cultural activities.
- Prisoners with mental disorders should be detained and managed separately.
- There should be a special focus on the post-release management of prisoners with mental disorders.

Inspections

To ensure compliance with minimum standard guidelines there is no substitute for a physical inspection of a prison or community corrections facility. Inspectors need to use a checklist and have access to all areas of the prison, subject to safety and security processes. Inspections should also include interviews with staff and inmates on both a scheduled and impromptu basis. Additionally, inspectors should review prison policies, on discipline and programs, for example, and also observe programs in action and interview program staff and participants (see Kennedy, 1988, p. 51; Nagle, 1978, p. 382.)

The membership of inspection teams is variable. Corrective services departments should operate their own inspection teams on a regular basis — such as annually or biannually. Some degree of independence from local staff can be achieved by using inspectors from the department's central office. However, as we have seen repeatedly throughout this book, independence is vital for confidence that judgments are not biased. From time to time then correctional facilities should be inspected by experts external to the organisation and government. Mixed international teams are particularly valuable in providing high-profile expert perspectives and a high level of independence. A cross-section of members of parliament will add to democratic accountability.

Official Visitors

Official visitors are used by corrective services departments as a mechanism for dealing with prisoner grievances that is partly independent of the department (Kennedy, 1988, p. 52). Official visitors are somewhat like an ombudsman who comes to your place of residence. They do not have adjudicative powers and are limited to making recommendations to the department. There are two main types of visitors: (1) lawyers and (2) community representatives (e.g., Indigenous official visitors). Visitors attend prisons on a regular basis and prisoners can book meetings. The visitor hears the prisoner's complaint and makes an official report to the department that includes a recommendation. The visitor may conduct an investigation of sorts, by interviewing relevant staff, for example, before making an assessment.

Professionalisation

Many inquiries into prisons have condemned low levels of education and training of staff, the anti-prisoner culture of cynicism among staff, and the lack of staff commitment to their work as a means to improve society and improve the lives of prisoners (Kennedy, 1988; Nagle, 1978). Professionalisation entails the following processes:

- Adoption of an enforceable code of conduct that addresses the full range of ethical issues in the occupation and sets out universal standards of behaviour expected of professional officers.

- The application of principles of appointment by merit in the selection, promotion and assignment of staff to ensure the best available staff are in place.

- The introduction of post-secondary educational requirements, especially for senior and management positions. The curriculum should include critical analysis of the social role of corrective services and the roles and behaviours of corrective services officers. Subjects should include law, ethics, sociology, psychology, politics and government, and research methods and critical thinking.

- Engagement in policy-oriented research and application of scientific findings to continuous improvement.

Cross-sectional Boards

Significant opportunities for bias and corruption are presented in decision-making about parole — or early release — and compliance with probation and other orders. It is essential therefore that these decisions are not made by one person who can monopolise the decision-making process and act corruptly or according to personal prejudices. Probation and parole boards should include community representation, including an independent lawyer and representatives of any major ethnic minorities in the jurisdiction. The same principle of community representation should apply to overall management of a corrective services department. A management board or advisory board should include prominent community representatives who can provide diverse perspectives on ongoing policy and key operational decisions (Kennedy, 1988, p. 51; Nagle, 1978, p. 382).

Parole Criteria and Review

Discretion also provides opportunities for corruption and bias unless there are clear criteria for decisions and a requirement that evidence is presented — such as evidence of participation in and completion of programs or evidence of violations of bans on drug use. Minutes of meetings need to be maintained and be open to scrutiny. Applicants should have due process rights of appearance, rebuttal and appeal where they can present at least a prima facie case of an error in reasoning or evidence. Again, there is a danger that these systems become overly complex, with appeals to magistrates and beyond. What is essential though is that there is timely and clear communication with applicants, an open process and avenues for review. Applicants will need assistance with their applications, and they should expect written reasons for decisions — there needs to be a clear paper trail in relation to decision-making that can be accessed by third parties as required (Kennedy, 1988, pp. 123–124). While security issues might preclude full disclosure in some cases — in regard to informants, for example — the reasons should be available to an independent authority.

Grievance Committees

Prisoner grievance committees can provide a useful line of communication between prisoners and prison management about prison conditions. Elected representatives from among prisoners can meet on a regular basis and consider complaints and requests from prisoners and pass them on in robust meetings with management. Apart from being a tool for improving or maintaining conditions, grievance committees can also serve as a safety valve to reduce prisoner dissatisfaction and resentment that can lead to violence. However, it has also been argued that prisoner grievances should be dealt with on an individual basis and that committees may try to assert a role in management that is not appropriate (Kennedy, 1988, p. 193).

Prisoner Rights Groups

Abuses in prisons and policy issues have given rise to community-based prisoner rights groups who primarily (1) advocate on behalf of prisoners with particular issues and (2) lobby governments for improvements to prison conditions and prisoner rights. These groups are often affiliated with religious groups and with prison ministries that organise priests and other members of a church or similar to visit prisoners. Prisoner rights groups can include specialist groups, including those concerned specifically with issues for women prisoners, ethnic or racial minorities, or political prisoners. These organisations need to be free from political repression and interference.

Privatisation?

The privatisation of prisons is sometimes touted as a way of improving accountability, especially where prison management or prison unions are intransigent (Kennedy, 1988, p. 88). In theory, the threat of non-renewal of a contract for underperformance by a private firm is a major motivating factor. Critics argue, however, that a profit-driven delivery of correctional services motivates contractors to reduce costs by cutting corners and hiding substandard services. In theory, the lack of direct line management between corrective services and the private prison can limit accountability. However, an evaluation of privatised prisons in Australia indicated that privately run prisons can be run well in terms of conditions, security and programs as long as the contract terms are carefully crafted and there is very close scrutiny and regulation of performance (Harding, 1997).

Conclusion

Corrective services and prisons are high-risk areas for corruption and for neglect and malign neglect in the treatment of offenders. A standard anti-corruption infrastructure is essential in the form of internal and external integrity management units, complaints investigations and discipline, ethics training, an enforceable code of conduct, due process procedures, whistle-blower legislation, and intelligence and risk management mechanisms.

Standards for prison conditions can be readily set using international guidelines. There are costs involved to taxpayers that will be particularly challenging for impoverished jurisdictions. Nonetheless, humane and productive sentencing can involve lower-cost alternatives to prison. Corrective services also need to commit to continuous improvement through a professional development program for staff. Cross-sectional community input is also important for accountability through community membership on parole and management boards. Genuine political commitment is the key final ingredient required for genuine integrity and accountability, and humane conditions, in corrections.

Australian Bureau of Statistics. (2008). *2008 year book Australia*. Canberra, Australia: Author.

Academics for Justice. (1991). The conviction of Timothy Wedward Anderson for the Hilton bombing: Verdict unsafe. In K. Carrington, M. Dever, R. Hogg, J. Bargen & A. Lohrey (Eds.), *Travesty! Miscarriages of justice*. Sydney, Australia: Author.

Alain, M., & Grégoire, M. (2008). Can ethics survive the shock of the job? Quebec's police recruits confront reality. *Policing and Society, 18,* 169–189.

American Bar Association. (2002). *Model rules of professional conduct*. Chicago: Center for Professional Responsibility, American Bar Association.

American Probation and Parole Association. (2008). *Code of ethics*. Retrieved February 20, 2009, from www.appa.org

Anatomy of an integrity test. (1997, December 23). *The Daily Telegraph* (Australia), p. 4.

Anderson, J., Kling, J., & Stith, K. (1999). Measuring inter-judge sentencing disparity before and after the federal sentencing guidelines. *Journal of Law and Economics, XLII*(April), 271–299.

Anozie, V., Shinn, J., Skarlatos, K., & Urzua, J. (2004). *Reducing incentives for corruption in the Mexico City Police Force*. Madison, WI: La Follette School of Public Affairs, University of Wisconsin–Madison.

Armstrong, K., & Possley, M. (1999, January 11). The verdict: Dishonor. *The Chicago Tribune*. Retrieved February 24, 2009, from http://truthin justice.org/prosecutors.htm

Australian Broadcasting Authority. (2000). *Commercial radio enquiry: Final report of the Australian Broadcasting Authority*. Sydney, Australia: Author.

Australian Broadcasting Corporation. (1985). *Out of sight, out of mind: The keepers and the kept*. Sydney, Australia: Author.

Australian Broadcasting Corporation Radio National. (2008, September 20). The ethics of keeping your mouth shut — The case of the buried bodies. *The Philosopher's Zone*. Sydney, Australia: ABC Radio National.

Australian Broadcasting Corporation Television. (1993). *Lawyers, drugs and money* [*4 Corners* report]. Sydney, Australia: Author.

Australian Government. (2008). *APS values and code of conduct in practice*. Canberra, Australia: Australian Public Service Commission.

Australian Institute of Judicial Administration (AIJA). (2001) *Litigants in person management plans: Issues for courts and tribunals*. Melbourne, Australia: Author.

Australian Law Reform Commission. (1994). *Equality before the law: Women's equality, Part 2.* Sydney, Australia: Author.

Ayling, J., & Grabosky, P. (2006). When police go shopping. *Policing: An International Journal of Police Strategies and Management, 29*(4), 665–690.

Bangalore Principles of Judicial Conduct. (2002). Available at http://www.unodc.org/pdf/crime/corruption/judicial_group/Bangalore_principles.pdf

Barker, T. (1983). Rookie police officers' perceptions of police occupational deviance. *Police Studies, 6*(2), 30–38.

Barron, S. (2007). *Police officer suicide: A review and examination using a psychological autopsy.* Retrieved March 10, 2008, from http://barronpsych.com.au/resource.html

BBC News. (2002, July 10). *Flashback: Rodney King and the LA riots.* Retrieved May 16, 2008, from http://news.bbc.co.uk/1/hi/world/americas/2119943.stm

Bennett, R. (1984). Becoming blue: A longitudinal study of police recruit occupational socialization. *Journal of Police Science and Administration, 12*(1), 47–58.

Bentham, J. (1996). *An introduction to the principles of morals and legislation.* Oxford: Clarendon Press.

Bermúdez, M. (2005). *Central America: Gang violence and anti-gang death squads.* Retrieved March 16, 2008, from http://ipsnews.net/news.asp?idnews=30163

Bita, N. (2009, January 29). Former childcare minister Larry Anthony lobbied for ABC Learning. *The Australian,* p. 5.

Brants, C. (2008). The vulnerability of Dutch criminal procedure to wrongful conviction. In C. Huff & M. Killias (Eds.), *Wrongful conviction: International perspectives on miscarriages of justice* (pp. 157–182). Philadelphia: Temple University Press.

Brereton, D. (2002). Monitoring integrity. In T. Prenzler & J. Ransley (Eds.), *Police reform: Building integrity* (pp. 115–130). Sydney, Australia: Federation Press.

Bryson, J. (2000). *Evil angels: The disappearance of Azaria Chamberlain.* Sydney, Australia: Hodder.

BStU. (2009). *Ministry for State Security.* Berlin, Germany: Office of the Federal Commissioner. Retrieved February 18, 2009, from http://www.bstu.bund.de

Buerger, M. (1998). The politics of third party policing. *Crime Prevention Studies, 9,* 89–116.

Burke, A., & Ducci, S. (2005). *Trafficking in minors for commercial sexual exploitation: Thailand.* Torino, Italy: United Nations Interregional Crime and Justice Research Institute.

Campbell, K. (2008). The fallibility of justice in Canada. In C. Huff & M. Killias (Eds.), W*rongful conviction: International perspectives on miscarriages of justice* (pp. 117–136). Philadelphia: Temple University Press.

Carrington, K., Dever, M., Hogg, R., Bargen, J., & Lohrey, A. (Eds.). (1991). *Travesty! Miscarriages of justice.* Sydney, Australia: Academics for Justice.

Chan, J. (1992). *Doing less time: Penal reform in crisis.* Sydney, Australia: Institute of Criminology, University of Sydney.

Charette, B. (1993). *Early identification of police brutality and misconduct: The Metro-Dade Police Department model.* The Florida Criminal Justice Executive Institute. Retrieved June 12, 2008, from http://www.fdle.state.fl.us/FCJEI/SLP/SLP%20papers/Charette.pdf

Christopher, W. (1991). Report of the Independent Commission on the Los Angeles Police Department. Los Angeles.

Claster, J. (Ed.). (1967). *Athenian democracy: Triumph or travesty.* New York: Holt, Rinehart and Winston.

Collins, S. (2008, March 14). Assault tape detectives escape time behind bars. *The Age,* p. 3.

Commissioner for Law Enforcement Data Security. (2007). *Standards for Victoria Police law enforcement data security.* Melbourne, Australia: Author.

Commonwealth Human Rights Initiative. (2005). *Police accountability: Too important too neglect, too urgent to delay.* New Delhi, India: Author.

Conlon, G. (1993). *In the name of the father.* New York: Plume.

Cornwall, D. (1992, April 25). Anger over transfer of racist police. *The Sydney Morning Herald,* p. 3.

Cortazar, J. (2009, February 10). Mexico arrests police chief over general's murder. Reuters News. *Factiva.*

Council of Chief Justices of Australia. (2002). *Guide to judicial conduct.* Melbourne, Australia: Council of Chief Justices of Australia, Australian Institute of Judicial Administration.

Council of Europe. (2000). *Code of conduct for public officials.* Strasbourg, France: Council of Europe Publishing.

Criminal Justice Commission. (1992). *Report of an investigation into possible misuse of parliamentary travel entitlements by members of the 1986–1989 Queensland Legislative Assembly.* Brisbane, Australia: Author.

Critchley, T. (1976). *A history of police in England and Wales 900–1966.* London: Constable & Company.

Daley, R. (1978). *Prince of the city: The true story of a cop who knew too much.* Boston: Houghton Mifflin.

Danforth, J. (2000). *Final report to the Deputy Attorney General concerning the 1993 confrontation at the Mt. Carmel Complex Waco, Texas.* Washington, DC: Department of Justice.

Davids, C. (2008). *Conflicts of interest in policing: Problems, practices and principles.* Sydney, Australia: Institute of Criminology, University of Sydney.

Dawkins, R. (2006). *The God delusion.* Boston: Houghton Mifflin.

Death Penalty Information Center. (2009). *Innocence and the death penalty.* Retrieved February 20, 2009, from http://deathpenaltyinfo.org/innocence-and-death-penalty

Devlin, P. (1986). *Easing the passing.* London: Faber and Faber.

Dixon, D. (2006). A window into the interviewing process? The audio-visual recording of police interrogation in New South Wales, Australia. *Policing & Society, 16*(4), 323–348.

Dodd, C.H. (1967). Recruitment to the administrative class 1960–1964. *Public Administration, 45*(1), 55–80.

Doneman, P. (1996, March 30). Review for sex favour cases. *The Courier-Mail,* p. 8.

Donnelly, J. (2007, May 18). Wolfowitz resigns from World Bank. *The Boston Globe,* pp. 3, A.1.

Eades, D. (2008). *Courtroom talk and neocolonial control.* Berlin, Germany: Mouton de Gruyter.

Ede, A., & Barnes, M. (2002). Alternative strategies for resolving complaints. In T. Prenzler & J. Ransley (Eds.), *Police reform: Building integrity* (pp. 115–130). Sydney, Australia: Federation Press.

Federal Election Commission. (2001). *2000 Presidential electoral and popular vote.* Washington, DC: Author. Retrieved July 20, 2008, from http://www.fec.gov/pubrec/fe2000/elecpop.htm

Findlay, M. (2004). *An introduction to policing.* Melbourne, Australia: Oxford University Press.

Finn, P. (2001). *Citizen review of police: Approaches and implementation.* Washington, DC: National Institute of Justice.

Fitzgerald, G. (1989). *Report of a Commission of Inquiry pursuant to orders in Council.* Brisbane, Australia: Government Printer.

Freeman, J. (1995, February 6). The Hilton bombing. *The Sydney Morning Herald,* p. 1.

Friedrichs, D. (2007). *Trusted criminals: White collar crime in contemporary society.* Belmont, CA: Thomson Wadsworth.

Gabor, T. (1994). *'Everybody does it!': Crime by the public.* Toronto, Canada: University of Toronto Press.

Gado, M. (n.d.). *Robert Garrow.* Retrieved February 21, 2009, from http://www.trutv.com/library/crime/serial_killers/predators/robert_garrow/1.html

Gaes, G., Wallace, S., Gilman, E., Klein-Saffran, J., & Suppa, J. (2001). *The influence of prison gang affiliation on violence and other prison misconduct.* Washington, DC: Federal Bureau of Prisons.

Gendreau, P., & Andrews, D.A. (1990). Tertiary prevention: What the meta-analysis of the offender treatment literature tells us about 'what works'. *Canadian Journal of Criminology, 32*, 173–184.

Glenny, M. (2000, October 6). Police and priests join workers' revolt — Yugoslavia. *The Times*, p. 3.

Goffman, E. (1968). *Asylums: Essays on the social situation of mental patients and other inmates.* Harmondsworth, United Kingdom: Penguin.

Goldenberg, S. (2008, December 10). Illinois governor tried to sell Obama's Senate seat to highest bidder, says FBI. *The Guardian*, p. 3.

Gornik, M. (2001). *Moving from correctional program to correctional strategy: Using proven practices to change criminal behavior.* Washington, DC: National Institute of Corrections.

Griffiths, C. (2000, September 16). CJC uncovers rorts in prisons. *The Courier-Mail*, p. 16.

Haney, C. (2001). *The psychological impact of incarceration.* Washington, DC: US Department of Health and Human Services.

Harding, R. (1997). *Private prisons and public accountability.* New Brunswick, NJ: Transaction.

Hayes, H., & Geerken, M.R. (1997). The idea of selective release. *Justice Quarterly, 14*(2), 353–370.

Hofer, P., Blackwell, K., & Ruback, R. (1999). The effect of federal sentencing guidelines on inter-judge sentencing disparity. *Journal of Criminal Law and Criminology, 90*(1), 239–321.

Hoffman, G. (2003). *Police pursuits: A law enforcement and public safety issue for Queensland.* Brisbane, Australia: Crime and Misconduct Commission.

Home Office. (2003). *A new deal for victims and witnesses.* London: Author.

How fair is the legal system? (1991, June 7). *The Sydney Morning Herald*, p. 14.

Huff, C.R. (2008). Wrongful convictions in the United States. In C. Huff & M. Killias (Eds.), *Wrongful conviction: International perspectives on miscarriages of justice.* Philadelphia: Temple University Press.

Huff, C.R., & Killias, M. (2008). Wrongful conviction: Conclusions from an international overview. In C. Huff & M. Killias (Eds.), *Wrongful conviction: International perspectives on miscarriages of justice.* Philadelphia: Temple University Press.

Human Rights Watch. (1998). *Shielded from justice: Police brutality and accountability in the United States.* New York: Author.

Human Rights Watch. (2007). *World report: Events of 2006.* New York: Author.

Human Rights Watch. (2008). *Briefing on the Counter-Terrorism Bill 2008, second reading in the House of Lords, No. 1.* London.

Independent Commission Against Corruption. (1992). *Report on investigation into the Metherell resignation and appointment.* Sydney, Australia: Author.

Independent Commission Against Corruption. (1994). *Investigation into the relationship between police and criminals.* Sydney, Australia: Author.

Independent Commission Against Corruption. (1998, November). *Press release*. Sydney, Australia: Author.

Independent Commission Against Corruption. (2008). *Investigation into tendering and payments in relation to NSW Fire Brigades capital works projects*. Sydney, Australia: Author.

Innes, M. (2004). Reinventing tradition? Reassurance, neighbourhood security and policing. *Criminal Justice, 4*(2), 151–171.

Insideprison. (2006). *The psychological effects of supermax prisons*. Retrieved March 3, 2009, from http://www.insideprison.com

International Association of Chiefs of Police. (2002). Law enforcement code of conduct. In *Police chiefs desk reference* (pp. 34–39). Washington, DC: Author and Bureau of Justice Assistance.

Jail psychologist on inmate sex charges. (1996, March 13). *The Courier-Mail*, p. 14.

Johnston, L. (1992). *The rebirth of private policing*. London: Routledge.

Jones, B., & Mathers, S. (2006). Los Angeles County Sheriff's Department risk management and civil litigation management programs. In J. Cintron Perino (Ed.), *Citizen oversight and law enforcement* (pp. 115–126). Chicago: ABA Publishing.

Jones, M. (1997). Police officer gratuities and public opinion. *Police Forum*(October), 8–11.

Kant, I. (1996). *Metaphysics of morals*. Cambridge: Cambridge University Press.

Kant, I. (2002). *Groundwork for the metaphysics of morals*. Oxford: Oxford University Press.

Kappeler, V., & Potter, G. (2005). *The mythology of crime and criminal justice*. Long Grove, IL: Waveland.

Kennedy, J.J. (1988). *Commission of review into Corrective Services in Queensland: Final report*. Brisbane, Australia: Government Printer.

Kessler, I. (2008). A comparative analysis of prosecution in Germany and the United Kingdom: Searching for truth or getting a conviction? In C. Huff & M. Killias (Eds.), *Wrongful conviction: International perspectives on miscarriages of justice* (pp. 213–247. Philadelphia: Temple University Press.

Kinnell, H. (2000). Serial homicide by doctors: Shipman in perspective. *British Medical Journal, 321*(23–30 December), 1594–1597.

Kirby, M. (2005) .*Tackling judicial corruption — Globally*. Sydney, Australia: St James Ethics Centre. Retrieved August 15, 2006, from http://www.hcourt.gov.au/speeches/kirbyj/kirbyj_stjames.htm

Kleinig, J. (1990). Teaching and learning police ethics: Competing and complimentary approaches. *Journal of Criminal Justice, 18*, 1–18.

Kleinig, J. (2008). *Ethics and criminal justice: An introduction*. New York: Cambridge University Press.

Knapp, W. (1972). *Report of a commission to investigate allegations of police corruption and the city's anti-corruption procedures.* New York: The City of New York.

Kohlberg, L. (1976). Moral stages and moralization. In T. Lickona (Ed.), *Moral development and behavior* (pp. 31–52). New York: Holt, Rinehart and Winston.

Kolts, J. (1992). *Los Angeles County Sheriff's Department: Report by Special Counsel.* Los Angeles.

Krone, T. (2007, June). *From appalling vista to appalling vista: Twenty years of evidence law reform.* Paper presented at the International Society for the Reform of Criminal Law Conference, Vancouver, Canada.

Landuyt, R., & T'Serclaes, N. (1997). *Enquete parlementaire sur la manière dont l'enquête, dans ses volets policiers et judiciaries a ètè menèe dans 'l'affaire Dutroux-Nihoul at consorts'* (Summary and selected translations by B. Bouhours). Brussels, Belgium: Chambre des Représentants de Belgique.

Langdon, J., & Wilson, P. (2005) When justice fails: A follow-up examination of serious criminal cases since 1985. *Current Issues in Criminal Justice, 17*(2), 179–202.

Law Council of Australia. (2002). *Model rules of professional conduct and practice.* Canberra, Australia: Author.

Lawson, G., & Oldham, W. (2006). *The brotherhoods: The true story of two cops who murdered for the mafia.* New York: Simon and Schuster.

Leaver, A. (1997). *Investigating crime: A guide to the powers of agencies involved in the investigation of crime.* Sydney, Australia: LBC.

Lee, H. (1979). *To kill a mockingbird.* London: Pan.

Legosz, M. (2007, October). *A cameo of recent research about police ethics at the Crime and Misconduct Commission.* Paper presented at the Australian Public Sector Anti-corruption Conference, Sydney, Australia.

Lewis, C. (1999). *Complaints against police: The politics of reform.* Sydney, Australia: Hawkins Press.

Maas, P. (1973). *Serpico.* New York: Viking Press.

Macintyre, S., & Prenzler, T. (1999). The influence of gratuities and personal relationships on police use of discretion. *Policing and Society, 9,* 181–201.

Macintyre, S., Prenzler, T., & Chapman, J. (2008). Early intervention to reduce complaints: An Australian Victoria Police initiative. *International Journal of Police Science and Management, 10*(2), 238–250.

Maguire, M., & Corbett, C. (1991). *A study of the police complaints system.* London: Her Majesty's Stationery Office.

Makkai, T., & Prenzler, T. (2009). The nature and prevalence of crime. In H. Hayes & T. Prenzler (Eds.), *An introduction to crime and criminology* (pp. 54–75). Sydney, Australia: Pearson.

Marx, G. (1992). When the guards guard themselves: Undercover tactics turned inward. *Policing and Society, 2*(3), 151–172.

McGowen, R. (1998). The body and the state: Early modern Europe. In N. Morris & D. Rothman (Eds.), *The Oxford history of the prison: The practice of punishment in western society* (pp. 71–99). New York: Oxford University Press.

McKenzie, N., & Berry, J. (2006, September 23). Brute force. *The Age*, p. 1.

McSherry, B., Keyzer, P., & Freiberg, A. (2006). *Preventive detention for 'dangerous offenders in Australia.* Canberra, Australia: Criminology Research Council.

Metcalf, F. (1997, June 19). Borbidge orders review of PS travel rules amid conflict of interest row. *The Courier-Mail*, p. 3.

Mexico nets seven-tonne cocaine haul. (2009, February 17). *The Australian*, p. 8.

Mieczkowski, T., & Lersch, K. (2002). Drug-testing police officers and police recruits. *Policing: An International Journal of Police Strategies and Management 25*(3), 581–601.

Mill, J.S. (1966). *John Stuart Mill: A selection of his works.* Toronto, Canada: Macmillan.

Miller-Potter, K. (2005). Capital punishment: The myth of murder as effective crime control. In V. Kappeler & G. Potter (Eds.), *The mythology of crime and criminal justice.* Long Grove, IL: Waveland.

Mollen, M. (1994). *Commission report.* New York: Commission to Investigate Allegations of Police Corruption and the Anti-Corruption Procedures of the Police Department (New York City).

Murphy, K., Hinds, L., & Fleming, J. (2008). Encouraging public cooperation and support for police. *Policing and Society, 18*(2), 136–155.

Murray, D. (2004, June 13). Inquiry into perks for senior police officials. *Sunday Mail*, p. 21.

Murton, T., & Hyams, J. (1969). *Accomplices to the crime: The Arkansas prison scandal.* New York: Grove Press.

Nagle, J.F. (1978). *Report of the Royal Commission into New South Wales prisons, Volumes I, II, and III.* Sydney, Australia: Government Printer.

National Center for Women and Policing. (2001). *Equality denied: The status of women in policing.* Beverly Hills, CA: Author.

National Institute of Justice. (2005). *Enhancing police integrity.* Washington, DC: Author.

New South Wales Department of Corrective Services. (2005). *Guide to conduct and ethics.* Sydney, Australia: Author.

New South Wales Ombudsman. (2002). *Improving the management of complaints: Identifying and managing officers with complaint histories of significance.* New South Wales, Australia: Author.

Northcote, S., & Trevelyan, C.E. (1854). *Report on the organisation of the permanent civil service.* London: Her Majesty's Stationery Office.

Ombudsman. (1998). *Operation BART: Investigation of allegations against police in relation to the shutter allocation system.* Melbourne, Australia:

Ombudsman Victoria. Retrieved February 25, 2009, from http://www. paccoa.com.au

Orwell, G. (2002) *Nineteen eighty-four*. New York: Rosettabooks.

Padraic, S. (2005). *Sympathy for the devil*. Sydney: ABC Books.

Palk, G., Hayes, H., & Prenzler, T. (1998). Restorative justice and community conferencing: Summary findings of a pilot project. *Current Issues in Criminal Justice, 10*(2), 138–155.

Paparozzi, M.A., & Gendreau, P. (2005). An intensive supervision program that worked: Service delivery, professional orientation, and organizational supportiveness. *The Prison Journal, 85*(4), 445–466.

Parker, C., & Evans, A. (2007). *Inside lawyers' ethics*. Melbourne, Australia: Cambridge University Press.

Parks, B., & Smith, A. (1999). *The 1992 Los Angeles riots: Lessons learned, changes made*. Retrieved July 3, 2002, from http://www.lapdonline.org

Party video sparks 'police racism' uproar in Australia. (1992, March 14). *Straits Times*.

Paterson, A. (1951). *Paterson on prisons: Being the collected papers of Sir Alexander Paterson*. London: Frederick Muller.

Perry, T., & Marosi, R. (2005, July 19). 2 San Diego officials guilty in strip-club graft scandal. *Los Angeles Times*, p. A-1.

Peters, E.M. (1998). Prison before the prison: The ancient and medieval worlds. In N. Morris & D. Rothman (Eds.), *The Oxford history of the prison: The practice of punishment in western society* (pp. 3–43). New York: Oxford University Press.

Police Education Advisory Council. (1998). *Police for the future: Review of recruitment and selection for the Queensland Police Service*. Brisbane, Australia: Author.

Police Integrity Commission. (2004). *Operation Florida: Report to Parliament on corrupt conduct by former and serving NSW police officers including soliciting and receiving bribes from drug dealers, Volume 1*. Sydney, Australia: Author.

Police Integrity Commission. (2005). *Operation Abelia: Research and investigations into illegal drug use by some NSW police officers, Volume 1, summary report*. Sydney, Australia: Author.

Pollock, J. (2007). *Ethical dilemmas and decisions in criminal justice*. Belmont, CA: Wadsworth.

Pope Osborne, M., Hinton, S.E., Handler, D., & Curtis, C. (2008). *What kids are reading: The book reading habits of students in American schools*. Wisconsin Rapids, WI: Renaissance Learning.

Pratt, J., Brown, D., Brown, M., Hallsworth, S., & Morrison, W. (Eds.). (2005). *The new punitiveness*. Devon, United Kingdom: Willan.

Prenzler, T. (1997) Is there a police culture? *Australian Journal of Public Administration 56*(4), 47–56.

Prenzler, T. (1990). Christianity and law. *Social Alternatives, 9*(1), 20–23.

Prenzler, T. (2000). Civilian oversight of police: A test of capture theory. *The British Journal of Criminology, 40*(4), 659–674.

Prenzler, T. (2002). Stuart, John Andrew (1940–1979). *Australian Dictionary of Biography, Volume 16.* Melbourne, Australia: Melbourne University Press.

Prenzler, T. (2006). Ethics and accountability in law enforcement. In S. Hayes, N. Stobbs & M. Lauchs (Eds.), *Social ethics for legal and justice professionals* (pp. 124–139). Sydney, Australia: Pearson.

Prenzler, T. (2009). *Police corruption: Preventing misconduct and maintaining integrity.* Boca Raton, FL: CRC Press Taylor and Francis.

Prenzler, T., & Lewis, C. (2005). Performance indicators for police oversight agencies. *Australian Journal of Public Administration, 64*(2), 77–83.

Prenzler, T., & Mackay, P. (1995). Police gratuities: What the public think. *Criminal Justice Ethics, 14*(1), 15–25.

Prenzler, T., & Ronken, C. (2001). Police integrity testing in Australia. *Criminal Justice: The International Journal of Policy and Practice, 1*(3), 319–342.

Prenzler, T., & Sarre, R. (2009). The criminal justice system. In H. Hayes & T. Prenzler (Eds.), *An introduction to crime and criminology* (pp. 259–273). Sydney, Australia: Pearson.

Probation and Community Corrections Officers' Association. (2009). *Code of ethics.*

Puddington, A. (2008). *Findings of freedom in the world 2008 — Freedom in retreat: Is the tide turning?* Retrieved March 1, 2009, from http://www.freedomhouse.org/template.cfm?page=130&year=2008

Ransley, J., Anderson, J., & Prenzler, T. (2007). Litigation against police in Australia: Policy implications. *Australian and New Zealand Journal of Criminology, 40*(2), 143–160.

Ransley, J., & Prenzler, T. (2009). Defining crime. In H. Hayes & T. Prenzler (Eds.), *An introduction to crime and criminology* (pp. 18–33). Sydney, Australia: Pearson.

Reuss-Ianni, E. (1983). *Two cultures of policing: Street cops and management cops.* New Brunswick, NJ: Transaction Books.

Roberts, C. (2005). *Displaying effectiveness: Evaluation report on the IRIS Project.* Oxford, United Kingdom: Centre for Criminology and Probation Studies Unit, University of Oxford.

Ross, Y. (2005). *Ethics in law: Lawyers' responsibility and accountability in Australia.* Sydney, Australia: LexisNexis Butterworths.

Royal Commission. (1993). *The Royal Commission on criminal justice: Report.* London: HMSO.

Rozenberg, J. (1992). Miscarriages of justice. In E. Stockdale & S. Cassales (Eds.), *Criminal justice under stress* (pp. 91–116). London: Blackstone.

Runciman, W. (1993) *Report of the Royal Commission on Criminal Justice.* London: HMSO.

Russell, J. (2007). *Terrorism pre-charge detention comparative law study.* London: Liberty.

Sarre, R. (1989). Towards the notion of policing 'by consent' and its implications for police accountability. In D. Chappell & P. Wilson (Eds.), *Australian policing: Contemporary issues* (pp. 102–119). Sydney Australia: Butterworths.

Sarre, R., & O'Connell, M. (2009). The criminal courts. In H. Hayes & T. Prenzler (Eds.), *An introduction to crime and criminology* (pp. 292–310). Sydney, Australia: Pearson.

Scarman, L.G. (1986). *Scarman report.* London: Penguin.

Scher, R., & Weathered, L. (2004) Should the United States establish a Criminal Cases Review Commission? *Judicature, 88*(3), 122–125, 145.

Schorr, D. (2001, January 1) Clinton's last scandal. *The New Leader, 84*(1), 4.

Sherman, L. (1977). Police corruption control: Environmental context versus organizational policy. In D. Bayley (Ed.), *Police and society* (pp. 143–155). Beverley Hills, CA: Sage.

Sigler, R., & Dees, T. (1988). Public perceptions of petty corruption in law enforcement. *Journal of Police Science and Administration, 16*(1), 14–20.

Skolnick, J. (1994). *Justice without trial: Law enforcement in democratic society.* New York: Macmillan.

Slayer's 2 lawyers kept secret of 2 more killings. (1974, June 20). *The New York Times,* p. 81.

Smith, A. (1993). *Neddy: The life and crimes of Arthur Stanley Smith.* Sydney, Australia: Kerr.

Stevens, D. (2008). Forensic science, wrongful convictions, and American prosecutor discretion. *The Howard Journal, 47*(1), 31–51.

Sutton, C., & Warnock, S. (1993, December 5). The fall from grace. *Sun Herald,* p. 16.

Targett, T. (2001, January 13). The sinner circle. *The Courier-Mail,* p. 27.

Three Ex-cops get prison terms in Key West cocaine case. (1985, August 8). *News,* p. a10.

Tonry, M. (2002). Setting sentencing policy through guidelines. In S. Rex & M. Tonry (Eds.), *Reform and punishment: The future of sentencing.* Devon, United Kingdom: Willan.

Transparency International. (2007). *Global corruption report.* Cambridge: Author and Cambridge University Press.

Transparency International. (2008). *National household survey 2007 on corruption in Bangladesh.* Dhaka, Bangladesh: Author.

Trueheart, C. (1998, December 24). Ex-NATO chief Claes convicted in bribery scandal. *The Washington Post,* p. A13.

Truth and Reconciliation Commission. (1998). *Truth and Reconciliation Commission Report, Volume 3*. Pretoria, South Africa.

United Nations. (1948). *Universal declaration of human rights*. Geneva, Switzerland: Author.

United Nations. (1977). *Standard minimum rules for the treatment of prisoners*. Geneva, Switzerland: Author.

United Nations. (1979). *Code of conduct for law enforcement officials*. Geneva, Switzerland: United Nations, Office for Democratic Institutions and Human Rights.

United Nations. (1996). *International code of conduct for public officials*. Geneva, Switzerland: Author.

United Nations. (2005). *Human rights and prisons: A pocketbook of international human rights standards for prison officials*. Geneva, Switzerland: Author.

United Nations. (2006). *Meeting the need: strengthening family planning programs. United Nations Population Fund and Program for Appropriate Technology in Health (PATH)*. Geneva, Switzerland: Author.

United Nations. (2007). *Global environment outlook*. New York: United Nations Environment Program.

US Courts. (1998). *Travel and hotel expenses — Judge and a family member*. Washington, DC: Author.

US Courts. (2000). *Code of conduct for United States judges*. Washington, DC: Author.

US Senate Armed Services Committee. (2008). *Inquiry into the treatment of detainees in U.S. custody*. Washington, DC: Author.

van Delden, B., Van de Wouw, F., & Van der Veer, J. (2008). The Amsterdam integrity system. In L. Huberts, F. Anechiarico & S. Frédérique (Eds.), *Local integrity systems: World cities fighting corruption and safeguarding integrity* (pp. 187–228). The Hague, the Netherlands: BJu Legal.

Van Dijk, J. (2008). *The world of crime*. Los Angeles: Sage.

Venkatraman, A. (2007). Religious basis for Islamic terrorism: The Quran and its interpretations. *Studies in Conflict and Terrorism, 30*(3), 207–227.

Walker, C. & McCartney, C. (2008). Criminal justice and miscarriages of justice in England and Wales. In C. Huff & M. Killias (Eds.), *Wrongful conviction: International perspectives on miscarriages of justice* (pp. 183–211). Philadelphia: Temple University Press.

Walker, S. (2003). *The disciplinary matrix: An effective police accountability tool?* Omaha, NE: University of Nebraska.

Walker, S., Alpert, G.P., & Kenney, D.J. (2001). *Early warning systems: Responding to the problem police officer*. Washington, DC: National Institute of Justice.

Weatherburn, D. (1994). *Sentencing disparity and its impact on the NSW Criminal Court.* Sydney, Australia: New South Wales Bureau of Crime Statistics and Research.

Weatherburn, D. (2004). *Law and order in Australia: Rhetoric and reality.* Sydney, Australia: Federation.

Weitzer, R. (2004). Public perceptions of police misconduct and reform. In M. Hickman, A. Piquero & J. Greene (Eds.), *Police integrity and ethics* (pp. 190–208). Belmont, CA: Wadsworth.

Wells, W., & DeLeon-Granados, W. (1998). 'Do you want extra police coverage with those fries?' An exploratory analysis of the relationship between patrol practices and the gratuity exchange principle. *Police Quarterly, 1*(2), 71–85.

White, R. (1998). Curtailing youth: A critique of coercive crime prevention. *Crime Prevention Studies, 9*, 17–140.

White, R., & Perrone, S. (1997). *Crime and social control.* Melbourne, Australia: Oxford University Press.

Whitton, E. (1987, April 29). How Australian justice can be manipulated. *The Sydney Morning Herald*, p. 4.

Whitton, E. (1990, March 10). Diary of a disgraced cop. *The Sydney Morning Herald*, p. 71.

Wilson, P. (1991). Miscarriages of justice in serious criminal cases in Australia. In K. Carrington, M. Dever, R. Hogg, J. Bargen & A. Lohrey (Eds), *Travesty! Miscarriages of justice.* Sydney, Australia: Academics for Justice.

Woffinden, B. (1987). *Miscarriages of justice.* London: Hodder & Stoughton.

Wood, J. (1997). *Royal Commission into the New South Wales Police Service: Final report.* Sydney, Australia: New South Wales Government Printer.

Zalman, M. (2008). The adversary system and wrongful conviction. In C. Huff & M. Killias (Eds.), *Wrongful conviction: International perspectives on miscarriages of justice* (pp. 213–247). Philadelphia: Temple University Press.

Legislation

Commonwealth of Australia Constitution Act
Explosive Substances Act
Police and Criminal Evidence Act 1984
Prevention of Terrorism Act
Racketeering Influenced and Corrupt Organizations Act

CPSIA information can be obtained
at www.ICGtesting.com
Printed in the USA
LVHW042126130123
737045LV00002B/235